Contents

Disaster Risk Management Series No. 2

Managing Disaster Risk in Emerging Economies

Edited by
Alcira Kreimer and Margaret Arnold

The World Bank
Washington, D.C.

Photo credits:
Cover, Turkey earthquake, 1999, photographer, Catherine Stevens; page xiv, workers after Turkey earthquake, 1999, photographer, Catherine Stevens; page 8, street flooded fromHurrican Mitch, Nicaragua, 1998, photo, PAHO/WHO page 52, reinforcing a building with sheer wall and cladding, Vanadzor, Armenia, 1996, photographer, Eric N. Patterson; page 100, fallen freeway due to Kobe earthquake, Japan, 1995, photographer, Fouad Bendimerad.

ISBN 0-8213-4726-8
ISSN 1020-8135

Cover design by Communications Development Incorporated.

Library of Congress Cataloging-in-Publication Data

Managing disaster risk in emerging economies / Alcira Kreimer and Margaret Arnold, editors.
        p. cm. — (Disaster risk management series)
    Includes bibliographical references.
    ISBN 0-8213-4726-8
    1. Emergency management—Economic aspects—Developing countries.   2. Emergency
management—Developing countries—Planning.   3. Disaster relief—Economic
aspects—Developing countries.   4. Disaster relief—Developing countries—Planning.   I.
Kreimer, Alcira.   II. Arnold, Margaret, 1965– III. Series.

    HV551.5.D44   M35   2000
    363.34↔09172↔4—dc21   00-035920

Acknowledgments

This volume presents papers connected to several events organized by the World Bank's Disaster Management Facility (DMF). The events focused on creating strategic partnerships to reduce the impacts of disasters on developing countries. The first event was a June 1999 consultation of the international community and private sector on how to collaborate on disaster risk management. The second event comprised workshops connected to the DMF's Market Incentives for Mitigation Investment (MIMI), which explores public-private partnerships to provide incentives for disaster mitigation investment. The third occasion was a February 2000 workshop cosponsored with the United Nations Development Programme (UNDP) to explore microfinance instruments to help the poor manage disaster risk.

These events and related initiatives led to the February 2000 launching of the ProVention Consortium. The Consortium is a global coalition of governments, international organizations, academic institutions, private sector, and civil society organizations aimed at reducing disasters in developing countries. The Consortium is based on two premises: (1) we all must take responsibility to make this new millennium a safer one, and (2) it is the intersectoral links—for example, among the scientific community and policymakers, and among the private and public sectors—that will facilitate risk assessment, risk reduction, and risk education activities in developing countries. The ProVention Consortium is an international network to share knowledge and connect and leverage resources to reduce disaster risk. By involving all stakeholders, the Consortium intends to promote innovative solutions for reducing disaster risk. It focuses on synergy and coordination, so that efforts, and benefits, are shared.

The Disaster Management Facility (DMF) team expresses its thanks to UNDP for its cosponsorship of the launch of the ProVention Consortium, and to the Government of Norway for the leadership it has demonstrated in the initiative. Thanks go also to the other governing members of the ProVention Consortium. A full listing of the governing members of the ProVention Consortium can be found at www.worldbank.org/dmf. The editors also would like to thank all of the contributing authors to the volume for their careful consideration of the topics.

The DMF team would like to express special thanks to several members of the World Bank staff who provided essential support to the goals of the Facility. These include President James Wolfensohn; Nemat Talaat Shafik, Vice President for Private Sector Development and Infrastructure; Manuel Conthe, Vice President of the Financial Sector; David de Ferranti, Vice President for Latin America and the Caribbean; Eduardo Doryan, Vice President for Human Development; Ian Johnson, Vice President for Environmentally and Socially Sustainable Development (ESSD); Jean-François Rischard, Vice President for External Affairs, Europe; Frannie Léautier, Director of Infrastructure; John Flora, Sector Director for Transport; Robert Watson, Chief Scientist and Director for ESSD; Andrei Raczynski, Director of Infrastructure, International Finance Corporation; Jeffrey Gutman, Sector Manager for Transport in the Latin America and Caribbean Region; Anthony Pellegrini, Sector Director of Urban Development; and Nicholas Van Praag, Principal External Affairs Officer for ESSD.

Partial funding for the two chapters on the Argentina case study was provided by the Government of the Netherlands, as part of the World Bank/Netherlands Environment Program. The World Bank's Disaster Management Facility thanks the Netherlands for its generous support. These two chapters were translated from Spanish by Aracely Barahona-Strittmatter, with additional editing by Melanie Zipperer. Alicia Hetzner was editorial consultant for this volume, and Gaudencio Dizon was the desktop publisher. The editors express their gratitude for their professionalism and excellent work. The editors also extend their thanks for the support provided by Livia Mitchell and Maria Eugenia Quintero.

Acronyms

ASCAs	Accumulating Savings and Credit Associations
AHPS	Advanced Hydrologic Prediction System (U.S.)
ALERT	Automated Local Evaluation in Real Time
AWIPS	Advanced Weather Interactive Processing System
BRAC	Bangladesh Rural Advancement Committee
CARICOM	Caribbean Community
CAS	Country Assistance Strategies (CASs)
CAT	catastrophe bond
CBO	Congressional Budget Office
CDMP	Caribbean Disaster Mitigation Project
CEA	California Earthquake Authority
CGE	computable general equilibrium
CHF	Cooperative Housing Foundation
CRED	Center for Research on the Epidemiology of Disasters
DHA	now OCHA
DMRS	disaster mitigation and relief strategies
EMA	Emergency Management Australia
ENSO	El Niño and the Southern Oscillation
EU	expected utility
FEMA	Federal Emergency Management Agency (U.S.)
FIA	Federal Insurance Administration (U.S.)
FIFMTF	Federal Interagency Floodplain Management Task Force (U.S.)
FIRM	Flood Insurance Rate Map (U.S.)
FPC	Federal Power Commission (U.S.)
GCI	Getty Conservation Institute
GCM	General Circulation Models
GDP	gross domestic product
GHG	greenhouse gas
GIS	Geographic Information System
GoT	Government of Turkey

ICCROM	International Center for the Study of the Preservation and Restoration of Cultural Property
ICOM	International Commission on Monuments
ICOMOS	International Council on Monuments and Sites
IDNDR	International Decade of Natural Disaster Reduction
IFI	international financial institutions
IFM	Integrated Fire Management
IFRC	International Federation of Red Cross and Red Crescent Societies
IGM	Instituto Geografico Militar (Argentina)
IIASA	International Institute for Applied Systems Analysis
IIPLR	Insurance Institute for Property Loss Reduction
IPCC	Intergovernmental Panel on Climate Change
ISCT	Integrative Social Contracts Theory
ISO	Insurance Services Office
ITFPMRC	Interagency Floodplain Management Review Committee (U.S.)
LFWS	Local Flood Warning System (U.S.)
MEGS	Maharashtra Employment Guarantee Scheme
MIMI	Market Incentives for Mitigation Investment
NFIP	National Flood Insurance Program (U.S.)
NOAA/OGP	National Oceanic and Atmospheric Administration, Office of Global Programs
NGO	nongovernmental organization
NRC	National Research Council (U.S.)
NRDF	National Research and Development Foundation (St. Lucia)
NWC	National Water Commission (U.S.)
NWS2000	National Weather Service improved forecast systems (U.S.)
OCHA	United Nations Office of the Coordinator for Humanitarian Assistance
OECS	Organization of Eastern Caribbean States
OFDA/USAID	Office of Foreign Disaster Assistance of the U.S. Agency for International Development
OTA	United States Office of Technology Assessment
PML	Probable Maximum Loss
RMM	risk mitigation measure
ROSCA	rotating savings and credit association
SCS	Soil Conservation Service (U.S.)
SFH	Special Flood Hazard Area (U.S.)
SPREP	South Pacific Regional Environment Program
SPPO	South Pacific Program Office
SUC	Standard Unit Contract
TFFFCP	Task Force on Federal Flood Control Policy (U.S.)
TVA	Tennessee Valley Authority (U.S.)
UIC	UNITED Insurance Company (Barbados)
UNDHA	United Nations Department of Humanitarian Affairs
UNDP	United Nations Development Programme
UNEP	United Nations Environment Programme
UNESCO	United Nations Educational, Scientific and Cultural Organization
UNFCCC	United Nations Framework Convention on Climate Change

USACE	United States Army Corps of Engineers
USAID/OFDA	United States Agency for International Development, Office of U.S. Foreign Disaster Assistance
USBR	United States Bureau of Reclamation
USGPO	United States Government Printing Office
WRC	Water Resources Council (U.S.)
WRDA	Water Resources Development Act (U.S.)
XOL	excess-of-loss

Contributors

William A. Anderson
Senior Advisor
Disaster Management Facility
World Bank
1818 H Street, NW, Room 4K-270
Washington, DC 20433
USA
Tel.: 202-473-6495
Fax: 202-522-2125
E-mail: wanderson@worldbank.org

Charlotte Benson
Senior Research Associate
Overseas Development Institute
Mulberry House
Station Road
East Sussex TN31 6QA,
United Kindgom
Tel.: 44-1797-252-954
Fax: 44-1797-252-954
E-mail: cbenson321@aol.com

Ian Burton
Consultant
72 Coolmine Road
Toronto, Ontario
CANADA M6J 3E9
Tel: 416 739 4314
Fax: 416 739 4279
Email: Ian.Burton@ec.gc.ca

Edward J. Clay
Senior Research Associate
Overseas Development Institute
Portland House, Stag Place
London SW1E 5DP
United Kingdom
Tel.: 44-1273-723-101
Fax: 44-207-393-1699
E-mail: e.clay@odi.org.uk

Nora Clichevsky
Architect
Instituto de Geografía
Universidad de Buenos Aires
Argentina
Tel.: 54-11-4772-9775
Fax: 54-11-4833-2488
Email: noraclic@satlink.com

Maxx Dilley
Geographer
Disaster Management Facility
World Bank
1818 H Street, NW, Room F 4K-264
Washington, DC 20433
USA
Tel: 202-473-2533
Fax: 202-522-2125
Email: mdilley@worldbank.org

Thomas W. Dunfee
Kolodny Professor of Social Responsibility
The Wharton School, University of Pennsylvania
3620 Locust Walk
Philadelphia PA 19104-6369
USA
Tel.: 215-898-7691
Fax: 215-573-2006
E-mail: dunfeet@wharton.upenn.edu

Paul K. Freeman
Senior Research Scholar
International Institute for Applied Systems Analysis
  (IIASA)
A-2361 Laxenburg
Austria
Tel.: 43-2236-807-471
Fax: 43-2236-807 466
E-mail: freeman@iiasa.ac.at

Hilda María Herzer
Professor and Researcher
Instituto Gino Germani
Facultad de Ciencias Sociales
Universidad de Buenos Aires
Argentina
Tel. 54-11-4542-8543
Fax: 54-11-4382-7040
Email: centro@datamarkets.com.ar

J. G. M. (Hans) Hoogeveen
Vrije Universiteit
De Boelelaan 1105
Room 4A-29
1081 HV Amsterdam
The Netherlands
Email: hhoogeveen@econ.vu.nl

Frederick Krimgold
Director of Joint Center for Disaster and Risk Management
Virginia Polytechnic Institute and State University
Northern Virginia Center
7054 Haycock Road
Falls Church, VA 22043-2311
USA

Tel: 703-538 8366
Fax: 703-538 8383
Email: krimgold@vt.edu

Howard Kunreuther
Cecilia Yen Koo Professor of Decision Sciences
  and Public Policy
The Wharton School
University of Pennsylvania
Philadelphia, PA 19104-6366
USA
Tel.: 215-898-4589
Fax: 215-573-2130
E-mail: kunreuth@wharton.upenn.edu

Robert Litan
Director, Economic Studies Program,
  and Cabot Chair in Economics
The Brookings Institution
1775 Massachusetts Ave. N.W.
Washington, DC 20036-2188
USA
Tel.: 202-797-6120
Fax: 202-797-6184
E-mail: rlitan@brook.edu

Ronald S. Parker
Senior Evaluations Officer
Operations Evaluation Department
World Bank
1818 H Street, NW
Washington, DC 20433
USA
Tel.: 202-473-1688
Fax: 202-522-3123
E-mail: rparker1@worldbank.org

Héctor Sejenovich
Consultant
Economia y Ambiente
Uriarte 2462 5 A - 6 A
Argentina
Tel/Fax: 54-1 773-4653
Email: hsejenovich@sion.com

Alan Strudler
Professor, Legal Studies Department
2204 Steinberg - Dietrich Hall
The Wharton School, University of Pennsylvania
Philadelphia, PA 19104
USA
Tel.: 215-898-1221
Fax: 215-573-2006
E-mail: strudler@wharton.upenn.edu

June Taboroff
Cultural Resource Specialist
   and Consultant
World Bank
526 Fulham Road
London SE5 8EA
United Kingdom
Tel.: 44-207-736-8212
Fax: 44-207-736-0784
E-mail: jtaboroff@worldbank.org

Juan B. Valdés
Professor and Department Head
Department of Civil Engineering
   and Engineering Mechanics
The University of Arizona
Tucson AZ 85721-0072
USA
Tel.: 520-621-6564
Fax: 520-621-2550
Email: jvaldes@u.arizona.edu

Maarten K. van Aalst
Institute for Marine and Atmospheric Research
   Utrecht (IMAU)
Utrecht University
PO Box 80005
3508 TA Utrecht
The Netherlands
Tel.: 31-30-253-7760
Fax: 31-30-254-3163
E-mail: M.K.vanAalst@phy.uu.nl

Krishna S. Vatsa
Consultant, World Bank,
   and Department of Engineering Management
George Washington University, Rm. 707 Staughton
22nd Street, NW
Washington, D.C. 20052
USA
Tel: 703-812 3966
Email: vatsa@gwu.edu

Jan Vermeiren
Chief, Caribbean Region
Organization of American States
1889 F Street, NW
Washington, DC 20006
USA
Tel.: 202-458-3006
Fax: 202-458-3560, 3168
E-mail: jvermeiren@oas.org

Workers after Turkey
earthquake, 1999.

Introduction

The revolutionary idea that defines the boundary between modern times and the past is the mastery of risk: the notion that the future is more than a whim of the gods and that men and women are not passive before nature.
> —Peter L. Bernstein, *Against the Gods:*
> *The Remarkable Story of Risk*

Natural disasters long have been considered a tragic interruption to the development process. Lives are lost; social networks are disrupted; and capital investments are destroyed. And when development plans are laid and disaster strikes, development funds are diverted to the emergency. Additional aid is directed to relief and reconstruction needs to get the country "back on track" toward economic and social development.

In recent years, however, the development community has been making the links between disasters and development. This evolution would seem inevitable when one considers the disproportionately high costs that developing countries pay for disasters.

The Development-Disaster Treadmill

In 1999 natural catastrophes and man-made disasters claimed more than 105,000 lives across the globe, and resulted in total losses of around US$100 billion (Swiss Re 2000). Developing countries bear the majority of these costs, accounting for more than 95 percent of

the deaths. The landslides in Venezuela alone caused around 50,000 fatalities; the Turkey earthquake claimed 20,000 lives; and the Orissa cyclone in India killed 15,000.

In 1998 close to half of the US$65 billion in economic losses caused by natural disasters were related to a single event in the developing world—the flooding of the Yangtze River. When the costs of Hurricane Mitch, the second largest catastrophic event of that year, are figured in, two-thirds of global losses occurred in the developing world. While the inter-regional distribution is variable, one thing is not: based on income disparities, the per capita burden of catastrophic losses is dramatically higher in developing countries (Freeman 1999).

Moreover, natural disasters impact developing countries in other ways not reflected in the figures above. Disaster losses include not only the shocking direct impacts that we see on the news, such as the loss of life, housing, and infrastructure, but also indirect impacts such as the foregone production of goods and services caused by interruptions in utility services, transport, labor supplies, suppliers, or markets.

Secondary losses include impacts on such macroeconomic variables as economic growth, balance of payments, public spending, and inflation. In a global economy changes in the perception of risk can adversely affect an economy if investors demand higher rates of return. If investors do not believe they are being adequately compensated for the risk they face, may decide to close a business or move to a less risky economy. The industry and businesses in the area of Turkey hit by the 1999 earthquake contribute to more than 35 percent of the country's gross domestic product (GDP). The destruction of these businesses is likely to effect the economic growth of Turkey for many years. The earthquake in Turkey had repercussions on the cotton producers in Africa as well, who were not able to export their production to the cotton manufacturers located in the devastated area.

As mentioned, another important impact that natural disasters have on developing countries is that funds targeted for development are reallocated to finance relief and reconstruction efforts, jeopardizing long-term development goals. Natural disasters, therefore, impede progress towards social and economic growth, as they wipe out investments made and divert resources from federal, state, and municipal budgets and aid agencies to recovery activities.

A Development Imperative: Reducing Disasters to Reduce Poverty

In its mission to reduce poverty the World Bank offers loans, advice, and an array of resources to more than 100 developing countries and countries in transition to help each country onto a path of stable, sustainable, and equitable growth. The Bank's primary focus is helping the poorest people and the poorest countries. However, the Bank emphasizes the same priorities for all of its clients:

• Investing in people through basic health and education
• Protecting the environment
• Encouraging private sector development
• Strengthening governments' ability to deliver quality services efficiently and transparently
• Promoting reforms to create a stable macroeconomic environment conducive to investment and long-term planning (World Bank 1998).

Poverty and vulnerability to disasters are closely linked. Disaster risk management is essential to the fight against poverty, because the poor are dispropor-

tionately affected by disaster. As with any risk, such as the death of a bread winner or commodity price swings, the poor are much more vulnerable to disasters due to their lack of assets with which to smooth consumption and respond to catastrophic events. Moreover, the poor often are forced to accept a higher exposure to hazards. Typically, they live in unsafe areas on marginal lands such as flood plains, slopes of steep hillsides, and river beds. Although they live in more vulnerable areas, the daily struggle to survive takes priority over investment in mitigating the impacts of potential disaster events.

Therefore, poverty plays a big role in keeping people vulnerable to disasters. In the same fashion disasters serve as a powerful downward trigger to poverty by continually destroying the few assets of the poor and wiping out investments in infrastructure and services that serve the poor. Access to public infrastructure comprises a large component of the wealth of the poorest households. The annual direct damage to infrastructure due to natural disasters in Asia alone is estimated at US$12 billion. Rural infrastructure projects (roads, irrigation, and electrification) have been found to be highly effective in reducing poverty. Programs and policies to minimize natural catastrophic losses, to improve public and private responses, and to institute appropriate risk transfer mechanisms will have a high anti-poverty impact (MacKellar and others 1999).

The links between poverty and disaster vulnerability make disaster management an important part of the World Bank's central mission to reduce poverty. While the Bank has a long tradition of providing reconstruction assistance after a disaster event, its efforts are increasingly integrating more proactive measures to prevent and mitigate the impact of disasters in its client countries.

World Bank Disaster Assistance

The World Bank is the largest provider of disaster-related assistance. Since 1980 the Bank has lent about US$20 million for disaster-related projects. In the last two decades the Bank has approved 110 reconstruction operations amounting to nearly US$10 billion. However, actual Bank support for natural disaster reconstruction is probably nearly double that figure, since the figure does not include funds that were reallocated from "normal" operations to respond to a disaster emergency. Typically, redirection of funds from an ongoing portfolio is the first course of Bank action in a country hit by disaster, as it is the most rapid way to get urgently needed assistance to an emergency situation. Redirected funds usually are followed up with a stand- alone reconstruction project. In Turkey the Bank reallocated US$267 million from ongoing projects in health, education, and reconstruction from flooding and a previous earthquake to provide urgently needed funds to the 1999 emergency caused by the Marmara earthquake. In Venezuela 150 million was reallocated from the portfolio in response to the December 1999 flooding and landslides. After Hurricane Mitch struck in 1998, portfolio reallocations for the four most affected countries (El Salvador, Guatemala, Honduras, and Nicaragua) amounted to US$226 million.

Weather-related disasters—floods, storms and droughts—account for nearly three-fourths of the Bank's reconstruction projects. Typically, the projects are multisectoral, and implemented in both urban and rural areas. By and large Bank projects have focused on repairing infrastructure and damaged community facilities as well as on supporting economic recovery through emergency imports.

Increasingly, the Bank has learned that reconstruction projects are not just "normal" projects to be implemented quickly. Over the years more and more reconstruction projects have also supported measures to strengthen institutional capacity to respond to future emergencies—through information and early warning systems, for instance—as well as structural measures to mitigate the impacts of future natural events.

The World Bank and its borrowers have developed a greater awareness of the need to invest more heavily in disaster prevention and mitigation. Since 1980 more than 200 projects containing components aimed at mitigating potential disaster impacts have been approved, amounting to approximately US$12 billion.

About 90 percent of these projects have addressed three likely weather-related events—floods, forest fires, and droughts—all with long lead times against which mitigation can be most effective. Among the main components are forest fire prevention including fire breaks and flood protection measures ranging from coastal defenses to terracing. As part of institutional development, these projects have pursued the enforcement of land use and building codes to avoid settlement in hazardous areas or in vulnerable widely structures.

Since cost information is not readily available on each component dedicated to disaster mitigation within all projects identified, it difficult to determine an accurate figure for Bank investment in disaster mitigation. Therefore, the total loan amount of US$12 billion above probably overestimates the total investment in mitigation. However, there is a definite trend in the Bank toward increasing investment in mitigation. Of the more than 200 mitigation projects approved since 1980, 80 were approved in the last 5 years; 58 were approved in the last 2 years.

Integrating Disaster Management in Bank Activities: Disaster Management Facility

To respond to an increased demand in disaster reconstruction assistance and to build on the efforts to mitigate disaster impacts, in 1998 the Bank established the Disaster Management Facility (DMF). The facility serves as the institution's central resource for technical support, information, and lessons learned on disasters, as well as for strategic direction on disaster risk management.

The DMF's objectives are to help the Bank provide a more strategic and rapid response to disaster emergencies and, more importantly, to integrate disaster prevention and mitigation measures in all Bank activities. The unit provides operational support and training for Bank staff and clients, addresses strategy and policy issues, and cultivates productive partnerships with the international and scientific communities, private sector groups, and nongovernmental organizations (NGOs) to advance disaster reduction efforts. In carrying out these tasks, the DMF focuses on the three key components of disaster risk management: risk identification, risk reduction, and risk sharing/transfer.

Risk Identification: Assessing Hazards, Vulnerability, and Impacts of Disasters

Any effective strategy to manage disaster risk must begin with an identification of the hazards and what is vulnerable to them. In this way informed decisions can be made on where to invest and how to design sustainable projects that will withstand the impacts of potential disaster events. A more complete understanding of the full economic, financial, and social impacts of disasters on a country also helps to demonstrate the importance of including risk reduction measures in development plans.

Working with the World Bank operational complex and with local and international partners, the Disaster Management Facility has organized ongoing efforts to inform the priority-setting process of the Bank's Country Assistance Strategy (CAS) development, sectoral policies, and project design. Initiatives include (1) country case studies to generate detailed evidence of the economy-wide significance of natural disasters and the problems they pose for long-term development, (2) models of the impacts of natural catastrophes on macroeconomic projections and infrastructure, and (3) a vulnerability index to identify the highest priorities in member countries and to identify urgent issues that need to be covered through development assistance.

Risk Reduction: Avoiding Hazards and Reducing Vulnerability

Disasters result when an extreme natural or technological event coincides with a vulnerable human settlement. The DMF provides guidance and operational support on how best to integrate disaster risk reduction measures in project design. The unit also has capabilities for rapid response in the event of major

emergencies. DMF staff have provided technical support to the country teams on reconstruction efforts in Honduras, Nicaragua, and Venezuela; disaster risk management projects in Mexico and the Caribbean; earthquake reconstruction efforts in Turkey; flood recovery projects in Madagascar and Mozambique; and disaster prevention efforts in Vietnam.

Reducing disaster risk requires that all stakeholders change their perceptions and behavior to place a high priority on safety in planning and development. Consequently, the DMF places a high priority on undertaking research and pilot projects that demonstrate the value of disaster risk reduction and contribute to Bank strategies and operations. For example, in Bangladesh an initiative is underway to develop a Community-based System for Disaster Prevention. It builds on the experience of community-based financial institutions such as the Grameen Bank to broaden the understanding and direct participation of communities in disaster mitigation investment.

Risk Sharing and Transfer: Protecting Investments and Sharing the Costs

The private insurance sector contributes important funding for natural disaster reconstruction in developed countries, but it has made fewer inroads in developing country markets. In emerging economies the state and the individual carry much of the cost of disasters. As a result, ad hoc funds transfers to respond to disaster emergencies disrupt planned development activities. Such diversion of development funding postpones progress toward long-term economic and social improvement.

The DMF supports efforts that protect development investments and advance disaster risk awareness. One such activity is the Market Incentives for Mitigation Investment (MIMI) initiative. Begun in 1998, MIMI works to create public-private partnerships to provide effective incentives for institutional and individual investment in disaster mitigation measures. MIMI case studies document current disaster management capacity and the potential for positive development in insurance and financial markets to mobilize mitigation investment. .

The first case study was conducted in Mexico, and another was conducted in Argentina, focusing on flooding in the Buenos Aires Metropolitan Area. As a result of the Mexico case study the Government of Mexico requested that the Bank prepare a project addressing the needs of ex ante initiatives to reduce disaster losses.

The DMF is also exploring the development of tools to assist the very poor to more effectively manage disaster risk. Since the poor are disproportionately affected by disasters and typically lack access to formal insurance mechanisms, the DMF is exploring Microfinance for Disaster Risk together with the United Nations Development Program (UNDP). This project aims to identify and disseminate effective microfinance mechanisms that can deal with covariate risks such as disasters and that build social capital and encourage risk mitigation for the very poor.

Stepping off the Treadmill: Partnerships for Prevention and Mitigation

The development community has learned a critical lesson from past disasters: we can continue to build vulnerability, thereby exacerbating disasters, or we can lessen their impacts. The creation of the DMF and its activities are enabling the Bank to shift to a more preventive mode, to shift from response to preparation and from the ex-post mobilization of resources to ex-ante programs of risk reduction and risk transfer. The need for this shift was echoed by the leaders of the Central American countries in the 1999 Stockholm donors meeting to pledge recovery assistance for Hurricane Mitch. These leaders called for a "transformation" of the region rather than mere reconstruction, or a return to the same state of vulnerability.

As the largest provider of development assistance, the World Bank can play a leading role in the necessary transformation to a new paradigm that puts comprehensive disaster risk management at the core of development. However, the Bank is still one among many development institutions, and does not pretend to have all the answers nor expertise to address the serious problem of disasters. For this reason, the DMF promotes strategic alliances with key private, government, multilateral, and nongovernmental organizations to ensure the inclusion of disaster risk reduction as a central value of development.

ProVention Consortium

The most important of these partnerships was launched in February 2000. The ProVention Consortium is a global coalition of governments, international organizations, academic institutions, the private sector, and civil society organizations. The Consortium is based on the premise that we all must take responsibility for making the new millennium a safer one and that it is the inter-sectoral links—among the scientific community, policymakers, and the private and public sectors—that will facilitate the promotion of risk assessment, risk reduction, and risk education activities in developing countries.

The Consortium's objectives are straightforward and attainable:

- To promote a culture of safety through education and training among leaders and citizens of developing countries
- To support public policy that can reduce the risk of natural and technological disasters in developing countries
- To support pilot projects and to disseminate information about "best practices" proven to mitigate the scope and frequency of disasters
- To develop governments' ability to minimize disasters and to respond effectively when they occur
- To forge links between public and private sectors, between the scientific community and policymakers, between donors and victims, so that all stakeholders work together to strengthen the economy, reduce pain and suffering, and promote the common good.

The ProVention Consortium functions as a network to share knowledge and to connect and leverage resources to reduce disaster risk. It focuses on synergy and coordination so that efforts, and benefits, are shared. Partners include the Government of Norway, Government of Japan, Organization of American States, International Federation of the Red Cross and Red Crescent Societies, Pan-American Health Organization, UN Development Programme, UN Environment Programme, UN Office for the Coordination of Humanitarian Affairs, UN World Food Programme, World Meteorological Organization, African Development Bank, Asian Development Bank, Inter-American Development Bank, World Institute for Disaster Risk Management, World Conservation Union (IUCN), International Institute for Applied Systems Analysis, Wharton School of the University of Pennsylvania, and private sector groups such as CEMEX, Munich Reinsurance, and Swiss Reinsurance.

As a new initiative, the Consortium holds promise as a coalition with governments to assist them in taking charge to identify and reduce the risks they face and in bringing in the participation of their citizens. It will be a coalition with civil society and communities to mobilize grassroots support for disaster preparedness and mitigation measures. It will be a coalition with the private sector, which has a major role to play in the promotion of risk awareness, risk prevention, pre-emergency planning and risk pre-financing. Finally, the Consortium will be a coalition of development community members to end duplication of effort and waste.

Organization of This Volume

This volume contains work that was produced over the first two years of operation of the Disaster Management Facility and led to the establishment of the ProVention Consortium. A draft publication was distributed at the February 3-4, 2000 launch of the ProVention Consortium in Washington, D.C. Many of the chapters were presented at that conference. The volume is organized in three parts, corresponding to the three main components of effective disaster risk management: risk identification, risk reduction, and risk financing and transfer.

Part I on risk identification contains chapters on the economic impacts on natural disasters in developing countries, including flooding, with the example of Buenos Aires; and time scales of climate and disaster.

Part II explores aspects of reducing disaster risk, such as the relationship of infrastructure, natural disasters, and poverty; flooding issues in the United States, incentives for risk management and mitigation concerning cultural heritage; issues related to single-family housing, women, and children; and climate change from a development perspective.

Part III looks at strategies for developing countries to more effectively share and transfer disaster risk from the angles of risk and insurance by the poor in developing countries; financing disaster mitigation for the poor; moral dimensions of risk transfer and reduction strategies; incentives for mitigation investment and risk management to encourage public-private partnerships; and linking catastrophe insurance and mitigating disaster losses.

Each chapter was selected to provoke thought and explore options on how best to integrate disaster risk management in sustainable development efforts. Reducing disaster vulnerability in developing countries may very well be the most critical challenge facing development in the new millennium. As the earth's natural environment continues to be degraded or destroyed, vulnerability grows along with population growth and the frequency and magnitude of disasters increase. Their most deadly impacts are on the lives and environment of the poor.

Development efforts have focused on helping the poor deal with many of the risks they face in daily life, such as in employment, health care, transport, clean water and sanitation, and education. Perhaps it is the "natural" nature of hazard events that have helped to perpetuate the myth that disasters are a "whim of the gods" and outside of human control. This fatalistic attitude in turn kept disaster risk from becoming a priority issue in development. However, one must remember that these events are natural, recurrent phenomena of our physical environment. It is always human actions leading up to and immediately following them that makes them disasters.

Frederick Cuny stated it very simply when he compared the 1971 San Fernando, California earthquake, which killed 58 people, with the 1973 earthquake in Managua, Nicaragua, which killed more than 6,000. Cuny asserted it was the level of development of the two cities that made the San Fernando event an "earthquake" and the Managua event a "disaster" (Cuny 1994).

A similar comparison was made by World Bank Vice President for Europe Jean François Rischard in comparing the December 1999 floods and landslides in Venezuela with the storms that hit France at the about the same time. While the amount of direct economic losses was similar in magnitude in both cases—approximately US$10 billion in damage to infrastructure—50,000 people died in Venezuela compared to 123 in France. And while Venezuela will be dealing with the effects of the disaster for years to come, France is already recovering through an astute system of public and private crisis response system and burden sharing. In the end, it is an issue of basic development. It is doing development right, and making sure that human activities contribute to reducing disasters rather than exacerbating them.

References

Bernstein, P. L. 1998. *Against the Gods: The Remarkable Story of Risk*. New York: John Wiley and Sons, Inc.

Cuny, F. C. 1994. *Disasters and Development*. Dallas, Tex.: Intertect Press.

Gilbert, R., and A. Kreimer. May 1999. *Learning from the World Bank's Experience of Natural Disaster Related Assistance*. Urban and Local Government Working Paper Series no. 2. Washington, D.C.: World Bank.

Ingleton, J., ed. 1999. *Natural Disaster Management*. Leicester, United Kingdom: Tudor Rose.

Kreimer, A. October 1991. "Lessons on Emergency Recovery from Past Experience." *Land Use Policy* 8 (4): 310. Oxford: Butterworth-Heinemann Ltd.

Kreimer, A., and others. 1999. *Managing Disaster Risk in Mexico: Market Incentives for Mitigation Investment*. Washington, D.C.: World Bank.

MacKellar, L., T. Ermolieva, and P. K. Freeman. 1999. "Simulating Macroeconomic Impacts of Natural Catastrophic Shocks with the World Bank's 'RMSM' (Revised Minimum Standard Model)." Draft. Disaster Management Facility, World Bank.

World Bank. 1998. *The World Bank: Knowledge and Resources for Change*. Washington, D.C.

Street flooded from Hurricane Mitch,
Nicaragua, 1998

PART I

RISK IDENTIFICATION

Chapter 1

Developing Countries and the Economic Impacts of Natural Disasters

Charlotte Benson and Edward J. Clay

Available data suggest that natural disasters can cause considerable damage, with potentially severe economic consequences. During 1990-98, natural disasters resulted in economic losses averaging an estimated US$76bn per year (in real 1998 prices) (Munich Re 1998).[1] Moreover, there is clear evidence that the costs of disasters are increasing. Real annual economic losses averaged US$4.9bn in the 1960s, US$9.5bn in the 1970s, and $15.1 bn in the 1980s. Record losses of US$191bn were recorded in 1995, the year of the Kobe earthquake. The second highest ever losses occurred in 1998, with a series of disasters around the world causing estimated economic damage of US$90bn and some US$15bn insured losses.

Such figures are dramatic. However, the full economic costs of disasters are probably even higher. Estimated figures are largely based on "direct" physical impacts, or losses of fixed capital and inventory (box 1). Meanwhile, many "indirect" and "secondary," or flow, effects on economic activity—such as changes in fiscal policy or the long-term consequences of the reallocation of investment resources—go unrecorded. This loss of information in part reflects difficulties in isolating the impact of natural disasters from other factors on economic performance; or of capturing such impacts in a single monetary figure.

Those assessing the costs of a disaster are also typically most concerned with meeting the short-term humanitarian needs of affected communities and funding reconstruction, so they concentrate on physical damage.

The emphasis on direct, physical losses has engendered a widespread perception that the absolute cost of disasters increases, and their relative cost as a percentage of gross domestic product (GDP) declines, as a country develops and, thus, as the value of capital assets rises.[2] However, recent analysis of the relationship between the structure and stage of development of an economy and its hazard vulnerability suggests a far more complex picture (Benson and Clay 1998). This analysis highlights the particular problems that disasters pose for middle- as well as low-income countries. It also underlines the importance of examining natural disasters not as singular events but rather as a series of successive random shocks which may have had a long-term impact on the pace and nature of development of particular countries. However, the analysis clearly indicates that there is considerable scope, both at a macro and household level, to influence the extent and nature of hazard vulnerability.

Determinants of Economic Hazard Vulnerability

The scale and nature of the economic impacts of a natural hazard depend on a range of factors, including:
- Type of hazard
- Geographical area and scale of impact
- Structure of an economy
- Prevailing economic conditions
- Stage of development of a country
- Stage of technical and scientific advancement.

Box 1   Measuring the economic impacts of a disaster

Direct costs relate to the physical damage to capital assets, including buildings, infrastructure, industrial plants, crops, and inventories of finished, intermediate, and raw materials destroyed or damaged by the actual impact of a disaster.

Indirect costs refer to damage to the flow of goods and services including lower output from damaged or destroyed assets and infrastructure; loss of earnings due to damage to marketing infrastructure such as roads and ports and to lower effective demand; job losses; and the increased costs associated with the use of more expensive inputs following the destruction of cheaper usual sources of supply. They also include the costs in terms of both medical expenses and lost productivity arising from increased incidence of disease, injury, and death. Indirect costs can be difficult to estimate, in part because of their "knock-on" effects. For example, disruption of the provision of basic services, such as telecommunications or water supply, can have far-reaching implications. Gross indirect costs are also in part offset by the positive knock-on effects of the rehabilitation and reconstruction efforts, such as increased activity in the construction industry. The complexity of indirect impacts can create problems of double-counting.

Secondary effects concern both the short- and long-term impacts of a disaster on overall economic performance, such as deterioration in trade and government budget balances and thus, perhaps, increased indebtedness. They can also include shifts in government monetary and fiscal policy, for example, to contain the effects of increased disaster-induced inflation or to finance additional government expenditure; and impacts on the distribution of income and scale and incidence of poverty.

The potential implications of a natural disaster for public finance and related fiscal and monetary policy provide an illustration of the complexity of indirect and secondary effects. Natural disasters may have several important impacts on public finance, resulting in either additional expenditure or partial redeployment of planned expenditure. Disasters can also reduce government revenue since lower levels of economic activity, including possible net falls in imports and exports, imply reduced direct and indirect tax revenues. Although such losses may be partly offset by increased flows of official external assistance, these flows are unlikely to offset completely increased levels of expenditure. Public enterprises may also experience disaster-related losses, placing an additional burden on government resources.

In consequence, a government may face increasing budgetary pressures which it will be obliged to meet by increasing the money supply, running down foreign-exchange reserves, or increasing levels of domestic and/or external borrowing. These financing options, in turn, have potentially significant knock-on effects. The creation of base money is inflationary. Domestic borrowing exerts upward pressure on interest rates and can result in a credit squeeze. Foreign borrowing can result in an appreciation of the exchange rate, reducing the price of imports and increasing that of exports. It can also place future strains on the economy via higher debt-servicing costs. Another option, the run-down of foreign-exchange reserves, is limited by the very size of those reserves and entails an appreciation in the exchange rate, with possible associated risks of capital flight and a balance-of-payments crisis (Fischer and Easterly 1990).

Type of Hazard

The type of hazard is relevant from three perspectives. Most obviously, different types of hazard cause varying nature and scale of damage. They are also associated with varying typical rates of frequency, in turn influencing perceptions of risk and behavioural responses; and with varying technical forecasting capabilities.

Different types of hazard cause varying levels of physical damage to infrastructure and agriculture, with implications for their indirect and secondary impacts. For example, droughts can result in heavy crop and livestock losses over wide areas of land, often affecting several neighboring countries simultaneously, but typically leave infrastructure and productive capacity largely unaffected. Earthquakes have little impact on standing crops, excluding localized losses occurring as a consequence of landslides but can cause widespread destruction of infrastructure and other productive capacity over relatively large areas. Floods can also cause extensive physical damage to both infrastructure and agriculture, depending on their timing relative to the agricultural cycle. However, the area affected can vary enormously, in part dependent on topographical features. As compared to earthquakes, a much larger share of the damage may also be repairable rather than requiring total reconstruction.

The relative frequency of various hazards in particular regions of the world also plays an important role in determining the scale and nature of disaster mitigation and preparedness measures and, thus, subsequent financial and economic losses. Even strictly scientific, objective information on the probability of occurrence of a particular hazard of varying levels of severity over a specified period of time may be largely lacking. Moreover, where information does exist, it may not be widely disseminated. Perceptions of risk, therefore, play an important role in determining behavior. Perceptions are strongly influenced by the length of intervals between events and the resulting extent of experience with disasters, both within communities at risk and among policymakers and the donor community more broadly. For example, the Caribbean island of Montserrat was severely damaged by Hurricane Hugo in 1989, with an estimated 98 percent of the island's housing stock, as well as the main jetty, damaged or destroyed. Total damage was estimated at some US$240m (IFRC 1997). During reconstruction hurricane proofing features were introduced into the design of houses and other buildings. However, little regard was paid to available volcanological risk maps as there had not been a major eruption for over four centuries and the risk of a severe event was perceived as low. The subsequent eruption, which began in 1995, has since devastated the island's capital, located only four kilometers from the volcano. Much of the infrastructure repaired or replaced post-Hugo has been destroyed.

Conversely, predictable flooding or even annual dry periods may be used to economic advantage. For example, in the early 1960s, sugar cane production in Fiji was deliberately moved to the west of the country,

where the drier climate ensured a higher sugar content. More generally, the widespread cultivation of deep-water rice types in south and southeast Asia is ecologically tied to areas of relatively extended annual inundation from 1 to 5 meters (Catling 1993).

Finally, forecasting and warning capabilities play some role in determining the extent and nature of shorter term preparedness measures and thus the impact of a hazard, assuming they are supported by effective dissemination systems. However, theoretical forecasting capabilities also vary significantly among hazard types. For example, in the case of droughts and floods there is some scope for long-term forecasting to the extent that such events are linked to El Niño weather variations. To some degree, it is also possible to respond to droughts as they evol.ve, reflecting their slow onset. Such warnings could prompt measures such as restrictions on water use or switch in the choice and type of crop planted. Short-term cyclone warnings can also be issued, reducing loss of life and physical damage if threatened communities undertake certain measures, such as securing windows and doors, tying down roofs, cutting tree branches, and relocating to cyclone shelters. In contrast, even in the two countries with the most advanced monitoring capacities, the United States and Japan, the timing and precise location of an earthquake remain extremely difficult to pinpoint, as illustrated by the unanticipated January 1995 Kobe earthquake. Broad known areas of seismic activity can be monitored, permitting the identification of locations where a build-up in tensions is occurring. Some more major earthquakes are also preceded by minor tremors, precipitating increased monitoring, but few earthquakes have been successfully predicted.[3]

Geographical Area and Scale of Impact

The proportion of a country and the particular region affected by a hazard has obvious implications. At one extreme, natural hazards can have severe economic impacts in the case of small-island economies. In the microstate of Niue in the South Pacific, for example, the cost of repairing damage to government-owned buildings alone as a consequence of Cyclone Ofa, which struck the island in February 1990, was estimated at $4m, equivalent to a massive 40 percent of GDP (UNDHA/SPDRP 1997).

With the important exception of widespread drought, however, recent natural disasters have not had measurable short-term impacts on national economic aggregates—such as levels of GDP, the balance of payments or the rate of investment—in geographically larger countries. Instead, their effects are perhaps best conceived in terms of development opportunities foregone at a national level although they can still cause serious economic disturbances locally. For example, in the Philippines only modest achievements in efforts to improve the country's transportation systems and increasing difficulties in meeting the social infrastructural needs of the country's rising population are attributed to the fact that a large proportion of available public resources earmarked for such purposes have had to be redirected in response to calamities (Benson 1997c). Readily accessible data on relief and rehabilitation expenditure alone indicated annual expenditure of 1.5 percent to 3.5 percent of total national government expenditure and of 3.9 percent to 8.3 percent of discretionary expenditure in 1991–94, while the full cost is probably higher.[4] Additional expenditure on the relief and rehabilitation program associated with the July 1990 Luzon earthquake probably pushed total relief and rehabilitation expenditure as a percentage of discretionary spending into double figures in 1991.

Relative hazard risks can also influence the choice of location of investments, whether within or, in the case of multinational corporations, between countries. In Vietnam, for example, this phenomenon is contributing to widening regional disparities as some of the more hazard-prone regions have received disproportionately small shares in both private and public investment and external assistance (Benson 1997b). Farmers in such regions have also been less well placed to take advantage of higher yielding but less hazard-tolerant strains of rice.

Economic Structure

Some countries exhibit a high degree of dualism, with a large capital-intensive extractive sector which features significantly in the trade account but is weakly linked with other sectors of the economy. In such economies the impact of a hazard event is in part determined by its impact on the extractive sector. For example, the economic impact of an earthquake will differ significantly depending on whether the extractive sector is affected. Similarly, unless the extractive sector is water intensive and fails through lack of investment or poor management to insulate itself from fluctuations in water supply, the economic impact of drought in dual economies is likely to be limited to variability in the agricultural sector, with only limited multiplier effects.

If the extractive sector is not affected, the macroeconomic impact of a natural hazard may thus appear small in a dual economy. For example, levels of exports and the broad revenue base may be largely sustained although, particularly in less developed countries, hazard events can still have potentially profound impacts for large segments of the population. For example, in Botswana in 1982-87 (Drèze and Sen 1989) and Namibia in 1992-93 (Thomson 1994), the macroeconomic aggregate and trade account effects of drought were modest. The respective governments had sufficient resources of their own to finance substantial relief programs, reflecting the importance of extractive mining sectors in both countries.

More generally, other factors such as the choice of crops grown and the composition of the manufacturing and service sectors also play important roles in determining the extent of hazard vulnerability. For instance, in countries highly dependent on hydroelectric power for a significant share of their electricity supply, droughts can severely disrupt electricity supply, potentially causing extensive damage to some industrial plants and equipment. In another example, many traditional root crops and coarse grains are more drought tolerant than newer crop varieties whereas hybrid coconut trees can be more vulnerable to typhoons than more traditional varieties, which typically have longer rooting systems. In Fiji, for instance, the increased economic impact of natural hazards in the 1980s over the 1970s largely reflected the expansion of the country's important sugar industry onto more marginal lands, where crops are more vulnerable to hazards. A second factor was the increasing senility of the country's coconut trees, again weakening their hazard tolerance (figure 1).

Prevailing Economic Conditions

Myriad other factors, both coincidental and deliberate, offset or amplify the economic impacts of hazard events, whether explicitly or implicitly. In terms of the balance of payments, for example, a number of developing countries rely on a handful of commodities for a significant part of their export earnings. Contemporaneous fluctuations in the prices of such commodities, as well as of major imports such as oil, can exacerbate or minimize the impacts of natural disasters, usually by random timing. For example, in 1984 high coffee and tea prices helped Kenya sustain its export earnings at a time of severe drought. In some cases, world market dominance also plays a role. For example, the Philippines has effectively benefited because of its position as a major coconut product

exporter, with temporary disaster-related declines in production offset by higher international prices. Commodity reserves have also been successfully used to maintain export earnings and prevent loss of export markets in the aftermath of natural disasters, as illustrated by Fiji's use of its sugar reserves (Benson 1997a). On occasion disaster-related reinsurance inflows have further boosted a country's balance of payments.

Countries already experiencing other adverse economic shocks typically are more vulnerable to natural hazards. For example, Ghana faced almost continual economic decline from the early 1960s to early 1980s, with per capita incomes a third lower in 1980 than in 1970. A subsequent drought was one of several factors forcing the economy to a crisis point, finally resulting in the adoption of a succession of structural adjustment programs. Meanwhile, in both Ethiopia and Mozambique, the effects of droughts in the late 1980s and early 1990s were amplified by ongoing internal conflict.

Figure 1   Fiji: GDP growth and natural disasters, 1982–94

Real annual GDP growth rate (%)

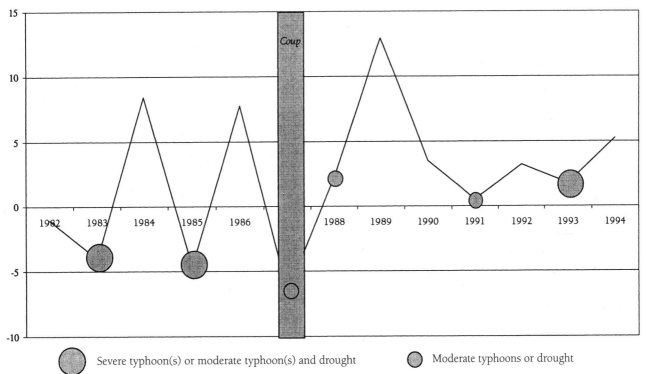

The existence and stage of a structural adjustment program can be another factor determining disaster impact. Disasters can exacerbate the short-term adverse impacts of reform, first and foremost via their effect on vulnerable groups. They may reinforce the inflationary impact of the removal of subsidies on basic food and other commodities, to the extent that governments continue this policy, and also contribute to job losses. Disasters can also intensify the short-term adverse economic impacts of reform more generally, for example, by prolonging tight monetary policy with implications for the rates of investment, as occurred in Zimbabwe in 1992-93.

The existence of reform programs and relationships with donors, particularly the international financial institutions (IFIs), more generally has also played an important role in determining the nature and level of the international response to disasters on some occasions, generating sometimes sizeable amounts of assistance to keep structural adjustment programs on course.

Disasters, in turn, can also impede the progress of reform. For example, in Zimbabwe the 1991-92 drought hampered government efforts to reduce the budget deficit and restructure the civil service and parastatals and, thus, to reduce domestic borrowing. In consequence, the expected domestic supply side response to the reform program, which was critical to its success, was partly curtailed. However, the drought shock also partly speeded up the restructuring of the manufacturing sector, as increased liquidity constraints forced enterprises to carry smaller stocks, shed surplus labor, and adopt less costly, efficiency-enhancing methods of production.

Stage of Development

The broader economic impacts of a disaster also need to be considered in the context of the stage of development of an economy, as defined in terms of factors such as the degree of sectoral and geographical integration, economic specialization, integration of financial flows, and government revenue-raising capabilities.

As already indicated, least-developed economies typically are perceived as most hazard vulnerable. Preliminary ongoing research indicates that over the past three decades more hazard-prone, low-income countries may have experienced a much slower pace of economic development than their less hazard-prone counterparts that had had similar levels of per capita income at the beginning of that period. In the former such economies the physical impacts of a hazard event may cause widespread destruction as there may have been little investment in hazard risks reduction measures. Loss of human life may also be high, in part reflecting poor warning capabilities, while disasters can exacerbate existing levels of poverty and indebtedness.

However, because of weak intersectoral linkages, a high degree of self-provisioning, and often poor transport infrastructure, the multiplier effects from the immediately affected regions and/or sectors through the rest of the economy may be fairly limited. Moreover, much of the relief and rehabilitation costs may be met through external grant and concessional assistance. Much of the economy may also revolve around rainfed agriculture, with little associated capital. For annual cultivation cycles, this implies that productive capacity can be restored relatively quickly if sufficient rehabilitation funds are made available to ensure the timely provision of seed, draught animals or agricultural machinery, other agricultural inputs, and tools.

Nevertheless, in its initial stages, increased development may not imply lower hazard vulnerability. Research at a household level suggests that poor and socially disadvantaged groups become more vulnerable to hazards in the initial stages of development due to the breakdown of traditional familial support as part of the disintegration of the old social fabric. Other factors include a decline in traditional coping measures, and rising land pressures, urbanization, and the increasing marginalization of poorer groups, forcing movement onto more hazard-prone lands (for example, SPREP/SPPO-UNDHA/EMA 1994; UN 1995). The decline in traditional coping mechanisms may result from planting less drought- or cyclone-resistant traditional crops as opportunities for marketing cash crops increase and older patterns of self-provisioning are eroded. Or it may result from constructing houses from "modern" materials, invol.ving structures that are both more vulnerable to hazards and more costly to reconstruct.

Such patterns may be mirrored at a macroeconomic level. An economy at an intermediate stage of development is more integrated than a simple one, among both sectors and geographical regions. Integration increases the multiplier effects of adverse performance in a particular sector or regional economy. For example, droughts impact on larger manufacturing as well as on the agricultural and livestock sectors because the lower domestic production of agricultural processing inputs reduces nonagricultural production while forcing up input costs. Intermediate (rather than final, as in simple economies) goods are also likely to form a larger share in total imports, implying that any drought-related import squeeze will have additional knock-on implications for domestic production.

The breakdown of traditional coping mechanisms also plays a role. For example, the increasing specialization of labor and the breakdown of community and extended family ties may reduce the ability of households to adapt to temporary shocks. Farmers increasingly engage in the market economy, perhaps replacing production of more hazard-tolerant traditional crops with cultivation of cash crops.[5] This can have implications for the macroeconomy as well as for individual households.

For example, in Zimbabwe, the relative shift in maize and cotton production from the large-scale commercial to the communal sector, the latter of which is heavily concentrated in lower-potential marginal areas, since 1980 has also been associated with increased rainfall- related variability in agricultural production. From 1982-83 to 1992-93, regression analysis indicates that an annual rainfall level 10 percent below the 1969-93 national mean would be associated with a 25 percent reduction in maize yields from the communal sector compared with only a 17 percent drop in commercial sector yields. Meanwhile, a 30 percent reduction in rainfall would be associated with declines of 62 percent in communal and 47 percent in com-

mercial sector maize yields.[6] These examples underscore the importance of a disaggregated approach in examining the sectoral impacts of drought, and of taking into account the effects of structural change in assessing the drought vulnerability of both individual sectors and the wider economy (Benson 1997d).

The structure of financial sectors and government financial policy are also likely to be more important in shaping the impact of a drought shock than in a simpler economy. Intermediate economies typically have more developed, economy-wide financial systems for the flow of funds, including small-scale private savings and transfers, which also diffuse the impact of disasters more widely. For example, again in Zimbabwe, the transfer of remittances from urban- to rural-based members of households was facilitated by the well articulated system for small savings in the aftermath of the 1991-92 drought. This mitigated the impact of the drought on the rural areas but at the same time spread its impact more widely, including into urban areas (Hicks 1993).

Meanwhile, the government is likely to meet a larger share of the costs of the relief and rehabilitation efforts, rather than relying almost entirely on international assistance. This will be financed by some combination of the reallocation of planned expenditure, government borrowing, and monetary expansion, with various indirect longer term implications, as discussed below. Large interannual fluctuations in economic performance, such as triggered by disasters, can also create economic management difficulties, for example, in controlling public expenditure.

Hazard-vulnerability of intermediate economies may be exacerbated by the fact that during the earlier stages of economic take-off, both governments and donors allocate considerable resources to new investment while recurrent costs are often underfunded, again potentially rendering a country more hazard vulnerable.[7] In some countries economic development may be accompanied by environmental degradation as already indicated, again increasing vulnerability to natural hazards.

In the later stages of development, evidence suggests that the economic impacts of disasters decline again, in part reflecting the smaller relative role of the potentially particularly hazard-vulnerable agricultural sector in GDP, as a source of employment and as both a source of inputs to other sectors and an end-user of other goods. More developed economies typically are both more open and have fewer foreign exchange constraints, facilitating the import of any normally domestically sourced items in temporary short supply as a consequence of the disaster without forcing a decline in other imports.

Other factors contribute to a decline in vulnerability in more developed economies, including increased investments in disaster prevention, mitigation, and preparedness measures; improved environmental management; and a reduction in the scale of absolute poverty and thus of household vulnerability.[8] Moreover, a greater share of economic assets is likely to be held by the private sector and adequately insured against disaster. Similarly, a higher proportion of damage sustained by individual households will be covered by insurance. Thus, the scale and cost of relief and rehabilitation programs will be limited and is less likely to necessitate a substantial increase in government domestic or external borrowing. However, the small segment of the population comprised of lower-income households may be severely hurt in terms of loss of income, assets, and savings.

Stage of Technical and Scientific Advancement

The impact of a hazard is time dependent, related to a country's stage of socioeconomic development and of technical and scientific advancement.

The role played by the latter relates most obviously to the stage of development of structural hazard mitigation techniques and forecasting technology and know-how. For example, between 1991 and 1997, there were considerable advances in short-term climatic forecasting for the Sahel and Southern African regions. Such information impinges on private and public decisions—for instance, pertaining to the management of water resources, choice of crops grown, and the level of exports and imports of grain. These in turn affect the relationship between climatic variability and economic performance. Similarly, considerable

advances in volcanological forecasting indicate how the impacts of volcanic events are in part determined by such factors. In 1976 predictions of a major eruption led to the temporary evacuation of part of the island of Guadeloupe at an estimated cost of over $50 million (Wood 1987). More recent improvements in monitoring of andesitic volcanoes made it possible to avoid a comparable scale of response on the neighboring island of Montserrat, which otherwise would have required complete evacuation during 1995 or 1996 (Young and others 1998).

Application of technical and scientific developments in other fields can influence the impact of a hazard. For example, flood-tolerant cultivars used in deepwater rice cultivation in south and southeast Asia are gradually being displaced by shorter-stemmed cultivars, which require more controlled, often irrigated water management but also permit more intensive production. Where, as in Bangladesh, this intensification is associated with a switch to dry-season irrigated, high-input rice, this change may reduce overall production variability and vulnerability to natural hazards. However, as the scope for substituting dry-season for monsoon-season cultivation is exhausted, future growth may again require investments in flood control to permit expansion of more intensive monsoon season cereal cultivation on naturally inundated flood plains. This, again, is an objective of several flood control projects for regions of Bangladesh under the controversial Flood Action Plan.

Implications for Government and Aid Policies

As indicated in the previous section, a complexity of factors determine a country's hazard vulnerability. Although the scale of direct physical damage typically increases as one moves along the spectrum from least to most developed countries, this does not imply that more developed countries are most vulnerable. Instead, high hazard vulnerability itself may be an obstacle to development.

More positively, high levels of hazard vulnerability are not inevitable. There is considerable scope for reducing hazard risk through the application of appropriately designed disaster mitigation, preparedness, relief, and rehabilitation efforts. Such measures should not be viewed as discrete activities undertaken by specialist government agencies but as measures that can be incorporated in development projects as well as in economic activities and government policy and planning exercises more generally. Indeed, in addressing both hazard vulnerability and post-disaster response, more attention needs to be paid to economic activities, rather primarily to the protection of economic assets.[9]

Current practices in many areas of economic activity can be adapted to reduce hazard vulnerability. For example, extension workers can promote techniques that reduce hazard-related agricultural losses, such as to encourage planting of early or late crop varieties that can be grown outside the main typhoon or flood season. Similarly, building codes can be used to promote the incorporation of hazard-proofing features into the construction of public and private buildings and infrastructure in earthquake- and hurricane-prone areas.

Broader government and donor policy and planning documents can also take greater account of hazard risk. Rather than ignoring natural hazards, as sometimes occurs, they should recognize the potential threat hazards pose to sustainable, equitable development and attempt to reduce overall economic hazard vulnerability. Indeed, even governments with relatively limited financial resources can do much to reduce hazard vulnerability. The degree of public sector and donor commitments to such issues should not be measured in financial terms alone.

Finally, in responding to the impact of a disaster, it is important to take account of underlying socioeconomic and technical changes to avoid inappropriate forms of assistance. For example, failure to recognize the hazard vulnerability-related impacts of changes in cropping patterns, such as in rice cultivation in south and southeast Asia, could lead to over-compensation for the expected impact of a flood disaster on aggregate food production. Programming of additional cereal imports, in turn, could negatively impact, through prices, producer incentives in the following dry season and beyond, amplifying the effects of a natural disaster shock in terms of output variability and lower agricultural growth.

Analyzing Economic Impacts of Disasters

Finally, the evidence presented in this chapter contains certain lessons about methodological approaches in the analysis of the economic impacts of disasters. It underlines the the importance of distinguishing between both type of hazard and economy in examining the impacts of natural disasters. Each disaster is unique, not only in physical impact but also in time, as in turn expressed in terms of the stage of technical and scientific advancement and the prevailing economic environment and circumstances within which a hazard occurs.[10]

In terms of methodological approaches for the analysis of the economic impacts of individual disasters, in theory computable general equilibrium models (CGEs) offer one of the best available tools. CGEs incorporate the socioeconomic structure of an economy, prices, and macroeconomic phenomena. CGEs have been used to simulate the economic and social consequences of a wide range of scenarios including exogenous shocks. In the specific context of natural disasters, however, there are certain constraints, in part reflecting the all-pervasive impact of many disasters on economic life. For instance, disasters can have highly complicated effects on productive sectors as well as on public and external sector accounts. The nature of such behavior may be fundamental in determining the outcome of a hazard event. Nevertheless, aggregated specification of different sectors may not reveal adaptive behavior, such as substitution among products and activities, or redeployment of government and private investment resources within particular sectors. More fundamentally, the current state of knowledge of the economic impact of disasters itself may be too limited to design appropriately constructed CGE models.

Instead, the evidence seems to point toward a more eclectic analysis, using a mixture of partial quantitative and qualitative techniques. Analysis of disaster impacts and assessment of strategies for hazard risk reduction need to explicitly consider socioeconomic and technical stages of development. This approach would place particular hazard events in their historical contexts, facilitating understanding of how impacts of future hazard events might differ and identification of appropriate responses before and after.

Notes

1. Munich Re's estimates of economic losses are based on figures released by governments and international agencies and on estimated ratios of insured to total economic losses. The latter are used to extrapolate the level of economic losses from reported figures on insured losses. For example, if insured windstorm losses in Germany are US$60m, then overall losses are usually estimated at around US$100m.

2. A third relationship commonly cited concerns a decline in the number of lives lost as consequence of disasters as one moves along the spectrum from least developed to highly developed economies. This reflects increasingly sophisticated meteorology and communications combined with downward revisions in acceptable levels of disaster risk. Improved technology provides both the means and the political impetus to improve the quality and timeliness of warnings and to ensure that appropriate action is taken to minimize loss of lives. The lower level of acceptable risk, in turn, reflects adjustments in household utility functions as improvements in levels of public health and other advancements reduce comparative risks in every day life (Coburn and others 1994).

3. A notable exception is the 1976 earthquake in Haicheng, Liaoning Province, China. The city evacuated before an earthquake measuring 7.3 on the Richter scale struck "almost certainly sav(ing) thousands of lives" (Alexander 1993, 43).

4. The Philippine Government faced very high nondiscretionary payments, accounting for 70 percent or more of total government expenditure, principally to meet debt-servicing and public sector wage bills.

5. This comment relates not only to drought-resistant crops—such as sorghum or millet—but to various crops and varieties better able to withstand floods or strong winds.

6. The results are sensitive to the choice of base and end years of analysis and to the rainfall indicator selected. The results reported, which are based on rainfall in critical winter months for selected stations in the various agro-climatic zones and include a time variable in the regressions, explain 88 percent

of variation in communal sector yields and 77 percent in commercial sector yields, with highly significant t-ratios for the rainfall variable.

7. For example, annual repairs to existing dikes may receive insufficient funding while considerable resources are allocated to the expansion of a country's overall water control system.

8. At the household level, poverty is the single most important factor determining hazard vulnerability, in part reflecting location of housing, choice of building materials, and primary types of occupation.

9. In a similar vein, Adger (1996) notes that various studies undertaken on the related issue of the socioeconomic implications of climate change have typically focused on the impacts on physical assets, such as land and economic assets, and the number of people potentially at risk. This has resulted in "a mechanistic approach leading to policy prescriptions which uniformly protect physical assets, rather than policy prescriptions which incorporates variability in social, economic and cultural constraints and opportunities."

10. Similarly, Otero and Marti (1995), for example, also conclude that: "in general and on the basis of experience accumulated in the Latin American and Caribbean region, there is no predetermined pattern as to the consequences of different disasters."

References

Adger, W. N. 1996. "Approaches to Vulnerability to Climate Change." *CSERGE Working Paper GEC-96-05*. Norwich: University of East Anglia, School of Environmental Studies, Centre for Social and Economic Research on the Global Environment.

Alexander, D. 1993. *Natural Disasters*. London: UCL Press.

Benson, C. 1997a. "The Economic Impact of Natural Disasters in Fiji." *ODI Working Paper* 97. London: Overseas Development Institute.

Benson, C. 1997b. "The Economic Impact of Natural Disasters in Viet Nam." *ODI Working Paper* 98. London: Overseas Development Institute.

Benson, C. 1997c. "The Economic Impact of Natural Disasters in the Philippines." *ODI Working Paper* 99. London: Overseas Development Institute.

Benson, C. 1997d. "Drought and the Zimbabwe Economy 1980-93." In *A World without Famine?* Ed. H. O'Neill and J. Toye. Basingstoke: Macmillan.

Benson, C., and E. J. Clay. 1998. "The Impact of Drought on Sub-Saharan African Economies: A Preliminary Examination." *World Bank Technical Paper 401*. Washington, D.C.

Catling, H. D. 1993. *Rice in Deep Water*. London: Macmillan for IRRI.

Coburn, A., R. J. S. Spence, and A. Pomonis. 1994. *Vulnerability and Risk Assessment*. Disaster Management Training Program. 2d ed. New York and Geneva: United Nations Department of Humanitarian Affairs and United Nations Development Programme.

Drèze, J., and A. Sen. 1989. *The Political Economy of Hunger*. Oxford: Clarendon Press.

Fischer, S., and W. Easterly. 1990. "The Economics of the Government Budget Constraint." *The World Bank Research Observer* 5 (2). Washington, D.C.

Hicks, D. 1993. "An Evaluation of the Zimbabwe Drought Relief Program 1992/1993: The Roles of Household Level Response and Decentralized Decision Making." World Food Program. Harare.

IFRC. 1997. *World Disasters Report 1997* Oxford: Oxford University Press.

Munich Reinsurance. 1998. "Annual Review of Natural Catastrophes 1998." December. Munich.

SPREP/SPPO-UNDHA/EMA. 1994. *Natural Disaster Reduction in Pacific Island Countries*, Report to the World Conference on Natural Disaster Reduction, Yokohama, Japan, 23-27 May 1994. South Pacific Regional Environment Program, South Pacific Program Office, United Nations Department of Humanitarian Affairs, and Emergency Management Australia. March.

Thomson, A. 1994. "The Impact of Drought on Government Expenditure in Namibia in 1992/93." Overseas Development Institute. London.

United Nations. 1995. *Yokohama Strategy and Plan of Action for a Safer World: Guidelines for Natural Disaster Prevention, Preparedness and Mitigation*. World Conference on Natural Disaster Reduction, 23-27 May 1994. New York and Geneva: United Nations.

UNDHA/SPDRP. 1997. *The Economic Impact of Natural Disasters in the South Pacific with Special Reference to Papua New Guinea, Western Samoa and Niue*. Suva: United Nations Department for Humanitarian Affairs/South Pacific Program Office.

Wood, R. M. 1987. *Earthquakes and Volcanoes*. New York: Weidenfeld and Nicholson.

Young, S., and others. 1998. "Overview of the Eruption of Soufriere Hills Volcano, Montserrat, 18 July 1995 to December 1997." *Geophysical Research Letters* 25 (18) (September 15): 3389–92.

Chapter 2

Economic Aspects of Floods: The Case of Argentina

Héctor Sejenovich and Guillermo Cock Mendoza

Floods, Catastrophes, and the Relationship between Society and Nature

Floods are catastrophic events that take place repeatedly in many countries, among them Argentina. Ample literature reveals the concern of our society to study these events and their different categories.

Concept of Catastrophe

The concept of catastrophe is often used to mean an unexpected, significantly harmful event affecting society in general and individuals. In this sense floods are natural catastrophes affecting people and their property. However, whether these are truly "natural" events is open for discussion. In general, a certain level of flood impacts can be anticipated when natural ecosystems are modified due to human activity. For example, modifying ecosystem properties for human settlements and the production of goods may result in certain indirect negative impacts on the environment, causing the impacts of a regular/normal flooding cycle to be catastrophic to humans.

The modification of ecosystems for development is similar to manufacturing goods in that it may entail a use-waste process. Along with production of goods comes deterioration of all the elements, which generally is not factored in: deterioration of raw materials, inputs, machinery, workforce, natural conditions for production, and of energy itself, which goes from use-

ful to dissipated energy. The elements involved and their environment can withstand part of this deterioration. Another part exceeds the load capacity of those elements and generates changes in the ecological system. If these changes take place gradually, they become part of a deteriorating environment. If the changes are abrupt, they become catastrophes. In the end, both scenarios adversely affect people's quality of life.

Natural systems have extended "memories." That is, major variations are not independent of small variations but have a unique relationship. In the case of rivers it means that the major flow variations causing what we know as floods are not independent of medium and small variations, nor of the frequency of occurrences. The records of the Nile River endorse this assertion.[1] Thus, the area for which the Buenos Aires floods need to be discussed is much larger than the area of the city itself.

Thus, in the case of floods, for example, the water occupies the river basin and the floodplain that belongs to it, if we expand the forecasting horizon. In this regard the economic and social impacts generated by a flood do not constitute a catastrophic element but are a natural part of the cycle. The time of a flood's occurrence as well as its impact can be foreseen—with a certain level of randomness. Taking into account the timeframe needed to build infrastructure, there is no doubt that in that particular period a recurrent flood can be predicted. Historical analysis show us that even a certain degree of vulnerability can be appraised, as shown below.

Every productive action implies a certain measure of destruction. In the case of Buenos Aires, however, the construction of settlements and infrastructure did not take into account the deterioration of the environment resulting from production. Substantial infrastructure, which in some cases benefits from being located close to the river, was located on the floodplain without considering the river's fluctuating water levels. Neither were structural measures built to deal with the runoff.

Such settlement becomes catastrophic, and the deteriorative aspects become visible only later, when the infrastructure has generated enough economic and social interest that a change of site cannot be considered seriously. Instead, the focus becomes "controlling" the river. As we can see, the river has not been smart enough to change its behavior and accept the intrusive actions of people that reduced or eliminated its floodplain.

At the same time, the economic push toward maximum cost reduction uses nature, but does not pay its sustainability costs. The sustainable use of the basin implies certain tasks for which the market does not take responsibility.

The concepts outlined above indicate that a different assessment process of natural resources is required for a city to achieve integrated basin management and to guide land development based on its sustainability and restrictions. To be sustainable, production should be maximized in a way that minimizes deterioration. We should use the floodplain differently, with other technologies and possibly also for other purposes. In this way adequate production could be achieved while minimizing or eliminating the problems caused by flood periods. Floods would no longer have catastrophic consequences.

Cost Minimization vs. Integrated Use of the Basin

In Buenos Aires settlement of the floodplains focused exclusively on the physical space, disregarding the floodplains' function as part of the ecosystem. Multiple alternative solutions could have been chosen when constructing large buildings and infrastructure. Multiple uses of the coast would have set the foundation for substantial improvement of the quality of life of the population in a city that, within three decades, lost its beaches and its coastal area.

In general, commercial sectors use the natural resources and the habitat, but do not ensure sustainability of the habitat. Agricultural activity degrades the soil, and erosion exhausts it. Forests are not restored. Rivers and their beds are used for production, but the watershed is not managed appropriately.

In recent years some industries have begun a different process, not yet prevalent, of taking a closer look at higher energy efficiency, recycling of waste, and an ecologically more friendly management of their facilities.

Floods and the Cost of Integrated Use

No restrictions were applied in the construction of housing settlements on the floodplains. Despite the studies that were carried out to improve the conditions of some rivers, the environmental degradation could not be stopped because the whole basin became more and more populated. The urbanization of the floodplain increased the runoff of the water and caused catastrophes.

In light of this situation, when discussing the economic issues related to floods, the emphasis essentially is placed on the damages they cause. The importance of the efforts made—especially by international organizations—to improve the calculation and to integrate all the variables, is undisputed.

To improve the role of the economy in the context of the environment and flood prevention, we have to analyze the management of natural resources and habitat. To do so, we need an integrated vision of the basin that determines the cost of its management and detects the potentials and restrictions of the basin area. In this way some activities can be relocated, and others can be promoted.

Floods, Disasters, and the Concept of Society
and Nature

Scientific Links to Understand Complex Systems

Most flood-related literature analyzes floods as natural disasters. In contrast the social sciences consider floods as a social category. Neither concept is broad enough to encompass the vast complexity of the issue. Floods are actually a link between society and nature, in the same way that natural resources and environmental problems are.

It is important to understand the interactions between social activities and nature. Investment planning is done on a short-term basis and defines the production scope. To put this into perspective, let us analyze the difference between the implicit schedules of ancient and contemporary societies concerning their task organization. The Nile floods, for instance, were not actually seen as dangerous events; instead, society was organized to anticipate their occurrence, aware of their positive aspects. The modern-day perception of floods as catastrophic events is undoubtedly related to the enormous push of economic development, which, as is well known, has a productive and a destructive aspect at the same time. Lester Brown points out that human output from the 1950s to the 1990s was roughly equivalent to what humankind produced from the beginning of time until 1950.

*Consideration of Production and Destruction
in Water Basin Use*

Every economically productive action implies, in a different sense, a certain measure of destruction. The extent of the destruction may disturb the homeostatic capacity of the natural systems.

Use of space and water as raw materials for production. To use the self-cleansing capacity of a river or water stream and its tributaries implies contaminating the course to a certain extent and partly destroying the natural habitat. The extent of ecosystem deterioration will depend on the level of pollutants and the capacity of the river to cleanse itself. The same

process occurs with respect to fishing, depending on the technique used, or to navigation, depending on its intensity. Negative impacts either can be absorbed by the homeostatic capacity of the natural system or a change will occur in the system. When it can be absorbed, it can be called sustainable production.

Development and infrastructure construction (housing, industrial, and urban services). Either directly or indirectly, development of human habitat and infrastructure for living and production implies concurrent construction and destruction of the ecosystem. In most cases building human settlements does not integrate concerns for environmental degradation.

Frequently, infrastructure is sited in Buenos Aires without taking into account the river's flood area or flood recurrence. Occupation of this land "reclaimed" from the river leads to negative consequences. However, this need not be the case, as there are many examples of appropriate development of urban river courses. In those cases floods are expected from the river. There is also a rich experience with river destruction and construction and subsequent reviving of marine life, as in the case of the Thames and the Ruhr.

A common mistake is the assumption of productive criteria without analyzing their destructive aspects. For example, calculation of the gross national product (GNP) adds all production activities, without deducting the destruction they cause, a systemic miscalculation.[2] Flood damage reveals the deterioration caused by previous production of infrastructure and other human settlements.

When calculating agricultural production, land production is generally exposed in terms of tons of output per hectare without considering soil loss by erosion, nutrient balance (extraction/replacement), and/or water use indicators.

The oversimplification of considering production without taking into account the destruction and floods it causes prevents the evaluation of the appropriate and necessary changes to minimize the consequences. It also affects any cost-benefit analysis. Conservation of nature is not considered in the costs. The possibility of establishing the benefit of sustainable natural resource management is not considered. In a way the establishment of insurance policies to at least plan the occurrence of these catastrophes is solving the problem.

Integrated Use and Wasteful Use of Natural Resources

Natural resources can be used either comprehensively or only to a limited extent. In general, the use of resources is limited, resulting in immense waste of trees, fish, fruits, harvests, and energy.

The river as a developed space also reveals large waste of potential uses. This waste is not only obvious when considering all the uses that could be possible in an agricultural area. Neither does the way the river is developed in the city take into account its many possible uses for recreation, landscape, transportation, and entertainment.

The River, Floods, and Quality of Life

Natural resources are used to improve the quality of human life. But quality of life cannot be defined without the active involvement of the population in solving its environmental problems. Quality of life is an historical and ever-changing concept embedded in the culture and in the specific goals of each social group. Summarized development indicators do not incorporate the effects of development on the social structure. Currently, human development indicators have begun a positive foray on a path awaiting deeper inroads.[3]

The comprehensive management of the river is embedded in popular culture. In Buenos Aires progressive development and effacing of the river is taking away all the positive aspects the river held in the social imagery. The river, especially the de la Plata River, had a coastline that allowed recreational uses for the whole population. Its beaches were popular spots for holidays and year-round recreational activities, especially for the poor. Recreational activities also took place in the rivers and streams of the basin of the city of Buenos Aires. These opportunities contributed to

quality of life. Currently, lands reclaimed from the river, even when they are part of the social endowment, are not available for popular use except to very high-income sectors. In comparison, the concept of flood is related to fear of loss: loss of workdays, of housing and furniture, or settlement instability.

Alternatives for an Ecological, Economic, and Social Concept of Floods

Social occupation of land is geared towards short-term productivity that, in the case of river and flooding areas, leads to deterioration and waste. This focus generates negative externalities that affect nature and quality of life, and it constitutes a core cause of environmental problems. In view of these problems the population has a certain perception that generates different reactions; thus, social and environmental movements are organized. Theoretical movements are constituted to interpret these new phenomena. The State usually intervenes, establishing various policies to influence the process.

Environmental policies mainly use incentives or restrictions to improve the management of natural resources. They make possible a better accommodation of the price structure based on sustainable development. The implementation of environmental regulations should operate in the same manner to guide land occupation. It is essential to generate and disseminate environmental awareness. What are required are work in the fields of formal and nonformal education, and the involvement of all social actors to come up with appropriate alternatives within the framework of sustainable development. With these policies, it is possible to generate change to maximize the sustainable use and productivity of natural resources, and minimize degradation, waste, and misuse.

To this end it is necessary that the economy adopt a more committed plan of action. Assessing the damages and the economic and social effects of economic production is very important. By assessing not only the damages caused directly but also the overall systemic impact of damage on the economy and society, we can assess the real impact of these floods and consider the benefits of preventing them.

However, the necessary calculations should be supplemented with the comprehensive assessment of natural resources, providing a more comprehensive framework in which economics interacts with ecological and social issues to constitute a model of interaction enabling joint intervention in the management of a city's metabolism. The city constitutes a technical structure that interacts with the agricultural ecosystem and the broader natural ecosystem of which it is a part. Understanding their interactions can lead to a wide range of actions designed to handle more appropriately the physical, biotic, infrastructural, economic, social, and political factors in a city.

Patrimonial Accounts

The economic sectors in Buenos Aires use nature, but do not consider within their costs the costs to conserve nature. This is consistent with the traditional belief of the economic schools (partially changing) that assumed that nature was infinite and would reproduce itself.

We now realize that this is not so. Natural resources are finite. The capacity to absorb greenhouse gases has been largely exceeded, creating the basis for climate change. The economic sectors draw down resources and natural habitat, but do not develop activities to replenish these resources. Degradation and waste are severe. By this time reclamation of nature has become a necessity to set up a new economic sector. The objective is to create an *ecological systemic supply* to be used as sustainable raw material by the economic sectors.

To achieve this, a series of tasks need to be accomplished:
- Research natural resources and analyze their dynamics
- Research *ecological systemic relations of natural resources*
- Perform market studies to ensure product use
- Set up controls and participation of the population
- Develop activities that foster reclamation.

Expenditures on these tasks and their costs could constitute the preprimary sector aimed at the generation of such ecological systemic supply. This systemic supply would be made up of the following elements:
- Annual flow of renewable natural resources, consistent with both their quantitative and qualitative conservation
- Load capacity of water, soil, and air to absorb gaseous, solid, and liquid effluents
- Annual usage of nonrenewable resources in a proportion that can be replaced by establishing renewable resources
- Natural conditions for the placement of habitat for the population and productive activities.

How are sustainability costs calculated to achieve the development of ecological systemic supply? Through the following:
- Identification of reasonably homogeneous units (a forest, grasslands, a river) working as *natural mills*. These mills are designed to produce many products but carry a production cost. This production cost is the management cost. Considering all the natural resources that can be used, the comprehensive management cost is taken into account. The Input Product Matrix can be used as a methodological instrument, renamed by us as the Natural Resources Intersectoral Relations Matrix. For each resource the total cost of management is divided by the ecological systemic production expressed in the measurement unit corresponding to the type of resource. This will yield the unit management cost. On the basis of this unit cost and knowledge of the total physical inventory of each resource, we multiply by the unit cost to obtain the value of natural resources supplies measured against sustainability cost.

From there, we apply the patrimonial accounts scheme. As does any account, it has debits and credits. We quantify the value of the supplies of a single resource and of the overall resources on the debit side. We record all the increases leading to an increase of the initial wealth during one year. On the debit side we record all losses. The main increases refer to the growth of trees and plants. The main item in the debit side is the withdrawal. Applying the sustainable development principles, the same rate of growth should be drawn. In that case the natural capital would be maintained. It would be as if an amount of money were deposited in the bank earning interest, and only the interest earnings were withdrawn. On the basis of the knowledge of how the ecological area operates, it is possible to draw alternative scenarios to evaluate the ecological, economic, and social impacts of different management alternatives. For that evaluation we require the use of *Regional Basins*.

• The economic regional accounts allow recording the evolution of the different productive sectors and also inferring the social impacts that eventually will be generated in light of the different natural resource management alternatives. Very frequently, to achieve the maximal benefit in the short term, a greater proportion than the capacity of regeneration is used, or industries exceed the load capacity of water, soil, and air, generating degrading processes. These approaches result in higher profits in the short term, but reduce the natural capital, jeopardizing future income. The sustainable management of natural resources makes it possible, in many cases even in the short term, for sustainable management to compete with squandering management.

Ecozones of the City

Ecological areas are reasonably homogeneous areas that can be seen as natural factories. Their operation requires quantitative and qualitative sustainability. The goal of these factories is to generate maximum sustainable supply. A city's goal is to operate the natural and infrastructural elements to provide an adequate quality of life for the population and adequate conditions for the productive activities.

Which is the ecological area of the city? What is its relationship with the area of its administrative jurisdiction? To analyze the city, we should ideally regard it as an area in which significant processes are trying to make the city ecologically sustainable. However, strict observance of this principle would cause many problems due to the spatial ambiguity and heterogeneity it encompasses. Productive activities of human

settlements in a city create multiple strong flows that often spill over into urban sprawl. In this regard the basins and sub-basins on which the urban sprawl has an impact should be reviewed frequently. Naturally, this decision depends on the type of natural space and the ecological system in question. But, in principle, the basin scheme can serve for the analysis of the city territory.

In special cases the first discriminatory criterion should be taken into account, since the main objective should be to focus on all major city processes. For example, if there were a factory outside the basin whose discharges reach the city and definitely pollute the watercourse, this facility should be taken into account. But in other cases, the difficulties of analysis and of action are much greater. For instance, emission of gases generated by a city, especially cities in which heavy industrial activity is concentrated, may necessitate the study of very broad territories. A similar broad study would be required to consider the place where the raw materials required by the city's industries are generated. These flows are of great interest, but specific studies should be undertaken in this regard.

Ecozones of the Autonomous City of Buenos Aires

An ecological "study area" to analyze, describe, and design actions and policies aimed at overcoming environmental degradation, particularly floods, brings to the fore once again the traditional issues between the land area of the water basins and the area covering the political and administrative jurisdiction. Studies of floods in the City of Buenos Aires seldom incorporate the city's tributary water basins. Thus, the analytical model excludes key aspects both in considering the problems and in their solution.

Similarly, problems are described in the environmental analysis of the city without systemic consideration of the existing ecological relations in the overall territory in which the city's significant problems are expressed. To understand all the phenomena, especially floods, the scope of such studies should include the entire ecological area.

The Autonomous City of Buenos Aires plus the 19 municipalities of the Buenos Aires Province form a functional unit known as the Buenos Aires Metropolitan Area (BAMA), to which 6 additional municipalities of the same province also contribute. The indiscriminate occupation of land and the changes of the runoff guidelines for the water basins and rainwater absorption have contributed to the growing problems. To analyze environmental problems in general, and flooding issues in particular, we need to include the land covered by the above units.

Water Basin Ecozone in the City of Buenos Aires

Characteristics. This area consists of the basins of the Matanza-Riachuelo Rivers, the Reconquista River basin, and the basins located in the City of Buenos Aires. According to the 1991 Census, the area comprises 4,110 km2, and a population of 9,050,000. These are flat-land rivers with little gradient and are highly polluted due to the discharge of industrial effluents and wastewater, mainly untreated, in the upper part of the ecological area.

Overall ecological area output and flood-related output. The main output of this ecological area is to guarantee a habitat adequate for human life and for production. Given the characteristics of this work, the emphasis is placed on the floods caused by tributary rivers of the de la Plata River along the coastline of the City of Buenos Aires.

To reaffirm the comprehensive consideration of the phenomena occurring in all the major city areas and its tributary basins, it should be stressed that the simple study of water flows may show the need for a joint analysis of the basins as essential to include both the current operation as well as the proposals for change. It should also be recalled that in recent years, although with major difficulties, the systemic relations of other features of the city and its surroundings have been strengthened. Generally, the city is taking into account environmental issues, but as separate aspects. Global studies have yet to be consolidated.

The treatment of the interactions requires two correlated procedures: to delve further into aspects and specific functions taking place in certain sections of the analyzed ecological area, and to maintain the interrelationships held by each of these areas. This requires constructing three subecological areas and indicating the differential outputs and externalities that each one grants or receives from others.

Floods and Environmental Problems of the Autonomous City of Buenos Aires

Floods in the City of Buenos Aires and its environmental problems have long been debated. However, economic evaluation and analysis of the interrelationships throughout the city have been very limited. We would like to stress the fact that "in the indiscriminate occupation of land and the changes of the runoff guidelines in the water basins and rainwater absorption," the rainfall, geomorphology, hydrology, and topography (with above sea level ranging from 4 to 24 meters) were not taken into account. This is a fact that "has given way to growing flood-generated problems," affecting extensive areas of the city. These problems are "aggravated by the pollution of waters originating from the Greater Buenos Aires municipalities" (due to the run-off of agricultural chemicals used in agricultural activities and to fluid effluents discharged by industrial plants) "and by the degradation of the coastlines and of de la Plata River waters, whose negative comprehensive impacts have not yet been studied."[4]

It should be noted that the areas recording greater frequency of floods, generally are very poor.

Albini and Costa (1988) developed an economic and social evaluation of great importance. They point out the unfavorable conditions created by the location of the city with respect to the surface runoff toward the de la Plata River. This runoff should have been subject to mitigation through an adequate drainage system. The current system was originated during the construction of the "450 km network constructed in the period 1925-1939," encompassing the city and part of the compound that operates as a tributary. The network was "planned under the assumption of an open structure city," with a significant density of permeable green spaces that would enable the infiltration of part of the rainfall. Since the inauguration of those works, the system has not been enlarged, despite the fact that since 1939 the population almost quadrupled from little more than 3 million to almost 11 million people.

The paving of natural drainage areas in the Municipalities constituting the Greater Buenos Aires also increased the frequency and the level of floods. The city became an impermeable unit with negligible or no capacity for infiltration of water, which concentrates in the lower and flood-prone areas. The "coastal landfills in the de la Plata River caused the disappearance of the reinforced coast, affecting the runoff of the emitting channels of the drainage network," which now end in trenches of nonconsolidated banks.

Federovisky (1985) states that

> the degree of urbanization in the tributary areas of the city streams led to an important increase in the volumes to be drained during periods of major rainfalls, for which the original infrastructure was not ready. The cleaning and maintenance system of 27, 000 storm drains and an 8 km duct was privatized. State control on the companies' efficiency is very weak....

due to short supply of staff at the City Water Authority.

Hilda Herzer and Raquel Gurevich (1996) raised a series of questions that we consider appropriate for the purpose of the evaluation:

• What is urban environmental deterioration?
• What scale is required to analyze urban deterioration processes?
• Is the urban area enough as a unit of analysis?
• Is it necessary to incorporate the region affected by environmental degradation?
• How is disaster related to urban environmental deterioration?
• What social stakeholders are involved in the deterioration and disaster processes?
• How are relationships between urban environment and disaster in central and suburban areas of a city revealed?

In reflecting on the floods occurring in the Buenos Aires Metropolitan Area, those authors identify as triggers "the rains associated with the inadequate sanitary and sewerage infrastructure," and the expanding area waterproofed by paving and development. The shantytowns of Greater Buenos Aires yielded results of major importance for their work. These shantytowns have the lowest indexes of health and schooling, thus verifying the highly significant relation between urban poverty and vulnerability to disasters.

Albini and Costa (1988) analyze the problem of "floods in the Buenos Aires Metropolitan Area, assuming that it covers an area of some 7,000 km2." Until the second half of the 1980s a fourth of the area was occupied by the urban network. The technical, social, and urban approaches to these problems focused on reviewing the negative impacts caused by 308 mm (one foot) of rainfall that fell in just 25 hours between May 31 and June 1, 1985. That rain necessitated the evacuation of approximately 100,000 people, damaged 2,500 dwellings and 14,000 automobiles, and affected the supply of drinking water, electric energy, and other services, in addition to a tragic number of victims and of large losses caused to public and private companies. "Since 1939 the drainage network remained practically without change," Albini and Costa say. But the change of land uses (increased construction of dwellings, paving, establishment of industries), both in the city and of the tributary basin areas of the Buenos Aires Province have continued without interruption until today.

Federovisky and Albini and Costa emphasize that "the industrial and derived wastes discharged in the drains entailed disasters that caused water degradation and the elimination of plant and animal life."

The 1985 flood gave rise to the spontaneous organization of victims in Flood Victim Boards, or their active involvement in existing Neighborhood Councils and Development Societies. Numerous public meetings led to a protest march to the Government House, the National Congress, and the Buenos Aires Province Office. There the marchers submitted proposals for a final solution to river floods and rejected the palliative measures provided by the Government.

During the last two decades "a large number of stations were deactivated, instead of being modernized and incorporated to a systematic registry network." These stations were responsible for the updated maintenance "of rainfall information." This, however, does not justify the delay in the implementation of measures aimed at overcoming flood-related problems.

In the Greater Buenos Aires Area rainwater is discharged into the de la Plata River and in the Matanza, Riachuelo, and Reconquista Rivers. Given their water profiles, we can conclude that during flooding, they act as water lids to the discharge of network waters, the opposing masses of water that hinder the release of rainwater. Storm drains were extended through trenches and bays lacking consolidated banks, of limited depth, and insufficiently dredged.

On the other hand, the lack of maintenance of storm drains, which should be carried out by the city garbage collection concessionary companies, contributes to a "significant reduction of the absorption capacity and evacuation of the drainage network." This is apparent upon observation of the patterns of the storm drains in the vicinity of major commercial centers. There is a high generation of garbage and no environmental education of the population (both from the operators of commercial booths and customers).

Gabriel Dupuy points out (1984) that "all the economic and social events of the city are absent in the dimensioning calculations" applicable to a network and to the overall urban infrastructure. He adds that "the economic dimension implies relating the cost of installing or expanding a network, with the social cost of not building it."

Albini and Costa analyze the urban sprawl or area affected by the floods that occurred in 1967 and 1985 in the City of Buenos Aires. They point out that around 30 percent of the affected population are living marginally and concentrated in the topographically low areas. The authors assert that "there are no natural disasters, but social situations of high vulnerability" and that the floods of 1985 in the municipalities surrounding the city can be classified as "poverty floods."

Albini and Costa conclude that water degradation results from the following:

- Industries discharge untreated effluents into rivers, streams, and drainage network.
- Shantytowns built on the flood-prone banks pollute the water sewage.
- Infrastructure to prevent floods does not exist.
- Installation of sewage ducts and drinking water supply in various municipalities of Greater Buenos Aires is deficient.
- Infrastructure, for example, massive highways, has expanded flood-prone areas.

The authors point out possible solutions:

- "Channeling all the river courses that directly or indirectly drain their waters in the de la Plata River."
- "Developing a massive and intense environmental education campaign" aimed at minimizing solid and liquid waste in river courses; "supplementing that education with effective and efficient policies concerning the control" to avoid the degradation of water in those river courses.

It is noteworthy that Law No. 2,797 was passed in September 1891, through which industrial plants were forbidden to discharge untreated hazardous waste, but a jurisdictional dispute between the Municipality of the City of Buenos Aires and the National Executive Branch rendered it ineffective to remedy the problem.

- Develop "environmental land regulation," that would relocate the dwellings in flood-prone or degradable areas, as well as reforest or enhance green areas.
- "Construct the necessary infrastructure to overcome the problems related to wastewater disposal, drinking water supply, sewerage pipes, and cost consolidation."

Finally, Albini and Costa develop an economic evaluation of the damages generated by the flood of 1985 on the basis of the expenditures made to pay for the damages.

Conclusions and Recommendations

- The economic aspects of floods are of fundamental importance. When considering them, it is necessary to incorporate the damages generated within a comprehensive framework such as evaluating ways to manage the city to reduce flood damage. From the analysis of the studies, it could be stated that the city and its surroundings could function as a "natural factory" that ensures sustainable natural and infrastructure conditions and social relations to generate a habitat appropriate to human life and to production.

- The literature reviewed suggests that to date few economic evaluations have been made in Argentina.

- The economic analyses that have been carried out are partial and excessively focused on the evaluation of damages. Actions taken to remedy the damage clearly are palliatives that do not attack the causes of the problem.

- We propose an economic evaluation that is closely integrated with an ecological and social analysis to demonstrate more clearly the interdependence of productive activities with one another and with the created bases.

- Evaluation of damages and permanent remedies can be achieved only when we consider the city not as a separate compartment but as an indivisible part of an ecological area. Comprehensive management of the ecological area is indispensable for a permanent solution.

- A more permanent solution to reduce floods requires that the City Government regulate new developments on the de la Plata River; that the current concessionaires carry out the necessary investments for the construction of works to consolidate the coast; and that adequate duct drainage, whose functions have been deteriorated by river development, will be reestablished.

- The riverbank should be structured as a recreation area with unrestricted access.

- The works underway to minimize flood damages should be part of an environmental management plan of the territory.

- The prior statement requires planning and actions agreed on by the political-administrative jurisdictions.

- The involvement of social sectors should not be considered as an additional requirement, but these sectors should be involved from the beginning. Grassroots organization should be encouraged to carry out activities aimed at reducing environmental damages. National universities, research centers, and nongovernmental organizations, with the authorities of the city and the province and the social organizations, should form a partnership that enables real consensus in changing the environmental conditions of the population. Within this organization, the development of flood contingency plans should be proposed.

Notes

1. J. Hurst, an English geophysicist, studied the water level variations of the Nile and found this unique time pattern that served as a basis for the development of the illustration of 1/f systems in nature.

2. The gross national product is a macroeconomic measure resulting from the sum of all the productive activities of a country in one year. In the text, when we refer to the methodology assumed to compute GNP, we refer to the "core" of the accounts. The new version of the National Accounts methodology includes an environmental "satellite account."

3. This area is formed by the continental surface that is part of the Greater Buenos Aires Metropolitan Area and by surfaces of islands and the water of the de la Plata River. The Greater Buenos Aires Metropolitan Area is made up of the city of Buenos Aires and 19 municipalities, comprising a total land area of 3,680 km2, in addition to 6 other municipalities that have a portion of their areas in the metropolitan area.

4. Studies carried out in 1997 by Aguas Argentinas, OSBA, Instituto de Limnología R. Ringuelet, and Servicio de Hidrografía Naval determined that the water quality of the southern coastal strip of the river is standard and that the quality is not appropriate for direct contact up to 500 meters from the coastline.

References

Editors' note: Full data not available by print date.

Chapter 3
Floods in Buenos Aires: Learning from the Past

Hilda María Herzer and Nora Clichevsky

Cities are the historical result of the interaction between nature and human activities. A flood-prone area is the manifestation of this relationship and of the conflicts among different areas and socioeconomic groups over time. Urban floods severely disrupt the daily life of the population and necessitate exceptional expenditures to return to normal conditions.

Social Causes of Floods

The objective of this chapter is, first, to investigate"how the flood risk in Buenos Aires is socially constructed. Second, we want to examine how the social structure continuously generates the framework in which, during the occurrence of a natural phenomenon, the hazard (intense rains in a given period of time) occurs.

Vulnerability plays a preponderant role in this social structure. The activities and aspects of the community and/or characteristics of the people that can increase the harm caused by certain threats will be discussed.[1] The vulnerability of people depends on age, sex, health conditions, and how society treats its members or different social groups. Vulnerability also depends on the quality and location of buildings, on land use, on the status of the infrastructure and services, and on lifestyles and political authority or government. Regarding the last two, vulnerability depends on the ethical, legal, and political frameworks in which a society develops. Vulnerability describes a potential

situation. It is precisely this vulnerability that combines with floods to produce disaster.

Description of the Area

From the topographical standpoint, the City of Buenos Aires and its suburbs are located in a periphery of the Undulated Grasslands, characterized by its limited slope toward the Rio de la Plata. The area was originally furrowed by small watercourses that drain in the de la Plata or in the two most important bodies of water in the area, Reconquista and Matanza-Riachuelo. All of them have the special characteristics of a plain region: short courses with little permanent flow, irregular routes, and broad flood valleys. As with every river, whatever happens in the low basin, that is, in the City of Buenos Aires, is also the result of what is caused upstream.

The layout of the watercourses defines flood-prone areas, flooding those tributary areas of piped streams: Maldonado (covering 5,050 hectares in Buenos Aires and 10,984 in total); Medrano, (covering 2,050 ha in Buenos Aires and 4,600 in total); White; Vega (covering 1,777 ha); and Cildáñez. Four of the important basins that pass through the city—Riachuelo, Cildáñez, Maldonado, and Medrano streams—have their river heads in the province of Buenos Aires, in the municipalities of Vincente López, San Martín, La Matanza, Morón and Tres de Febrero, and receive water in the municipalities of the Buenos Aires Metropolitan Area (BAMA), through them or their tributaries. As a result, the type of occupation of the land has an impact on the floods that occur in the City of Buenos Aires.

Cause of Floods

In recent decades Buenos Aires has been flooded at least twice a year (table 1). These floods are due to two causes: the condition of the drainage network, and strong winds from the southeast, *sudestadas*, which produce a rise of the de la Plata River high above its average. Its waters spill over the land, flooding the coastal areas, with greatest impact on the La Boca and Barracas neighborhoods (the southern area), which are inhabited by the poor.[2] The most dramatic recent flood happened in May 1985.

The city is constructed on a complex drainage system that discharges into the de la Plata River. These drainages, together with the drinking water supply network, were planned in two stages: the first one (1869) aimed at resolving the drainage of the central area, called the old radius. The second corresponds to the works for the new radius, which were planned in 1919 and were completed in 1953. Calculated for a population of 800,000, they solved the flooding problem until suddenly the urban population grew to an unexpected extent. This urban growth was not accompanied by adequate provision and maintenance of infrastructure, such as rain drainages, and confronted the city with immense urban problems.[3]

Apart from the central area of Buenos Aires, there are two other areas: one that is tributary of the Buenos Aires basins, and one that is not. With respect to the first one, in recent decades its high water contribution has disturbed the situation in Buenos Aires. In general the nontributary area lacks a rain drainage network, and only 22 percent of the population has this service.

The increased population densification of the city and its suburbs has to be seen in close relation to the floods.[4] The urban structure changed completely between 1895 and 1914. During the intense immigration that ended in 1930, a process of residential dispersion, redistribution of the population, and increased agglomeration, took place.[5] Between 1904 and 1909 some immigrants moved toward the suburbs, which gave them access to real estate and a place in the middle class. Through this suburbanization the neighborhoods that toward the turn of the century made up the new radius grew and were built based on the design of the new drainage network (Flores, Belgrano, La Paternal, and Chacarita. These neighborhoods are partially located in the basins of the Maldonado, Vega, and Medrano piped streams).

Two mechanisms enabled this suburbanization: "the extension of urban transportation with the almost complete electrification of the streetcar system which started in 1858, and the sale of lots in installments in new urban areas that extended gradually as the transportation networks advanced."[6] These mechanisms explain the progressive population density of the areas far from the city's downtown.

The main mechanism that facilitated the suburbanization of 1895-1914 was access to urban property by immigrants, who began to be integrated into the middle classes, and by incipient industrial employers.[7] In 1947 a new suburbanization period began. The 1914 crown of periurban neighborhoods (located on the basins of piped streams) had stopped being "suburbs" by 1947. The growth of new peripheral municipalities in the Buenos Aires Metropolitan Area transformed the City of Buenos Aires into what can be considered the central nucleus of the metropolitan agglomeration.

Between 1947 and 1960 the homeowners in the suburbs increased dramatically from 43 percent to 67 percent of the whole population living in the Buenos Aires Metropolitan Area. This was due, basically, to the potential facilitated by official credit plans of having access to housing ownership or to lots. In tandem, the densification of the central areas took place, a process that was facilitated by the approval of Law 13,512 on horizontal property (1952).

In the suburbanization period after 1947 Buenos Aires expanded its perimeter—through operations

Table 1 Floods in the City of Buenos Aires

Number	Date	Flooded neighborhoods
1	April 22, 1928	Saavedra-Belgrano-Nuñez-Va.Crespo-Palermo-La Boca-Barracas
2	February 27, 1930	Saavedra-Belgrano-Nuñez-Va.Crespo-Palermo-La Boca-Barracas
3	April 16, 1940	La Boca-Barracas and riverside areas
4	April 15, 1959	La Boca-Barracas and riverside areas
5	April 6, 1962	Saavedra-Belgrano-Nuñez-Va.Crespo-Palermo
6	December 19, 1969	La Boca-Barracas and riverside areas
7	January 25, 1974	Boca-Barracas-Va. Lugano-Riverside areas
8	January 26, 1985	Va. Crespo-Palermo-Saavedra-Belgrano-Va-Urquiza-Nuñez-Chacarita-Boca-Barracas-Va Lugano and riverside areas
9	May 31, 1985	Va. Crespo-Palermo-Saavedra-Belgrano-Va-Urquiza-Nuñez-Chacarita-Boca-Barracas-Va Lugano and riverside areas
10	June 28, 1985	Barrio Norte-Almagro-Barracas-Villa Crespo
11	November 14, 1985	Barracas-Boca-Villa Lugano-Saavedra
12	October 4, 1986	
13	March 23, 1987	Saavedra-Nuñez-Belgrano-Palermo-Va.Crespo-Chacarita-Boca-Barracas
14	March 25, 1988	Mataderos-Retiro-P.Patricios-Palermo-Saavedra-Belgrano-Boca-Barracas
15	April 8, 1989	Saavedra-Retiro-Palermo-Va. Crespo-Nuñez-Belgrano-Boca- Barracas
16	August 20, 1989	Retiro-La Boca-Palermo-Barracas-Nuñez-Belgrano-Pompeya
17	October 9, 1989	Saavedra-Palermo-Nuñez
18	November 11, 1989	La Boca-Palermo-Barracas-Belgrano-Nuñez-Saavedra and Retiro
19	December 16, 1989	Retiro-Liniers-Va. Urquiza-Saavedra-Barracas
20	February 2, 1990	Palermo-Belgrano-La Boca
21	February 24, 1990	La Boca-Barracas-Belgrano-Palermo
22	April 15, 1990	Va. Crespo-Palermo-Saavedra-Belgrano-Barracas-Boca
23	September 7, 1990	Barracas-La Boca
24	November 20, 1990	Barracas-La Boca
25	January 30, 1991	Palermo-Va. Crespo
26	October 22, 1991	Va. Crespo-Ba. River-Palermo-Almagro-Barracas-La Boca-Va. Lugano
27	January 2, 1992	Congreso-Palermo-Boedo-Caballito-Belgrano-Liniers-Va. Lugano
28	May 7, 1992	Va. Crespo-Chacarita-Belgrano-Palermo-La Boca-Barracas
29	June 15, 1992	La Boca-Barracas-Palermo-Va. Crespo-Belgrano
30	February 7, 1993	Nuñez-La Boca-Barracas
31	February 20, 1993	Boca-Barracas
32	April 3, 1993	La Boca-Barracas-Palermo
33	June 7, 1993	Saavedra-Boca-Barracas
34	March 15, 1994	Saavedra-Nuñez-Belgrano-Palermo-La Boca-Barracas
35	April 5, 1994	La Boca-Barracas-Belgrano-Palermo
36	December 13, 1994	Saavedra
37	March 31, 1995	Boca-Barracas-Palermo
38	April 14, 1996	Belgrano-Va. Urquiza
39	March 20 , 1997	Palermo-Boedo-Caballito-Flores-Va-Devoto-Liniers
40	April 24 , 1997	La Boca-Paternal
41	May 18 , 1997	La Boca-Palermo-Belgrano-Retiro
42	December 26, 1997	Saavedra-Palermo-Belgrano-La Boca-Barracas
43	February 6, 1998	Palermo-Belgrano-Va. Urquiza-Nuñez-La Boca
44	March 10, 1998	La Boca-Palermo-Nuñez

Sources: Desinventar, Inventory of Disasters in Argentina 1988-1998. Prepared by the authors based on periodical publications.

within the framework of the land and housing market and through illegal occupations. From 1960 to 1970 there was a greater spatial concentration of the population, both in central areas with better living conditions and in the most deficient areas in the suburbs. In this process periurban areas classified as "maximum registered flood" were occupied. These areas usually coincided with areas whose rain drainages were inefficient and with numerous homes lacking basic infrastructure. At the same time the infrastructure serving the central nucleus of the city became inefficient.

Urban policies and planning did not take into account the growing population. As a result within 20 years the designs for carrying out works were obsolete.

Once the low areas of the city were cleaned up, they were rapidly urbanized and became high-density areas. These low areas included the Belgrano, Núñez, Palermo, and Villa Crespo neighborhoods; the areas close to Riachuelo; and the Lugano developments. The planned safety margins were not kept. Thus, these areas are true hazard areas. Each new rainfall of certain intensity increases the vulnerability of Buenos Aires considerably.

In the 1970s the amounts earmarked for investment and maintenance of the urban infrastructure plummeted. From 1970 to 1980 the annual average investment throughout the country was almost US$350 million per year. In the following decade investment was cut to US $130 million and registered just US$69.9 million in investments in the sector by 1989. In practice, through this policy preventive actions were abandoned, while the utilities limited themselves to acting only during emergencies.

From 1985 to March 1998 Buenos Aires was flooded 26 times. The successive floods show the degree of vulnerability in which a population of more than 10 million inhabitants lives: 35 percent of the country's population—or almost 50 percent of its urban population (= 5 million—are supplied with a service originally planned for a medium- to low-density city.

With regard to the City of Buenos Aires (4.5 million inhabitants) two elements were not taken into account in the design of sanitation works in general, and of rain drainage in particular. First, the popula-

tion in the suburbs grew by nearly 700 percent: from 117,763 inhabitants in 1895 to 1,741,338 in 1947, to 3,772,411 in 1960, to 7,926,379 in 1991. This urbanization led to currently 48.4 percent of the surface of the metropolitan area (134,416 ha) being considered "densely populated."

Second, some supplementary works were not carried out, for example, the spillway channels of the piped streams. Their absence partly explains the recurrent floods that occur in certain basins of the Federal Capital (Maldonado, Vega, and Medrano). The obsolescence of the drainage network is also due to a lack of maintenance. It persists despite the fact that until 1992 the city government had a contract with the former Obras Sanitarias de la Nación—today Aguas Argentinas—and now contracted privatized companies.

It could be inferred that the appearance of serious floods in Buenos Aires is in close relation to the changes experienced in the suburbs. Urbanization and the lack of a settlement policy for low-income population, combined with the elimination of absorptive surfaces of the tributary areas (occupation of green spaces, paving of streets and around buildings), made the BAMA vulnerable.[8] This urbanization occurs in the manmade areas of the municipalities of the Buenos Aires Metropolitan Area in which the headwaters of the basins of the City of Buenos Aires (Maldonado, Cildáñez, and Medrano) are located.

Global paving of the federal district, together with the almost complete elimination of cobblestone paving in the city, eliminated the retention capacity of the soil and increased the speed of surface and fluvial runoff. The paving level conceals the characteristic accidents of the land, resulting in only 5 percent to 10 percent of fallen water's entering the soil through infiltration. In 1990 the city had only 80 unpaved blocks, with green spaces reduced to only 5 percent. Given the intensive use and inadequate maintenance, it is widely believed that even those green spaces are rainproof. In addition, the woodlands of the city, except in some neighborhoods, diminished in recent decades, and have begun to increase again for only a few years. Thus, the majority of the 500,000 trees in the city are too young to give significant foliage to slow rainfall and enable it to soak into the soil. Flood processes are worsened in some neighborhoods due to the elimination of curbs and ditches and the increased level of the streets.[9]

Landfill and occupation of coastal areas have been extensive. The city has been encroaching on the de la Plata River. Recently, a strip was filled with land reclaimed from the river for commercial uses; the outlets are through ditches.

More than the construction density of the city, the population became very mobile. This has increased consumption and the quantity of waste deposited in Buenos Aires. Average household waste is estimated to have increased by 50 percent in recent decades to 1.386 kg/person/day.[10] Inadequate cleaning of city streets, added to the population's habit of depositing waste directly on the street instead of on high sites or in special receptacles, increases the possibility of blockage of storm drains and floods from low-intensity precipitation.[11]

This set of causal processes means that there are few water-retention mechanisms. Consequently, the drained volume that has to be pumped out is almost the same or greater than the fallen water, which in turn finds restrictions in its journey and comes to the surface, causing floods.

State Regulations on Land Occupation

The State's intervention in the implementation of construction regulations for the private sector has been limited. It has not taken into account the flood risk in the City of Buenos Aires, nor in the municipalities belonging to the BAMA of the Buenos Aires province (Vincente López, San Martín, La Matanza, Morón, and Tres de Febrero). These will serve as examples in view of the fact that the basins of the Medrano, Maldonado, and Cildáñez streams originate there.

Drawings of the City of Buenos Aires
from the Beginning of the Century to Date

Since the plan prepared by Bouvard in 1909, the topography has not been taken into account in defining land use standards. Neither have the existence of the basins and the possibilities of floods due to overflows. The first important instrument that guided public investments was the Aesthetics Plan for the City of Buenos Aires, prepared by the Construction Aesthetics Commission.

The Code of 1925 defines densities and forms of patio construction—without establishing density differentials according to the topography of the city. The plan's proposals were to "reconquer" the river; complete the North and South crossways and Avenida Santa Fe; improve the Barrio Sur; Plaza de Mayo or Government Plaza; and create neighborhoods for the "working class."

The Municipality was to develop projects in low-income areas where the population accepts technologies of "more modern and practical application." Concern over improving the suburbs was indicated in the requirement for tree planting and enclosures of uncultivated land, with the imposition of stiff fines on nonwooded land.

In 1937-1938, in collaboration with Argentine specialists, Le Corbusier prepared a plan that was never implemented but has been an important ideological prop for subsequent planning developments.[12] The plan envisioned a city without the problems that Buenos Aires already had in those years and that persist to date.[13] Le Corbusier centered his analysis on the lack of solarization; the housing deficiency in the central areas; the displacement of residential areas toward the periphery, increasing travel time to the workplace; and the deterioration of both public and private administrative areas. Floods were not on his agenda.[14]

> The 1856 drawing shows a covered surface comprising 6 km[2]; in 1931 (75 years later) this constructed surface comprised 190 km[2], that is *thirty times* bigger. Just imagine a normal individual whose height is 1.75 m evolving into one with a height of 52 m, whose circulatory system remains the same, and whose essential organs remain grouped into the same region that corresponded to the 1.75 m individual....
>
> —*Le Corbusier Plan*[15]

Building Code, 1944-77

Toward the end of the 1930s the need to regulate city construction from purpose to implementation was brought to the fore when Buenos Aires offered living conditions below socially accepted guidelines for a city of over 2 million people. Both the national and the municipal authorities, as well as private organizations of professionals in the construction industry and the city, were aware of this. The idea of preparing a single instrument that would change even municipal provisions on restrictions to private ownership took form with the creation of the Building Code Commission. Public and private agencies involved in construction or its regulation and inspection participated in these decisions. The city's population had no right to participate in the decisionmaking. Technicians imposed the model for the city and its construction.

The main objective of the Building Code was to serve as a regulatory instrument for construction in the city. The bases of the third edition of the Code (1959) are very clear: "Legislation is the result of community life and, in a certain way, the purpose for future relations among people. The city is the highest example of community life, requiring, for biological reasons, regulated behavior to make living together possible."[16]

The guidelines for the development of the Code were collective social welfare, hygiene, health, and safety. The city was seen as a biological organism, completely independent of the social entity per se. The hygienist principles had originated during the industrial revolution. The zoning principles are present in different sections of the code. They have morphologically defined important areas of the city since the Code was implemented in 1944.[17]

The Building Code puts some order into the different construction uses, forms, masses, and heights. Thus, it corrects the drawbacks produced by the excess human density and contributes to improve living conditions in the city."[18]

With respect to zoning, the Code refers to the uses allowed in each area and strengthens the already existing uses. Maximum heights based on the widths of streets and land occupation possibilities overlap with this zoning, without taking into account the formal result or the population that the city could support if the Code were fully utilized. Later studies determined that the most advantageous use of the Code would apply to a city of 20 million inhabitants.

In spite of these characteristics of uses, allowed heights, and land use, the regulations on the works were inspired by building aesthetics. Toward the end of the 1960s the Code underwent a series of modifications. One of the most important changes refers to the possibility of tower building construction in the Belgrano neighborhood, as well as the mandatory construction of underground garages in horizontal property buildings. The impact both types of construction would have in the flood-prone areas of the city were not taken into account, especially in the Vega stream basin, an area in which an important number of tower buildings have been constructed. Neither did the modifications to the Code take into account the floods of 1959 and 1962.

No reference was ever made to the topography, nor to the characteristics of the land or the problems caused by floods in the area.

The Building Code regulated construction in the City of Buenos Aires from 1944 to 1977, when the Planning Code and the new Construction Code were implemented. The Building Code has had more direct influence on the city as a whole, particularly on the area of study.

The Code left it up to the land market to decide when and how to build. Horizontal property law regulations and the different periods in which housing credits have been instituted defined a construction typology whose results were quite damaging. The Code totally ignored flood-prone areas, even though there was full awareness of the floods at that time. The drainage works plan for the old radius was planned in 1869, and those for the new radius in 1919, as mentioned above.

Master Plan, 1958

From 1958 to 1960 the Master Plan for the City of Buenos Aires was prepared by a group of technicians from different disciplines. This exercise coincided with the worldwide development of urban and regional planning, at a time when all efforts based exclusively on the action of urban planners to diminish the urban problems had already failed.[19]

At the metropolitan level the main proposals were rationalization of density and occupation; banning occupation of flood-prone lands; controlling housing developments; regrouping industries; regulating coastal areas; constructing coastal and central highways; and coordinating all public works.

At the urban level the main proposals were to achieve a more balanced distribution of the population; equilibrium of the southern and northern areas; division of the city into planning units based on land use, density and social fabric; urban remodeling of the Alte. Brown, and Catalinas Sur and Norte areas; urban renewal of La Boca, Chacra Saavedra, Plaza Las Heras, Arsenal Esteban de Luca, and the Agronomía neighborhood; reorganization of the subway and the railways; and construction of incineration plants.

The proposal suggested high residential and commercial densities for some of the flood-prone areas, with an important subcenter in the city at Cabildo and Juramento in the Belgrano neighborhood. In other words it did not bear in mind the existing topography either, although the latter appears to have been studied during the analysis of existing conditions. The proposal did not take into account the previous floods, especially the floods that took place at the same time (1959) the studies for the preparation of the Master Plan were undertaken.

Planning Code of the Municipality of Buenos Aires, 1977

The Planning Code of the Municipality of Buenos Aires of 1977 was prepared by the municipal authorities.[20] It constituted an important modification on the use and occupation standards defined by the Building Code of the City of Buenos Aires before 1977. The most important instruments were

• Reduction of the FOT in relation to the Building Code, especially in residential areas where the FOT was specifically between 1 and 3.5

• Execution of a highway network extending 117 km
• Creation of recreational parks.

The 1977 Planning Code did not take into account the topography, the flood-prone areas in zoning delimitation, or the FOT. But since these instruments were quite restrictive with respect to construction in the highlands, exceptions to them have been very frequent since their approval.[21]

Starting in 1983, urban planning was oriented around the following principles: (1) to focus only on particular areas of the city, not on the whole metropolitan area; (2) to plan toward the economic recovery of Buenos Aires; (3) to make flexible standards for the private sector, which meant modifying the Planning Code, (4) incorporating public participation; and (5) developing cooperation between the public and the private sector.

There was no global plan for the BAMA or for the City of Buenos Aires, with the fundamental actions being modifications to the Planning Code of 1977, and implementation of specific projects. In 1989 the Code was made more flexible.[22] In practice the flexibility of the Code has meant setting up special standards for those who have greater economic power and/or greater quantities of land. For example, owners of more than 2,500 square meters of land can request individual standards.

The modified Code changed the construction dynamics of the city, without considering environmental impacts. For instance, the increase in density clogged the infrastructure without prior study of the capacity of the running water, sewerage, and rainwater systems and of the impact on the historically flood-prone areas of the city.[23]

Urban Planning in the Municipalities of the Buenos Aires Metropolitan Area from Mid-Century to Present

In the municipalities that have traditionally been part of the Buenos Aires Metropolitan Area, the first important instrument concerning planning was Decree No. 1,011/44.[24] It establishes that every development plan has to be approved by the Office of the Director of Geodesy, Cadastre and Lands.

In subsequent years the most important instrument was Decree N° 21.891/49. Its clauses describe the problems generated by the division of lots into urban units "whose planning and solution should be planned by the government." The decree points out that the process of dividing the land into lots and the sale "of land favors the actions of speculators, and increases inflation whose consequences fall on the most deprived sectors of the population." The decree then defines that the land to be divided into lots should have the necessary infrastructure. It also bans division of urban lots in flood-prone areas. This is the first regulation to influence the Buenos Aires Metropolitan Area, prohibiting the use of flood-prone land or unhealthful water.[25]

Decree No. 2,303/53 partially repeals Decree No. 21,891/49 in response to attacks in newspapers and bulletins of the Corporation of Auctioneers by those directly affected.[26]

Law No. 6,053/54 allows the construction of houses with piles in flood-prone areas of the Buenos Aires Metropolitan Area, since there was no obligation to fill flood-prone lands.

The legislation related to paving is found in National Law No. 5,139/47 and Provincial Law No. 6,301/48. Based on their application, the municipalities are responsible for providing the service. Ninety-five percent of the cost of paving is borne by owners of road-facing urban real estate and 5 percent by the municipality.

Decree No. 14,076/60 empowers the municipalities to prepare Regulatory Plans that modify provincial legislation concerning housing developments. In 1960 Laws Nos. 6,253 and 6,254 ban developments below the +3.75 level of the Instituto Geográfico Militar (IGM), as had been recommended in 1948. A reserve of flood-prone areas is declared.

Exceptions were granted to lands in which public or private sanitation works were carried out. But, given the lack of precise standards, these were only partial solutions, and flooding occurred subsequent to the completion of the works. On the other hand most of

the urban land incorporated into the BAMA had already been divided into lots.

Law No. 8,912, approved in 1977, bans developments without basic infrastructure: network water, sewerage and rain drainage, paving, and electric network. It also defines minimum dimensions: 300 m² for urban lots. A definition of areas for different uses is imposed on the municipalities, as well as regulation of lots set aside for "country clubs."[27]

However, this legislation was approved when a large supply of lots without infrastructure existed and demand for land from low-income sectors was strongly reduced due to the socioeconomic conditions prevailing in the 1970s. On the other hand restrictions on the supply of land without infrastructure encouraged the sale of clandestine lots, many of them in flood-prone areas.

Currently, the municipalities of the Buenos Aires Metropolitan Area have Master Plans or Planning Codes prepared in 1977, in view of the fact that Law No. 8,912 defines that these should be adapted to the particular situation of every municipality.

Historically, in the prior periods of greater land development and occupation of the 1950s and 1960s, these municipalities had lacked instruments that took into account the flood plains. (The province of Buenos Aires had defined a level in 1960, but many lots had already been developed.)

Even today, when defining their planning instruments, the municipalities of the Buenos Aires Metropolitan Area scarcely give importance to the floods issue.

Vincente López is one of the municipalities with the most up-to-date Code—approved by Ordinance 8,062/92. The new Code is still under discussion in public hearings; yet it does not take into account flood-prone areas. Similarly to many of the codes of the Buenos Aires province, it introduces the possibility of "awards" above the maximum FOT values and densities corresponding to each area, which cannot exceed 70 percent of their maximum values. In lots lacking a sewerage system, the density must not exceed 150 inhabitants per ha.[28]

The Gral. San Martín municipality approved the Code through Ordinance No. 2,971/86. It also introduced the concept of "award," whereby the maximum FOT values and net density established for the different areas of the municipality can be increased in accordance with "awards." Together these awards cannot exceed 70 percent of the afore-mentioned regulation maximum values, based on a classification included in the Code.

The Tres de Febrero municipality's Planning Code was approved in 1985. Among its objectives are to

- Preserve and improve the environment
- Preserve areas and sites of natural, historical, or architectural interest
- Implement legal, administrative, economic, and financial mechanisms to eliminate speculative excesses
- Ensure that standardization and urban renewal are carried out taking into account general interests of the community
- Prevent occupation of land that does not have adequate sanitation.

"Tres de Febrero" is the only Code in all the municipalities of the Buenos Aires Metropolitan Area that defines the elimination of "speculative excesses" as well as a series of issues related to the environment. It also requests the creation of parks in urban areas.

For developments that imply occupation by up to 2,000 inhabitants, the code sets aside 3.5 m²/person, increasing that parameter to up to 6 m²/person for more than 5,000 inhabitants. As do other municipalities, it defines that the allocation of green and free public areas can not be modified, since they constitute public goods owned by the State. Nor can they be deaccessioned for transfer to entities or private persons except in the case of exchange for other goods of similar characteristics that better fulfill the established allocation. However, the Code does not indicate how those objectives will be achieved.[29]

The Morón municipality approved Ordinance No. 10,832 in 1984. Although it adjusts to Law No. 8,912 in terms of areas, which are defined in the aforementioned ordinance, it places greater attention on issues related to environmental quality. This Code is the only one—of the Codes of the 19 municipalities constituting the suburbs—that has a special heading for flood-prone areas.

As defined by the municipality, the areas in this category will be subject to the following restrictions: (1) division of land into lots is banned until the works making the capacity of the soil feasible for urban uses are implemented; and (2) prior to the start of construction, a minimum level for the habitable sites should be requested from the planning agency.

In the municipality of La Matanza a series of ordinances define the potential for land development, use, and occupation. The most recent was issued in 1987. They correspond to Law N° 8,912, but none of the ordinances takes into account the special features of the municipality.

Conclusions

In the Buenos Aires Metropolitan Area

- There is no coordinating agency liaising between the city and the municipalities of the suburbs, or among the municipalities of the suburbs.
- The political-institutional practice concerning floods is characterized by a fragmentation between the hydrologic elements, and social and economic issues.
- Regulations vary in such a way (allowing and banning construction and settlement in low areas with flood risks) that it is difficult to integrate them. There is no integration of the types of area in the borders between the municipalities. This is most significant in the border between the municipality of Morón and the municipalities of Merlo, General Sarmiento, and La Matanza. Accordingly, an effort should be made to make this integration possible.

Common characteristics of existing regulations concerning physical urban planning in the municipalities of the Buenos Aires Metropolitan Area are

- Urban planning does not seem to be a priority for municipal administrations. Some municipalities have not even prepared a specific Urban Management Code for the municipal territory but have followed the general directives from the Buenos Aires province.
- Recommendations are prescribed but ways to implement them are not specified.

- The instruments do not involve the social actors in the planning process. Even the few Codes that mention the participation of the population in decisionmaking do not develop truly participatory alternatives, except the claims that citizens can make using the administrative-bureaucratic route.

- The legislation is primarily "spatial" or "physical," that is, its conceptual basis is the idea that the city is a part of the territory that needs to be "regulated." The legislation does not consider the social actors who make decisions in urban planning, live in the metropolitan area, and use it.

- The population density proposed by the Codes does not correspond to the real figures, which are higher. Impact assessments of these densities on the infrastructure of existing drainages have not been conducted. As a result the effects of these densities on flood-prone areas are unknown.

- Environmental problems, among them the settlements in flood-prone areas that were supposed to disappear with the application of the new regulations, are increasing.

The authors conclude that the proposed regulations are adequate from the technical, but not the social, standpoint.

Recommendations

When floods occur on a highly built and densely populated space, ways to prevent and mitigate the risk for flooding should be studied in depth. Buenos Aires completely lacks data on constructions by cadastral radius, which would enable detailed analysis of the construction density to find out how it affects flooding.

Furthermore, although the greater quantity and population density by cadastral radius provides an idea, it does not provide accuracy. The information on floods should be systematized.

It is important to produce a set of integrated standards that will enable mitigation of the flood risk. The infrastructure works that can be constructed will never be sufficient if nonstructural measures are not addressed. In other words urban regulations must be developed in accordance with the morphological and social characteristics of the area in question.

Nonstructural measures should include a clearly advertised and well-promoted warning system for the population of the areas affected by floods, enabling the vulnerable families to implement them. In addition, the adoption of mitigation measures by the community could be promoted.

In addition, it is necessary to

- Modify current regulations that permit and promote underground construction in flood-prone areas, such as garages in buildings. It is also important as a safety measure to free some of the ground floor spaces in the most critical areas.

- Publicize the flood-prone areas. The lack of valid information on the risks generates and accumulates new risks.

- Alter the solid waste disposal systems. This requires the placement of waste on high ground on the public thoroughfare, or in receptacles that allow the passing of water.

- Encourage not only the creation but also the maintenance of green spaces for their infiltration capacity. Replace and increase woodlands in the city.

- Regulate and supervise the repaving of city streets. Urban Plans and Codes to be developed and implemented should envisage

- Physical support (natural and manmade)

- Consequences of density increases on floods, since there are no systematic analyses of this aspect.

Notes

1. Kenneth Hewit, 1997.
2. In this work the authors will not examine the floods produced by the southeastern winds in the southern section of the city because in November 1998 a set of works was inaugurated to mitigate the flood risk in that area. Since these works were completed, southeastern winds significant enough to evaluate the result have not occurred.
3. For a complete review of the subject see Herzer and Federovisky, 1994; and Herzer and Di Virgilio, 1996.
4. The 24 municipalities surrounding the Federal Capital together with the Federal Capital constitute the Buenos Aires Metropolitan Area.

5. Germani, 1966.

6. Towers, 1975:285.

7. See Towers, 1992.

8. In the same way as settlements are created in low-lying areas, municipal or provincial governments in some BAMA municipalities encourage the settlement of people in low-lying and flood-prone areas. This has occurred in some settlements created through official programs such as Pro-Tierra, Pro-Casa, or Pro-Lote.

9. This actually masks the increase in profits of the contractors responsible for the repair of sidewalks, the lack of control of the corresponding municipal agency, and the lack of participation of local neighborhoods in controlling public works.

10. This average is based on the total production of waste in the City of Buenos Aires, which has considerably increased, and on the number of inhabitants, which has remained almost stable.

11. At present a new fashion has been added, encouraged by the press. Building janitors have disseminated a practice whose result is doubtful: to drive away dogs from their frontages, they place plastic bottles filled with water around the trees in the sidewalks. Rainfall of certain intensity would drag the bottles to the storm drains with negative effects.

12. Ferrari, Hardoy, and Juan Kurchan, Architects.

13. Economic growth coexists with the urban problems derived from it. Physical structures are not flexible so do not adjust to the rapid changes in concentration of population and location of new activities in the city and in the areas that will become the BAMA.

14. The most important proposals were to (1) Renew the southern area. The city is divided into two sectors, the north and the south, which need to be integrated. (2) Build an automobile circulation system, with the definition of highways: two cross streets north-south/east-west, and one beltway. (3) Concentrate the city and transform Belgrano, Flores, and Villa Urquiza into satellite cities. (4) Initiate the plan: first the downtown, since it is the most critical area, especially the road system. But none of this is being implemented.

15. Plan Le Corbusier, SCA, 1940, p. 20.

16. Building Code, 1959 Ed., p. 6.

17. It should be emphasized that implementation of an instrument such as the Code could not be carried out without the intervention of the National Executive Branch, since the City of Buenos Aires did not have the capability to impose the necessary restrictions to ownership. Through Decree 9,434 of 1944, the PEN authorized the municipality of Buenos Aires to establish restrictions to ownership related to heights, volume, and distribution of the buildings and the free surface that must be left at the rear of the lots; to ban construction in unhealthy areas; to impose zoning regulations in the city according to uses; and to execute agreements with border municipalities to address zoning issues jointly.

18. Building Code, 1959 Ed., p. 7.

19. The urban and metropolitan reality is sufficiently complex for it to be analyzed by different specialists and for the proposals to be the result of a multidisciplinary diagnosis.

20. Approved through Ordinance 33,387, becoming effective on May 1, 1977 by Ordinance 33,515.

21. For the poorer sectors the policy of the military government that implemented the Code consisted in eradicating the shantytowns in Buenos Aires (Oszlack 1991).

22. Several reform projects of the Planning Code of 1977 were proposed by the Municipal Executive Branch and rejected by the Deliberative Council (DC). On December 1, 1989 after 6 years of discussions and with the unanimous support of all the blocks, the DC approved the de facto standards and made the Code prepared in 1977 more flexible. The DC approved Ordinances 44.092/89, 44.094/89, 44.095/89, and 44.873/91. In those years an important series of partial modifications to the Code had been carried out as "concealed exceptions" (Clichevsky 1996).

23. No analysis was made of the draft Code, which was debated in Congress following its analysis at a public hearing last June (in addition to another proposal, also discussed in a public hearing in November 1997).

24. Although legislation on construction of towns has existed since 1913.

25. An Advisory Commission of the Buenos Aires Metropolitan Area had been created in 1948 through Decree 70. The decree specified, "There has been uncontrolled speculation, most of the time holding land without using it, as if the property title or the purchase-sale contract were a bond to be offered in the Stock Exchange." The report of the Municipality of Matanza stated, "The last years have

been characterized by unbridled speculation that has resulted in numerous developments and new housing blocks hastily prepared...." Real occupation of the developments in the Metropolitan Area was approximately 10 percent. An Immediate Urgency Plan was proposed, establishing a scheme of land use in all the area, and the draft "Urban and Regional Planning Law" was under study for the entire Province where the purchase of land through direct purchase, donations, exchange, or expropriations according to the 1947 Law was proposed. At the meetings of the municipalities at the end of 1948 and beginning of 1949, awareness arose of the severity of the land occupation problem, as well as of the makeshift dwellings in the Buenos Aires Metropolitan Area. By resolution of the commission a recommendation was made to ban new developments below the 3.75 IGM level in Avellaneda, E. Echeverría, Gral. San Martín, Sarmiento, Lanús, La Plata, Lomas de Zamora, San Fernando, and Vincente López, Matanza, and others that globally involved 100,000 ha. However, because of the restriction to ownership that it implied, this would be a temporary measure. The commission went into recess in 1950, and the measures taken by the government on the basis of the report were negligible.

26. In its clauses it was accepted that the Decree "implied a serious restriction to ownership," justified by the housing shortage that favored speculators. However, "after four years of its application, the inflationary process in real estate values has been stopped and due to the fact that the infeasibility of dividing certain land into urban-type lots bears heavily on the price increase of dwellings, it becomes necessary to partially repeal it."

27. In addition, minimum green areas, among other issues, are defined for the new urban developments.

28. The Code proposes the objectives for the city of Vincente López. The main objectives are, first, to implement a *continuous and dynamic planning process* (emphasis added). The second objective is to program urban development through proposals for promotional, regulatory, and planning actions and investments through short-, medium- and long-term operational methods. These would be endorsed by technical, legal, and administrative standards.

29. It defines acceptable reserves of green spaces. However, the current limited incorporation of urban areas in the land market, for reasons previously mentioned—shrinking demand, ample supply—implied that public green areas would not increase significantly, especially in a municipality adjoining Buenos Aires. The most peripheral municipalities presented a different situation, where incorporations of closed neighborhoods, country clubs, and farms were significant.

References

Albini, X., and X. Costa. 1988. "Las inundaciones en el área metropolitana de Buenos Aires." In *Medio Ambiente y Urbanización* 7 (23). Buenos Aires: IIED-AL.

Clichevsky, N. 1986. "Políticas urbanas para Buenos Aires 1900-1980." Report. CONICET. Buenos Aires. Mimeo.

_____. 1994. "Política urbana, normas urbanísticas y configuración de la ciudad de Buenos Aires 1984-1993." Informe de Investigación. Buenos Aires.

_____. 1996. *Política social urbana*. Buenos Aires: Editorial Espacios.

Código de Edificación de la ciudad de Buenos Aires. 1959 ed.

Urban Planning Council, MCBA. 1989. "Bases para la participación pública en la planificación territorial de Buenos Aires." Fondo Editorial de la Cooperación- EUDEBA. Buenos Aires.

Germani, G. 1966. *Política y sociedad en una época de transición*. Buenos Aires: Ed. Paidós.

Herzer, H., and S. Federovisky. 1994. "Las políticas municipales y las inundaciones en Buenos Aires." *Desastres y Sociedad*. Semi-annual magazine of the Social Studies Network in Disaster Preparedness in Latin America. 2 (2) (January-July). Lima, Peru.

Herzer, H., and M. Di Virgilio. 1996. "Buenos Aires Inundable. Del siglo XIX a mediados del siglo XX." In *Historia y Desastres en América Latina*, Virginia García Acosta (coordinator). Vol. 1. LA RED. Social Studies Network in Disaster Preparedness in Latin America and CIESAS Mexico. Tercer Mundo Editores.

Hewit, K. 1997. *Regions of Risk*. London: Addison Wesley Longman Limited.

Municipalidad de la Ciudad de Buenos Aires (MCBA). 1992. Temas Urbanos 1, Bs As.

Novaro and Perelman. 1993. "La pobreza en el Área Metropolitana de Buenos Aires (1974-1991)." In *Medio Ambiente y Urbanización* 11:45. Buenos Aires. IIED-AL.

Ordinances corresponding to changes to the Planning Code. 1983-1993.

Oszlack. 1991.

Plan Le Corbusier. 1940. SCA.

Smith, K. 1998. *Environmental Hazards*.

Stallings, R. 1991. "Feedback from the Field. Disasters as Social Problems?: A Dissenting View." In *International Journal of Mass Emergencies and Disasters* 9 (1) (March). University of North Texas, Denton, Tex.

Suárez, O. 1986. "Planes y Códigos para Buenos Aires-1925-1985." *Serie Ediciones Previas*, FADU-UBA.

Summa. 1977. "Código de Planeamiento Urbano de la Ciudad de Buenos Aires No. 113." June.

Torres, H. 1975. "Evolución de los procesos de estructuración espacial urbana. El caso de Buenos Aires." In *Desarrollo Económico* 15 (18):281-306. Buenos Aires. IDES.

Torres, H. 1992. "Cambios en la estructura socioespacial de Buenos Aires a partir de la década de 1940." In *Después de Germani. Exploraciones sobre estructura social de la Argentina*, R. Jorrat and R. Sautu, eds. Buenos Aires: Ed. Paidós.

Chapter 4
Climate, Change, and Disasters

Maxx Dilley

Hazards related to climate and weather affect more people and cause more economic damage worldwide than any other type of natural hazard by far. Over the past three decades disasters triggered by cyclones, droughts, and floods occurred 5 times as frequently, killed or affected 70 times as many people, and caused twice as much damage worldwide as did earthquakes and volcanoes, the two major geological hazards (table 1). When secondary impacts, such as landslides, epidemics, and pest infestations are also considered, it becomes all the more evident that climate and weather are primary concerns for natural disaster and risk management.

Fortunately (or unfortunately, depending on where one lives) hydrometeorological hazards are not randomly distributed, and different types of hazard events tend to occur in specific areas during specific seasons. The spatial and temporal distribution of hazard events is increasingly well documented, and the risks they pose are increasingly understood. This growing understanding and awareness makes it possible to take proactive measures to prepare for them and minimize their impacts in high-risk areas, many of which are in the developing world, where lack of resources contributes to a high degree of vulnerability.

High-risk coastal areas, flood plains, and marginal lands increasingly are being settled and developed. As a result disaster losses can be expected to mount in coming years, even if hazard frequency and severity rates were to stay constant. When global warming and the possibility of abrupt climatic changes are factored in, there is every reason to proactively integrate disaster reduction in sustainable development.

"Climate change" is often taken to refer to changes in climatic averages and variability brought about by global warming. In fact, "change" is an intrinsic characteristic of the climate system. The Intergovernmental Panel on Climate Change (IPCC) uses "climate change" to refer to any climate variation over time, regardless of whether it is naturally occurring or due to human activity (IPCC 1996, p. 3). In this sense "change" means variability, and establishing what constitutes a climate change requires defining a temporal frame of reference. For example, climate changes on seasonal, interannual, decadal, and multidecadal time scales. Actual and potential climatic extremes arising from the functioning of the climate system at these different time scales affect how disasters occur and will continue to occur. Understanding the physical factors that create climate extremes at these different time scales, as well as the social and economic forces that create societal vulnerability, are prerequisites for accurate risk assessment. By linking across timescales, immediate and longer-term vulnerability reduction efforts can be integrated to reduce the frequency and severity of climate-related disasters.

Sources of Climate Variability

The dominant source of climate variability is the earth-sun relationship that results in the seasons. Seasonal climate is so reliable that environmental and socio-economic systems tend to be well adapted, to the extent that the vastly important role that climate plays in maintaining these systems may be taken for granted. Nonetheless, because extreme climate events naturally occur and environmental or economic systems can get out of sync with prevailing climatic conditions, dozens of climate-related disasters occur annually worldwide.

Of the many sources of interannual variation in the quality of a given season at any given location, the largest and arguably the best understood is El Niño and the Southern Oscillation (ENSO). Frequent ENSO warm events (anomalous warming of the eastern Pacific sea surface) occurred throughout the 1990s, culminating in an extremely strong event from 1997-1998. Atmospheric perturbations associated with ENSO, while not so reliable as the seasons, tend to affect temperatures and precipitation in specific regions in specific ways. One result is that in some regions, such as the west coast of South America, Oceania, and southern and eastern Africa, climate extremes of such magnitude occur that the ability of affected populations to cope is consistently overwhelmed, leading to disaster (Dilley and Heyman 1995). The 1997-1998 event, for example, was directly responsible for 22 disaster declarations by U.S. Ambassadors to affected countries, signifying that the countries required international assistance (figure 1). Estimates of the worldwide cost of this event are on the order of $25-36 billion (NOAA/OGP 1999). World Bank loans to eight severely affected countries for prevention and reconstruction activities totaled $359 million (van Aalst and others 1999).

It remains to be seen whether the frequent and strong ENSO events of the 1990s signal the arrival of a new climate regime or whether Pacific sea surface temperatures and global atmospheric circulation patterns will continue to vary around historical averages. Either way, changing ocean temperature patterns on decadal scales are known to drive corresponding shifts in regional climates. These include a current tendency towards rising average July-September rainfall in the Sahel region of Africa (see Ward and others 1999 for a discussion of the physical mechanisms) and a decadal

scale increase in Atlantic hurricane frequency (Gray and others 1997).

The interaction of these climatic changes with society determines levels of disaster risk. Decadal scale low-rainfall extremes that occurred in the Sahel in the late 1970s and early 1980s were responsible for severe famine events affecting millions of people. Since then, seasonal Sahelian rainfall levels have returned to near their long-term averages, and drought-related disasters in the region have become more localized and less frequent. Similarly, there has been a pronounced decadal scale overall warming of the Atlantic Ocean, including the presence of warmer water up into the North Atlantic. The warming provides more energy and larger surface areas for storm formation, causing more intense and frequent storms affecting the United States, Central America, and the Caribbean. The last five years, 1995-99, have been among the most active in the climate record in tropical storm and hurricane frequencies. This is in spite of persistent El Niño activity, which tends to suppress Atlantic storm formation. Disasters like that caused by Hurricane Mitch in 1998 are reminders that these decadal scale changes have implications for climate-related risks and risk-reduction efforts.

Future climate changes expected to accompany global warming pose significant longer-term disaster risks. The average global temperature has increased appreciably since the 19th century, although "[t]here are inadequate data to determine whether consistent global changes in climate variability or extremes have occurred over the 20th century" (Houghton and others 1996, p. 30). Variability has increased in some regions and decreased in others (Houghton and others 1996). Nonetheless, increasing temperatures and retreating ice caps make sea-level rise a potential hazard well worth noting. Sea levels have already risen 10-25 cm over the past 100 years, and estimates of future rates of increase range from 13-94 cm over current levels by the year 2100 (Warrick and others 1995, p. 364). Increases in the middle of this range could have severe implications for small island states and heavily populated low-lying areas such as the Ganges and Nile deltas. Reduction in Arctic Sea ice extent over what would be expected from natural variability has already been observed (Johannessen and others 1999; Vinnikov and others 1999).

Furthermore, while reliable regional predictions are beyond current capabilities, climate models suggest that a general warming will lead to more frequent extremely high temperature events and "an enhanced hydrologic cycle," meaning more intense precipitation, more dry days, and longer dry spells (Houghton and others 1996, p. 44). Elevated probabilities of these kinds of events have implications for the frequency and severity of droughts, floods, and storm surges.

Vulnerability

Social vulnerability to climate and weather hazards is a function of such things as location, the extent and type of infrastructure, and the role of climate in the economy. The importance of climate for agriculture is well established, and countries that are highly dependent on primary production can show a climate signal in their economic data (Benson and Clay 1998). Drought affects food availability through secondary effects on wages and food prices (Sen 1981). Population migrations under drought stress lead to increased mortality from contagious diseases (de Waal 1989). High winds and flooding cause population displacement, loss of shelter, and other critical infrastructure. Flooding also contributes to the spread of waterborne diseases and increased mortality.

A number of trends can be identified as potential contributors to growing human vulnerability to climate hazards. Even if the frequency and severity of

climatic hazards were to remain constant, these trends suggest that the number and magnitude of climate-related disasters could continue to grow. Global population is increasing. The number of people exposed to climate-related risks is therefore also growing, magnifying the impacts of future hazard events. Settlement patterns also have implications for vulnerability. Population growth in low-lying coastal areas places more people at risk of flooding, wind damage, and storm surges. The growth of informal settlements around urban areas on sloping terrain increases the possibility of landslide casualties during heavy rains. Settlement on flood plains increases the likelihood of flood damage. In some areas there is increased dependency on the use of degraded or marginal lands, which increases the sensitivity of agricultural and other primary production to climate variations. In countries or segments of populations in which general economic levels are decreasing, declining resources mean fewer alternatives for coping with prevailing climate conditions or capitalizing on them.

In general, while economic development decreases disaster deaths, it tends to increase economic losses. Therefore, it is imperative that development efforts acknowledge and address disaster risks, as doing otherwise simply increases losses when disasters occur. As the data in table 1 and figure 1 make clear, frequent climate- and weather-related disasters are testimony that current development efforts have not adequately addressed vulnerability to the normal, and "natural" variations in the climate system. A logical (although not the only) starting point, therefore, is to use these catastrophes that occur annually as an

Table 1 Worldwide impacts of major hydrometeorological and geophysical hazards, 1970-1998

Trigger	Frequency	People killed	People affected	Damage (billions)
Cyclones (all)	1,770	597,704	265,627,230	231
Drought	484	1,069,912	1,296,096,628	37
Floods	1,721	186,736	2,002,201,949	286
Volcano	123	25,477	2,626,481	3
Earthquake	699	562,417	51,207,764	271
Total hydrometeorological	3,975	1,854,352	3,563,925,807	554
Total geophysical	822	587,894	53,834,245	274

Source: EM-DAT—The OFDA/CRED International Disaster Database, www.md.ucl.ac.be/cred.

Figure 1   Declared disasters related to the 1997/98 El Niño event

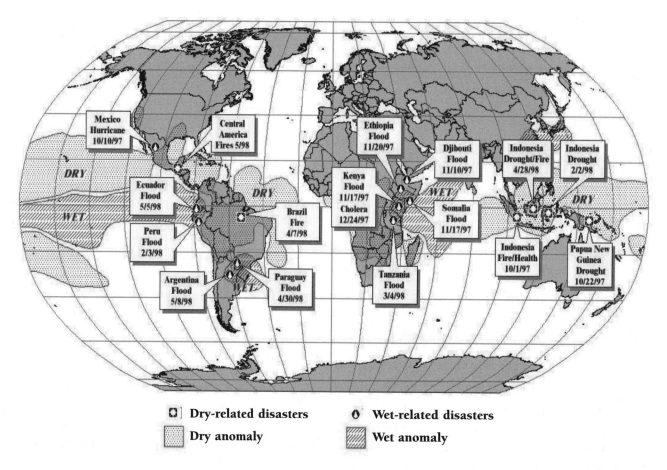

[] Dry-related disasters	◊ Wet-related disasters
Dry anomaly	Wet anomaly

Source: USAID/OFDA, "FY 1998 Annual Report," p. 13.

opportunity to develop flexible and effective counter-measures for addressing climate-related risks, immediate and longer term.

Risk Reduction

Given the strength of the physical forces involved, coupled with human economic interdependence on climate and the environment, it is unlikely that adverse impacts from extreme climate events will ever be totally eliminated. Nonetheless, numerous approaches and techniques have proven their utility in reducing negative climate impacts. Special efforts to identify and implement such measures may be necessary, however, in areas where they have not already

been instituted. As the needs are great and the range of possible measures is broad, it is helpful to have an analytical basis for guiding where and when disaster prevention and preparedness investments are likely to pay off.

If one knew for certain where the next hurricane would strike, or where the next flood would occur, it would be negligent not to act in advance. As this kind of certainty is usually not possible when dealing with natural systems, hydrometeorological hazard assessment relies on historical patterns as well as on predictive models to anticipate which events are most likely to occur, where, and when. This knowledge can be used to assign probabilities of certain types of hazard events occurring in a given area over a given period. Probabilistic forecasts of this nature were developed during the 1997-98 El Niño, for example, to provide guidance on whether seasonal precipitation was likely to be in the upper or lower portions of historical ranges for specific regions due to ENSO and other controls on regional climates (NOAA/OGP 1999b). Similarly, storm belts in tropical oceans are well delineated, and storm warning systems that track the development of individual storms can provide short-term estimates of probable landfall. Flood-prone areas, especially those with large populations, tend to be adequately modeled and mapped such that the probabilities of specified flood levels can be estimated.

What this type of information does make clear, however, is that large numbers of people over large areas potentially are exposed to these types of hazards. As an additional basis for enhanced disaster prevention and preparedness efforts, additional information on risks can be obtained by looking at societal vulnerability to these hazards. Vulnerability assessment is an intensive exercise that requires indepth knowledge of economic, social, and demographic factors that make people and groups more or less likely to experience negative impacts from the particular hazards to which they are likely to be exposed. High levels of vulnerability coupled with high probabilities of experiencing hazard events create high degrees of risk, and an impetus to act in advance of potential disaster rather than waiting until afterwards.

Prior to the prominence of the issue of global warming, it was thought that people's ability to influence climate hazards was minimal and thus that vulnerability reduction was the only viable means of reducing risk. Ironically, the prospect of human-induced climate change transfers a degree of responsibility for these hazards, as well as mitigation potential, into society's hands. If greenhouse gas emission levels can be held to lower levels and global warming abated, sea levels, for example, might not rise to the extent that they otherwise would. So efforts to reduce emissions are to some extent an exercise in hazard reduction.

The other means of reducing risk is vulnerability reduction. The list of effective prevention and preparedness measures is long, comprising structural and nonstructural approaches. Structural approaches involve building design considerations such as strapping on roofs to prevent them from being blown off during hurricanes or raising houses on stilts above typical flood levels. Nonstructural measures have to do with decisionmaking behavior and include a wide range of options from economic policies to planning evacuation routes.

Large uncertainties about future climates due to global warming tend to favor nonstructural disaster reduction strategies. In particular, the telecommunications and information revolution is creating tremendous opportunities for more effective use of information, not only by specialists but also as a means to coordinate public action.

Conclusion

Efforts to reduce disasters in the short term and to address longer-term climate changes have more commonalities than differences. In the short term, uncertainties are less but risk reduction alternatives are largely limited to vulnerability reduction measures. Over the longer term, patterns of future climatic extremes as well as vulnerability are uncertain, but there are opportunities to act to limit greenhouse gas emissions in an attempt to reduce probabilities of abrupt, high-magnitude climatic shifts. On the adaptation side, there is much to be learned from current extreme events about managing climate variability over the longer term. If today's climate-related disasters can be mitigated, there will be cause for optimism that society has developed the flexibility to deal with tomorrow's climate surprises.

References

Benson, C., and E. Clay. 1998. *The Impact of Drought on Sub-Saharan African Economies: A Preliminary Examination.* World Bank Technical Paper 401.

de Waal, A. 1989. *Famine That Kills: Darfur, Sudan, 1984-1985.* Oxford: Clarendon Press.

Dilley, M., and B. N. Heyman. 1995. "ENSO and Disaster: Droughts, Floods and El Niño/Southern Oscillation Warm

Events." *Disasters* 19 (3): 181-93.

Gray, W. M., J. D. Sheaffer, and C. W. Landsea. 1997. "Climate Trends Associated with Multidecadal Variability of Atlantic Hurricane Activity." In *Hurricanes: Climate and Socioeconomic Impacts*. Ed. H. Diaz and R. S. Pulwarty. Heidelberg: Springer-Verlag. 15-54.

Johannessen, O. M., E. V. Shalina, and M. W. Miles. 1999. "Satellite Evidence for an Arctic Sea Ice Cover in Transformation." *Science* 286: 1937-39.

Houghton, J. T., and others. 1996. "Technical Summary." In *Climate Change 1995, The Science of Climate Change. Contribution of Working Group I to the Second Assessment Report of the Intergovernmental Panel on Climate Change*. Ed. J. T. Houghton and others. Cambridge: Cambridge University Press. 2-7.

IPCC (Intergovernmental Panel on Climate Change). 1996. "Summary for Policy Makers." In *Climate Change 1995, The Science of Climate Change*. 9-49.

NOAA/OGP (National Oceanic and Atmospheric Administration, Office of Global Programs). 1999a. *Compendium of Climatological Impacts*. Washington, D.C.: NOAA/OGP.

_____. 1999b. *An Experiment in the Application of Climate Forecasts: NOAA-OGP Activities Related to the 1997-98 El Niño Event*. Washington, D.C.: NOAA/OGP.

Sen, A. 1981. *Poverty and Famines: An Essay on Entitlement and Deprivation*. Oxford: Clarendon Press.

USAID/OFDA (U.S. Agency for International Development Office of U.S. Foreign Disaster Assistance). "Annual Report, FY 1998." USAID/OFDA. Washington, D.C.

Van Aalst, M. K., and others. 1999. "The Role of Climate Information and Forecasting in Development. Lessons from the 1997/98 El Niño Event." 2d draft. A NOAA/OGP and World Bank. Washington, D.C.

Vikkikov, K.Y., and others. 1999. "Global Warming and Northern Hemisphere Sea Ice Extent." *Science* 286: 1934-37.

Ward, M. N., and others. 1999. "Climate Variability in Northern Africa." In *Beyond El Niño: Decadal and Interdecadal Climate Variability*. Ed. A. Navarra. Berlin: Springer-Verlag. 119-40.

Warrick, R. A., and others. 1996. "Changes in Sea Level." In *Climate Change 1995, The Science of Climate Change*. 359-405.

Reinforcing a buidling with sheer
wall and cladding, Vandazor,
Armenia, 1996.

PART II

RISK REDUCTION

Chapter 5

Infrastructure, Natural Disasters, and Poverty

Paul K. Freeman

This paper discusses natural catastrophes and poverty. Measuring poverty is important to describe its relationship to natural catastrophes.[1] A recent Overseas Development Institute (ODI) Poverty Briefing articulates nine methods used to describe poverty (Maxwell 1999). As with most other complex issues the definition of the problem invariably leads to conclusions about policy options. Here, the discussion is narrowed primarily to issues in which risk transfer may play an important role. Risk transfer for natural disasters in the developed world is directed primarily at transferring the risk of damage to private real property to the insurance industry.. In the developing world, with its high concentration of publicly owned infrastructure, an equivalent problem is the vulnerability of infrastructure to the sudden impact of major natural catastrophes.

Risk transfer provides a safety net for economic loss to property. Just as governments provide safety nets to people in times of need, risk transfer is the safety net for losses to property from unexpected events. For property damage, risk transfer provides resources to rebuild. Generally, rebuilding means restoring the damaged property. As a safety net, it reinforces original investment decisions, whether right or wrong.

The first section of this chapter will describe the worldwide economic costs of catastrophes, articulating the specific impacts on the developing world. It then will examine the relationship to poverty in the developing world from these natural catastrophe

costs. Finally, future directions of research will be discussed.

Worldwide Costs of Natural Catastrophes

Since the 1970s the two largest reinsurance companies in the world, Munich Re and Swiss Re, have maintained comprehensive records on the frequency and severity of natural catastrophes. For the past decade each firm has published comprehensive annual reports on the worldwide costs of natural catastrophes. Munich Re also has published reports examining trends over the past 10 and 25 years, as well as a map describing all natural catastrophes during the prior decade. Swiss Re publishes reports on natural catastrophes at least annually, with additional reports issued on specific issues. While the measurement tools used by each firm differ, the basic conclusions of their studies are quite similar. None of their reports specifically reviews the issues discussed in this paper. As a result, in some instances the statistics in this paper are calculations based on data or ratios provided in the referenced reports.

Over the past 10 years both the number and severity of natural catastrophes have been increasing. During the 1990s the number of catastrophes increased five-fold, and the damages increased by a factor of nine, contrasted to the decade of the 1960s (Munich Re 1999). From 1987 to 1997 the total direct economic loss from natural catastrophes was US$700 billion, for an average loss of US$70 billion. Catastrophes are a function of physical events affecting human settlement. Increasing concentrations of populations and fragile infrastructure in hazard-prone areas are the main causes of the increased costs of catastrophes (Munich Re 1998).

Natural catastrophes generally are defined in three main categories: windstorm, flood, and hurricane. Windstorms, including hurricanes, and flooding each account for approximately 35 percent of natural catastrophes and 30 percent of the annual damage caused by catastrophes. Earthquakes are responsible for 15 percent of the total number of events, and 30 percent of the total damage. The number of windstorms and flooding events have both increased in the past decade, while the number of earthquakes has remained relatively constant (Munich Re 1998a).

Despite the concentration of capital assets in the developed versus the developing world, the economic impacts of catastrophes are relatively evenly split between these groups of countries. While windstorms and flooding each account for approximately 30 percent of the annual average direct damage from catastrophes, their impacts on the developed and developing countries are significantly different. Windstorms are responsible for 70 percent of the private property damage from natural catastrophes in the United States (Swiss Re 1999). Floods primarily occur in Asia, which bears 70 percent of worldwide flooding damage (Munich Re 1998a). Earthquake damage during the past few decades has been more evenly split between the developed and the developing world. Consequently, the developed world primarily bears the costs of windstorm, the developing world the cost of flooding, and they divide the cost of earthquake damage. Ultimately, the developing world bears approximately US$35 billion in direct costs of natural catastrophes, the same as the developed world. However, based on the enormous disparity in the gross domestic product (GDP) between the two, in the developing world the per capita cost of natural disasters in relation to GDP is dramatically higher.

The damage variance between years is dramatic. During the past decade the range has been between a high of US$130 billion, and a low of US$30 billion (Munich Re 1998). In addition, the use of mean dam-

age amounts may significantly discount the severity of events for limited geographical regions. For example, in 1998 total worldwide economic losses are estimated at approximately US$65.5 billion (Swiss Re 1999). Over half of those losses, US$35 billion, were Asian flooding losses, with US$30 billion attributable to the losses in China from the immense flooding along the Yangtze River. The second largest single disaster was Hurricane Mitch, with losses of US$5 billion. As a result, 66 percent of 1998 losses were incurred by the developing world (Swiss Re 1999).

Global Warming and Natural Catastrophes

Continuing a long-term trend, 1998 proved to be the warmest year on record in terms of mean temperature (Munich Re 1998b). The implications and causes of worldwide temperatures increases are one of the important worldwide policy scientific debates of our time. In examining the implications of global warming, particular concern has arisen over the increased windstorms and floods. Both windstorms and floods are atmospheric events. Warmer surface and ocean temperature result in increased moisture absorption in the atmosphere. Increased moisture absorption leads to increased precipitation in the form of floods and windstorm events. As said in the *New York Times:*

> …experts have long said that one effect of global warming will be to alter precipitation patterns—increasing rainfall in some places while decreasing it in others. A warmer atmosphere, according to this view, causes more water to evaporate from the surface. Also, a warmer atmosphere holds more moisture, so that when a storm system comes through a given locality to make it rain, the rain is heavier. Data collected and analyzed by Federal scientists suggest that there is indeed a trend in that direction in the United States (May 18 1999).

The statistics maintained by Munich Re suggest that, worldwide, more atmospheric events of increased severity are occurring. The impacts of natural catastrophes will be of increasing concern for the foreseeable future.

Relationship of Natural Catastrophes, Infrastructure, and Poverty

A clear link of natural disasters to poverty is through infrastructure. The linkages can be described in at least three components: access to infrastructure is often a measure of poverty; infrastructure is a key component of economic growth; and the loss of infrastructure may have significant indirect and secondary costs that directly affect the poor.

In the *World Development Report 1994* the World Bank articulates the direct links of infrastructure to poverty. In fact, access to sanitation, electricity, and clean water, all supplied by infrastructure, are measures of poverty. As stated by the Bank, lack of access to infrastructure is a welfare issue. Furthermore, for the rural poor access to infrastructure—primarily irrigation and transportation—increases income that enables the poor to manage risk.

The maintenance of infrastructure is essential to maintain economic growth, the primary linchpin in reducing poverty. As it does every 10 years, in 1990 the Bank discussed its role in reducing poverty. In its report the Bank outlined the principles for its strategy in the 1990s for reducing poverty:

> (R)apid and politically sustainable progress on poverty has been achieved by pursuing a strategy that has two equally important elements. The first element is to promote the productive use of the poor's most abundant asset—labor. The second is to provide basic social services to the poor. A comprehensive approach to poverty reduction, therefore, calls for a program of well targeted transfers and safety nets as an essential complement to the basic strategy (World Bank 1991).

These principles have guided the Bank's lending activity.

The report also specified additional particular characteristics of the poor that are important to understand:

1. One third of the total population of the developing world are poor, and 18 percent of these are extremely poor.
2. Nearly half of the developing world's poor, and half of those in extreme poverty, live in South Asia.
3. Poverty is at its worst in rural areas.
4. Agricultural is still the main source of income for the world's poor. The livelihood of rural poor are linked to farming, whether or not they earn their income directly from it.

These facts lead to a strategy to reduce poverty would increase the income of rural poor through farming.

Infrastructure development plays an essential role in reducing rural poverty. Infrastructure projects with a direct impact on rural agricultural production, primarily transportation, irrigation, and electricity, have a particularly direct impact on poverty reduction. In a study examining the role of infrastructure and agricultural production, the Bank reported that greater infrastructure development for agricultural development was associated with a one-third increase in average household incomes, 24 percent increase in crop income, 92 percent increase in wage income, and a 78 percent increase in income for livestock and fisheries. These changes associated with greater infrastructure development largely benefited the poor (World Bank 1994). The Bank estimates that a 1 percent increase in the stock of infrastructure translates to a 1 percent increase in GDP. To reduce rural poverty, effective infrastructure projects related to agricultural have proven an essential policy tool.

Natural catastrophes destroy essential rural infrastructure. In Asia, which accounts for half of the natural catastrophes in the world and 70 percent of all floods, the average annual cost of floods over the past decade is approximately US$15 billion (Munich Re 1998). A high proportion of losses from flooding is due to infrastructure loss. By some estimates, infrastructure loss accounts for 65 percent of all flood loss (Swiss Re 1997). For Asia, this would account for average annual infrastructure loss of approximately US$12 billion for the past decade. As more infrastructure is developed in rural areas to combat poverty, and as the frequency and severity of natural disasters also increase, the impacts on the poor will become more critical.

The size of the loss to infrastructure can be compared to the worldwide lending activity of the World Bank. Over the past decade the Bank has annually loaned approximately US$25 billion (Kreimer 1998). The direct damage to infrastructure in Asia alone approximates nearly 50 percent of the total lending activity of the Bank.

Rural infrastructure loss in the developing world has impacted on the activity of the world's international lending institutions. The World Bank has estimated that it has loaned US$14 billion to developing countries in the last 20 years for damages from natural disasters. This is nearly 2.5 times the amount loaned by the Bank for relief from civil disturbances worldwide (Kreimer 1998). The Asian Development Bank (ADB) has estimated that, between 1988-98, 5.6 percent of ADF loans were for disaster rehabilitation. In 1992 nearly 20 percent of the ADF loans were for rehabilitative assistance from natural disasters (Arriens 1999). The World Bank has estimated internally that in Mexico during the past decade up to 35 percent of Bank infrastructure lending has been diverted to the costs of natural catastrophes.

Economic data generally available regarding costs of catastrophes is primarily for direct economic costs. To date, little work has been done to measure the indirect impacts of natural catastrophes on developing countries. While measuring indirect impacts is much more difficult than measuring direct property loss, implications of indirect costs can be much more severe. Some studies measuring the impacts of the loss of flows from infrastructure indicate that damage may be 2.5 times the cost of the direct losses (Shinozuka 1998).

The state of the art data tends to measure the direct economic loss caused by catastrophes. In fact, almost all the data referenced in this chapter are based on such data sources. This tendency often distorts disaster policymaking. For example, these types of analysis focus attention on disasters as singular events. For most countries harmed by them, disasters are repeated events that may strike at random but impact on both the rate and pattern of development (Arriens 1999).

Not considering catastrophes as patterns of events with indirect and secondary effects tends to minimize the costs of the events. As such, policy options such as mitigation and risk transfer do not receive their proper due as tools to reduce the long-range cost of catastrophes.

A new initiative is underway between the World Bank, the International Institute of Applied Systems Analysis, and Swiss Re to better understand the indirect costs of catastrophes to the developing world.

Strategies to Deal with Natural Catastrophes

Knowing the costs of catastrophes is not enough. The critical risk management issue is what steps are possible to effectively deal with the costs of catastrophes. Generally, risk management falls in two broad categories: risk reduction and risk transfer.

Risk Reduction

On a worldwide policy level, the causes of climatic change must be pursued. While the scientific links between human activity and increased global mean temperature continue to be explored, the international community must take into account increasing loss burdens for developing countries from natural catastrophes. This increasing burden will be fed by the dual trends of increasing concentration of vulnerable assets in hazard-prone regions, and the likelihood of increased severe natural atmospheric catastrophes.

Planning for catastrophe has a set of common tools employed in the developed world. The first tools deal with the reduction of risk prior to an event. These tools are generally classified as mitigation, and are directed at either reducing exposure to catastrophe events or increasing the ability of structures to withstand the impact of the catastrophes. Land use planning attempts to reduce construction on seismic fault lines, coastal regions subject to windstorm or storm surge damage, and river shorelines subject to floods. While among the most effective of risk reduction measures, land use planning has proven difficult to implement (Kunreuther 1998).

A second strategy reduces risk through engineering or ecological intervention. The creation of dams for flood control, dikes to reroute flood waters, and reforestation activity or seawalls to break storm surges are examples.

An additional engineering approach reduces the impact of catastrophes on individual structures. Proper construction techniques can substantially reduce the loss of life from earthquakes and flooding. The use of these measures requires weighing the comparative cost of the mitigation measure with the benefits to be gained.

Another planning tool combines pre-disaster planning with immediate post-disaster response. These activities fall under the general terminology of disaster emergency preparedness planning. Examples are the use of early warning systems, evacuation of hazard-prone regions, creation of temporary housing and life support systems, and other activities immediately around the disaster event. This disaster preparedness planning can dramatically reduce lives lost and property damaged from catastrophes.

Risk Transfer

Risk transfer is an important policy tool in the developed world to address the cost of natural catastrophes. These costs have increased for the developed world dramatically in the past decades. The increased concentration of populations and property values in the developed world, particularly the United States, has dramatically increased the economic costs of catastrophes to that part of the world. These costs have been spread through the use of risk transfer techniques.

The most common tool for spreading the risk associated with natural catastrophes is excess loss insurance coverage. This coverage spreads the risk of catastrophe loss to the world reinsurance community and through it to the world capital markets. During the past five years the coverage purchased by the developing countries has increased by 31 percent. The amount of catastrophe reinsurance purchased is approximately US$53 billion, or 50 percent more than the average annual damage of US$35 billion caused by catastrophes in the developed world. Through in-

surance and reinsurance, a substantial portion of the losses from natural catastrophes is borne by others than the victims and governments in those countries. In the United States nearly 70 percent of the catastrophe losses from natural disasters results from hurricanes. In the United States 85 percent of the losses to private property from hurricanes are insured. On average, in the U.S. the insurance industry absorbs 60 percent of the private property losses from natural catastrophes. By contrast, almost no insurance and reinsurance exist to absorb the cost of catastrophes in the developing world. In Asia, for example, less than 2 percent of the damage from natural catastrophe is insured. As a result, nearly all the losses from floods in Asia are absorbed by either the governments or victims (Swiss Re 1997).

In the developing world the lack of insurance for catastrophe is in contrast to the use of insurance for other risks. The developing world is responsible for 14 percent of the worldwide direct insurance business, and almost 19 percent of the demand for non-life reinsurance. The use of insurance, and especially reinsurance, therefore is not unknown to these countries. The failure of any effective market for catastrophe insurance has meant that the risk-spreading benefits and costs of catastrophe insurance have bypassed the developing world.

In addition to catastrophe reinsurance, in the past five years a new generation of tools for catastrophe risk transfer has developed. These tools capture the economic risk of catastrophe event and transfer them directly to the capital markets. Since 1996, US$2.7 billion of these instruments have been used to transfer risk as varied as earthquake and typhoon exposure in Japan, to hurricane risk in the United States (ISO 1999). To date, none of these innovative tools has been used for any risk in a developing country.

Risk transfer for natural disasters is primarily a tool to absorb cost of property damage. While some risk transfers for income replacement exists, crop insurance, for example, it does not have wide application. Risk transfer tools also tend to be developed and defined for markets that exist for the products. Consequently, a deep market exists for hurricane protection and a much smaller market exists for flood risk. The size of the market for earthquake coverage lies between these two markets. Not suprisingly, the risks that impact on the developed world are much more developed than the risks that primarily impact the developing world.

The tools to transfer catastrophe risk in the developed world are known. Flood risk is insurable, and programs for flood protection exist in some countries (Swiss Re 1998a, 1998b). Although technical issues exist for all insurance programs, those issues associated with flood programs in the developing world can be solved. Of course, no effort to solve those issues will occur unless demand for risk transfer in the developing world develops.

Future Directions

The first step is recognition of the impact of natural catastrophes on the effort to reduce poverty. The poverty debate now fails to account for the role of natural catastrophes as a development issue. Without this recognition, little progress can be made in dealing with the impacts of catastrophes.

Risk transfer in the developed world is based on complex models of catastrophic risk exposure. During the past decade these models have been essential for pricing and accumulating catastrophe risk (Swiss Re 1999). The outcomes of these models are compared to complex decisionmaking models for both the sellers and buyers of risk to compare the benefit of risk transfer to its cost. In the developing world, the essential decisionmaking tools to evaluate alternative policy options are missing. Key among those tools is a clear understanding of the total impact of catastrophes.

Currently, the costs of catastrophes in the developing world are borne by the victims and governments. When disasters occur, governments generally rely on reallocating domestic budgets, redirecting approved loans , or aid and new loans to restore lost infrastructure. So long as the international community is willing to provide needed resources to the developing world, often at substantially reduced cost, to replace lost infrastructure, no change in current policy may be necessary.

As the lending and aid community looks at the options for more efficiently dealing with costs of catastrophes, the issue of risk transfer will become more important. In some cases the use of risk transfer may be much more efficient than the use of lending after the fact. The equitable argument of allocating costs to activities may reduce the willingness of the international community to subsidize inefficient behavior. While risk transfer has proven an effective tool to deal with the costs of catastrophes in the developed world, its role in the developing world is still undefined. Even worse, the terms of the dialogue have not been subject to much discussion. Without developing the proper information, there can be no meaningful dialogue. At the same time the range of policy options available will be dependent on the long-term role that the international lending and aid agencies are willing to play to finance the losses from catastrophes in the developing world. The role of privatization, financial sector reform, devolution, and other policy objectives all will influence this discussion. This dialogue will be essential to develop any policy options.

The tug between governmental subsidies, direct or indirect, to support desired activity and the need to efficiently and fairly allocate capital to absorb the real risk associated with its expenditure has been one of the great recent policy debates. The discussions of environmental accounting and impact assessment are good examples of this debate. The increasing burdens of natural catastrophes on development may warrant its attention as an issue of comparable importance.

Note

1. Discussions with my colleagues at the International Institute of Applied Systems Analysis (IIASA), particularly Joanne Linnerooth-Bayer, Landis MacKellar, and Koko Warner-Merl, were helpful in preparing this paper. Discussions with Howard Kunreuther, Charlotte Benson, and Alcira Kreimer also contributed to my appreciation of the issues. As always, the views expressed are those of the author and not of any institution or organization, including IIASA.

References

Arriens, W. T. L., and C. Benson. 1999. "Post-Disaster Rehabilitation: The Experience of the Asian Development Bank." Paper before IDNR-ESCAP Regional Meeting for Asia: Risk Reduction and Society in the 21ˢᵗ Century, Bangkok, 23-26 February 1999.

Insurance Services Office (ISO). 1999. *Financing Catastrophe Risk: Capital Market Solutions.* New York, N.Y.: Insurance Services Office.

Kreimer, A., and others. 1998. *The World Bank's Experience with Post-Conflict Reconstruction.* Washington, D.C.: World Bank.

Kunreuther, H., and Richard J. Roth, eds. 1998. *Paying the Price: The Status and Role of Insurance against Natural Disasters in the United States.* Washington, D.C.: Joseph Henry Press.

Maxwell, S. 1999. "The Meaning and Measurement of Poverty." ODI Poverty Briefing 3 (February 1999).

Munich Re. 1998. Topics: Annual Review of Natural Catastrophes 1997. Munich.

____. 1998a. World Map of Natural Hazards. Munich.

____. 1998b. "Munich Re's Review of Natural Catastrophes in 1998." Press release, December 29.

____. 1999. "Climate Change and Increase in Loss Trend Persist." Press release, March 15.

New York Times. 1999. "New Focus of Climate Fears: Altered Air Currents." May 18.

Shinozuka, H.., and R. J. Roth, eds. 1998. *Engineering and Socioeconomic Impacts of Earthquakes: An Analysis of Electricity Lifeline Disruptions in the New Madrid Area.* New York: Multidisciplinary Center for Earthquake Engineering Research.

Swiss Re. 1997. "Too Little Reinsurance of Natural Disasters in Many Markets." *sigma* no.7/1997.

____. 1997a. "Learning from Disaster: The Floods in the Czech Republic, Poland and Germany in the Summer of 1997."

____. 1998a. *Floods—An Insurable Risk?* Zurich: Swiss Reinsurance Company.

____. 1998b. *Floods—An Insurable Risk? A Market Survey.* Zurich: Swiss Reinsurance Company.

____. 1999. "Natural Catastrophes and Man-made Disasters 1998: Storms, Hail and Ice Caused Billion-Dollar Losses." *sigma* no. 1/1999.

World Bank. 1991. *World Development Report 1990: Poverty.* Washington D.C.: Oxford University Press.

World Bank. 1994. *World Development Report 1994: Infrastructure for Development* Washington D.C.: Oxford University Press.

Chapter 6

Flooding Issues: The Case of the United States

Juan B. Valdés

Floods and their related damages play a very important role in the development of the United States. In spite of significant progress made with respect to weather forecasting, damages are increasing, a main economic concern both in developed countries and the developing world. In the United States annual economic losses caused by floods (in constant US dollars) have been increasing while loss of human life has not declined (figure 1). However, data on lives lost may reflect an improvement in the recent past: almost 90 percent of deaths are caused by flash floods and more than half to the crossing of river flows and other vehicular accidents. The damages from floods is the highest of all natural disasters in the country. Eighty percent of the areas declared as natural disasters by the president of the United States are due to floods (FEMA 1999).

In a detailed analysis of the impact of the 1993 floods, Pielke (1999) notes that one of the main reasons behind the lack of progress shown by society is due to erroneous perceptions about flood occurrences.

Figure 1 Evolution of economic losses and loss of human life due to floods in the United States

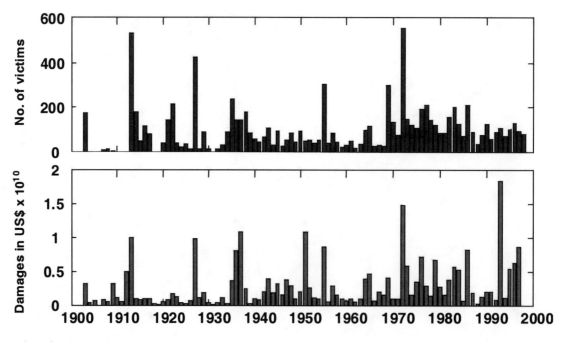

Source: National Weather Service 1999.

Pielke identifies nine myths in the treatment of flooding issues that hamper the development of new management policies.

Mitigating the impact of floods on society should be part of a comprehensive approach of the administration of water resources in a given country. In the United States, as in almost all countries, the government has taken the main responsibility of handling the resource given its importance to society. Generally, investment in water resources administration is one of the most important of a country's investments in infrastructure.

Management of Water Resources indicates four problems related to governmental actions in the sector (World Bank 1993).
1. Fragmentation of the public sector
2. Reliance on government agencies with poor coordination, thus poor financial control.
3. Poor programming of public investments and policy development
4. Over-reliance on technical characteristics; neglect of social, environmental, and legal priorities.

To manage water resources more efficiently, the Bank publication promotes the development of institutional policies and reforms balancing the efficiency of market forces while strengthening the capability of governments to carry out their important role in the administration of the natural resource.

This is the most important message of this World Bank document. It proposes adopting comprehensive policies and handling water as an economic asset, combined with a decentralized administration, higher reliance on the price of the resource, and full participation of the beneficiaries. This approach is consistent with other documents such as the Dublin Document (1992) of the International Conference on Water and the Environment as well as Agenda 21 of the United Nations Conference on the Environment and Development (1992).

With respect to floods these recommendations are similar to those proposed in the United States by the U.S. Interagency Floodplain Management Review Committee, which assessed the 1993 floods in the Midwest (ITFPMRC 1994). The ITFPMRC recommendations will be reviewed in greater detail in the section on examples of floods in this chapter.

Therefore, a comprehensive system to analyze policies and options may help administrators to manage water resources and resolve flood-related problems. This system should make it easier to review the relationship between the ecosystem and social activities in the water basin. It should also provide the mechanisms to develop policies for regulations, incentives, investment plans, and environmental protection as well as for relationships among these sectors (Valdés and others 1995b).

Characteristics of Water Infrastructure Investments

Water resources infrastructure projects generally are the responsibility of the public sector at all levels. These projects usually have the following characteristics (World Bank 1993):
*   Planning investments in the very long term.
*   Large initial investments and economies of scale.
*   Political interference in decisionmaking.
*   Interdependence of water uses.
*   Some actions such as flood forecasts and their mitigation are for the public good and cannot be quantified in terms of each individual.
*   Governments generally hold ownership of water resources given their importance to national security and to regional development.
*   Governments usually have control of water in areas with periodic droughts since water is the element that supports life.

Historical Evolution of Flood Administration and Mitigation in the United States

Management of water resources in the United States, especially with respect to floods and their mitigation, may be divided in four phases (Wurbs 1983):

*   Before 1936
*   1936-1966: Emphasis on structural actions
*   1966-1986: Structural and nonstructural actions
*   1986-present: Federal-regional consortia.

Before 1936

This period, in which a significant increase in the occupation of floodplains took place, was based on the proliferation of protection measures, both individual or at the community level, without taking into account their impact upstream or downstream of the works. The direct involvement of the federal government was minimal, and even resisted by some states, although there was increasing demand on the federal government to become involved in flood protection, particularly when local actions were inadequate. However, the federal government participated in flood protection and mitigation works, normally hidden in the works intended to promote navigation and commerce. In 1824 Congress authorized the president to undertake studies and works to ensure commerce and hire civil engineers and officers of the Corps of Engineers. The main intervention of the federal government, however, took place in the lower basin of the Mississippi River.

For instance, the 1849 and 1850 Acts took care of the floods at the lower basin of the Mississippi and transferred to state governments approximately 100,000 square miles of federal property with a view to use the revenues derived from such sales in the construction of protection measures such as longitudinal banks made by the States. In the debates over these works it was mentioned that federal taxes were used to favor a particular community and group of people. This debate continues to date.

In 1850 Congress sent the U.S. Army Corps of Engineers (USACE) to perform its first exercise in planning in which the Corps was to identify the "most appropriate plan" to control the Lower Mississippi floods. Two reports were submitted with strong differences between them. The first, prepared by Captain Humphreys, emphasized structural actions (levees-only), excluding other measures. The other report, charged to Engineer Ellet, recommended a wider strategy—strengthening the banks in the lower Mississippi with dams and increasing flows in the upper part. In 1861 the Corps decided to follow the recommendations of the first report. The Corps' activities were increased with the River and Ports Act of 1899, in which it was

authorized to control and/or ban the discharge of dredging material and other wastes in navigable rivers.

The Reclamation Act of 1902 established the Reclamation Service. This service was called the Bureau of Reclamation (USBR) in 1923, and was given authority in the basin headwaters and responsibility for the development of water resources for irrigation and hydroelectricity in the western United States. Subsequently, this agency notably increased its scope. The Federal Hydroelectricity Act of 1920 and the Rivers and Ports Act of 1925 gave to the Federal Power Commission (FPC) the responsibility of issuing licenses to private hydroelectricity providers and the funds to undertake the studies.

It is important to note that Congress did not authorize earmarked funds for flood control until the year 1917, when the Ohio and Mississippi Rivers floods gave way to the first project funded by the federal government.

1936-1966: Emphasis on Structural Actions

A series of catastrophic floods in the United States in 1935 and 1936, including of the Potomac River in Washington, D.C., forced Congress to pass the Flood Control Act in 1936, where the federal government assumed the responsibility for flood control and initiated an effort, at the national level, to construct hydraulic works intended to do that. Critics of the act noted that the philosophy of individual projects instead of a comprehensive view of the basin would lead to an increase in the development of the floodplains, giving at the same time the wrong idea on the safety of this development.

The primary federal government agency in charge of this task was the Army Corps of Engineers. Other federal agencies were created in individual jurisdictions to deal with the issue of floods, such as the Tennessee Valley Authority (TVA), the Bureau of Reclamation (USBR), and the Soil Conservation Service (SCS), established in 1954 to oversee works at basin headwaters.

During these 30 years these agencies embarked on a massive program of hydraulic works including dams, weirs, river walls, and channel improvements, with an approximate investment of 10 billion dollars (James and Lee 1971). By 1961 the Corps had built more than 9,000 miles of retaining walls and 220 dams while the development of the floodplains increased at a rate of 3 percent annually. At the same time, annual losses due to floods increased, reaching $1 billion in 1966. By the end of the 1970s more than 5 million acres had been developed for urban uses and had given rise to more than 6,000 communities with populations of more than 2,500. Population growth in the floodplains increased at a rate twice the population increase of the entire United States (American Rivers 1997).

Even though during this period emphasis on water resource management shifted from individuals and communities to the federal government, the philosophy of "control and/or tame Mother Nature" did not change. The emphasis was placed, therefore, on structural measures. This attitude was strengthened by the financing requirements, in which structural measures were paid fully by the federal government while States and communities had to provide the land for the works. The Flood Control Act spelled out the conditions under which the federal government would take care of flood control works: "if and when benefits are higher than estimated costs and if the social safety of individuals is being affected negatively."

The act required that the Army Corps of Engineers perform a cost-benefit analysis of all flood control projects. The Corps pioneered an approach to assess the benefits and use a discount rate to evaluate the projects. The method to estimate benefits was based on the expected value of avoided damages; the only uncertainty taken into account was the uncertainty in the flows. Currently, the Corps has adopted an evaluation system based on the explicit acknowledgment of economic and hydraulic uncertainties besides the hydrological uncertainties. This new method was implemented in the American River in California (USACE 1991), after which a debate ensued on possible biases in the estimate (NRC 1995). An analysis of the evolution of the USACE planning process may be seen in another NRC report (NRC 1999).

In spite of an increasing level of investments intended to protect communities and control floods, flood damages continued to increase, mainly because of the intensified development in the floodplains and the increase in the value of buildings and other construction in the floodplains. Because of this, in 1965 the Task Force on Federal Flood Control Policy (TFFFCP), was established. Its 1966 published recommendations noted the need to plan and regulate the floodplain and outline a combination of structural and nonstructural actions to mitigate damages.

1966-1986: Structural and Nonstructural Actions

The recommendations of the TFFFCP were adapted and emphasized by the National Water Commission (NWC). One of the recommendations of the report was implemented in the National Flood Insurance Program (NFIP), which was modified on several occasions. It concerns a joint program of the federal government, state governments, the communities, and the insurance industry, currently under the responsibility of the Federal Emergency Management Agency (FEMA). The NFIP allows communities that agree to regulate floodplains access to NFIP flood insurance through private companies.

During 1970-1985 there was an important change in USACE activities, because Congress did not authorize any major project in water resources. One of the reasons was the large variability of discount rates for the evaluation of water projects.

The switch from primarily structural actions to combination measures was continued by the Water Resources Development Act of 1974, which requires that federal government agencies review nonstructural actions in the planning and design of any project that has flood mitigation as one of its components. Several laws amended the 1974 act, but its main intent remained unchanged. One of the changes was related to the direct input of beneficiary communities by increasing their contribution to structural measures and allowing the federal government to contribute to the cost of nonstructural measures.

1986-Present: Federal-Regional Consortia

In 1994 the Unified National Program for Floodplain Management emphasized combining mitigation strategies, from structural measures to the restoration of floodplains (FEMA 1994).

The 1996 Water Resources Development Act (WRDA '96) significantly changed flood mitigation policies. In the WRDA '86 federal involvement ranged between 50 percent and 75 percent for structural measures and 75 percent federal for nonstructural measures. WRDA '96 increased the nonfederal participation to 35 percent for structural measures and for nonstructural measures. That is, the community is being asked for a greater share in the costs of both structural and nonstructural mitigation measures. This increased contribution should also be granted in the responsibility for floodplain management, by requiring that regional and local authorities design a system that reduces future flood impact on the area of the proposed project.

WRDA '96 also changes the previous reliance on ex≤post assistance to mitigating the risk of floods ex-ante (protection and/or elevation of dwellings, and purchase and relocation outside the floodplain). The act restates the principle that preventing and decreasing flood damages should be the first line of protection, to be supplemented with structural and nonstructural measures when necessary and with public awareness campaigns and insurance included as main components for the remaining flood risk. As mentioned it the U.S. Interagency Floodplain Management Review Committee (ITFPMRC), the 1996 act gives greater recognition to the role of nonstructural measures in damage mitigation.

The United States Government is involved in all aspects of water resources management, with more than 30 federal agencies within 10 departments, seven independent agencies, and several bilateral organizations. This federal government involvement is not evenly distributed in the States, reflecting the diversity of water-related issues.

National Flood Insurance Program

The National Flood Insurance Program (NFIP) has played an important role in developing alternatives to structural measures. The NFIP was established by the National Flood Insurance Act of 1968, which, backed by the federal government, made flood insurance available to communities that were willing to adopt and maintain floodplain administration with standards similar to or stricter than federal standards. NFIP's scope was expanded by the 1973 Flood Disaster Protection Act, in which the purchase of flood insurance was required as a condition to receive any type of federal or federal government-related assistance, such as mortgages. This two-part approach has been highly successful; more than 19,000 communities participate in the program. NFIP has established flood risk maps of these areas, with communities maintaining their floodplain law enforcement and management capabilities.

The federal standard is the definition of the flood area coverage with a 100-year recurrence period, that is, floods that have a 1 percent chance of being surpassed every year. This standard, now more appropriately called the 1 percent standard, defines the Special Flood Hazard Area (SFHA) displayed in the maps known as Flood Insurance Rate Maps (FIRMs). Communities must regulate the use of land in these areas.

An interesting analysis of the NFIP experience up to the 1993 Midwest floods, can be found in Kunreuther and White (1995). As a result of the lessons learned in those floods, the program was reformed through the Reform Act of the Flood Insurance Federal Program (1994). This act caused major insurance reforms and incorporated some of the recommendations of the Interagency Floodplain Management Review Committee (ITFPMRC) report. Communities and States have adopted floodplain management measures that exceed the NFIP standards.

The 1968 Act also required that the Executive Branch develop a consolidated floodplain management program. This report was updated in 1994 by the Federal Interagency Floodplain Management Task Force (FIFMTF). This report included national goals for floodplain regulation and placed more emphasis on the relocation and purchase of properties under risk.

Special programs for farmers exist within the Department of Agriculture, among them the Crop Insurance Program and the Crop Disaster Assistance Program. During the 1993 Mississippi floods approximately half of the payments were earmarked for farmers.

Current Status of the NFIP

In 1999, four years after the passing of the Flood Insurance Reform Act, significant changes have occurred in the implementation of the NFIP. Implementation has been facilitated by the publication of regulations of mortgage loan entities and the significant reduction of interest rates that encouraged owners to renegotiate their mortgages and, as a result, acquire insurance if they were in the floodplain. NFIP reported an increase of more than one million policies for dwellings in flood areas (SFHA) from October 1996 to December 1998 (NFIP 1999). It is estimated that 66 percent of these policies are due to mortgage requirements. Retention of policies has increased significantly to around 86 percent.

However, the Federal Insurance Administration (FIA) estimates that only 25 percent of the dwellings in the SFHA have flood insurance policies. FEMA and the NFIP have initiated advertising campaigns on flood insurance and on the risks and costs of the phenomenon. It has been estimated that the NFIP, together with the insurance industry and the communities, have reduced flood damage by approximately US$800 million per year. The system is self-sufficient for average annual losses but receives support from the federal government for catastrophic events.

Evaluation of Achievements Reached through Forecast, Alert, and Flood Mitigation Measures

In recent years the National Weather Service, in cooperation with other agencies, has made significant investments in the modernization and improvement of its hydrometeorological alert and climate forecast systems under the name NWS2000 (NWS 1999).

Some of these activities include the installation of a new network of Doppler meteorological radar; im-

provement of satellite systems; and automation of procurement, validation, and processing of information and forecast operations.

The Advanced Hydrologic Prediction System (AHPS) is the hydrologic component of the NWS modernization program. This system is not so sophisticated at the national level as, for example, the Advanced Weather Interactive Processing System (AWIPS), but it already has some basins in operation. The recent FY2000 budget request of the NWS includes an allotment of $2.2 million for the deployment of the AHPS system in the upper Midwest (including the States of Illinois, Michigan, Minnesota, and Wisconsin, and parts of Iowa, Missouri, and North Dakota) and tributaries to the upper Ohio River (NWS 1999). The system was validated in Des Moines (Iowa) in March 1997. The basin of the Des Moines River up to the Ottunwa station, which covers an area of 34,640 km^2, is one of the first in which the new AHPS system was implemented. The system there has been totally operational since 1997 (Fread and others 1999).

For urban floods the National Weather Service has supported the development of the so-called Local Flood Warning System (LFWS). The LFWS automatic systems were installed for the first time by the USBR in California at the beginning of the 1970s. The development of the Automated Local Evaluation in Real Time (ALERT) systems by the NWS noticeably facilitated the development of warning systems. There are more than 400 LFWSs in the United States, primarily in Arizona, California, and Texas.

Performance of U.S. Forecast, Alert, and Mitigation Systems before Modernization

Two examples make it possible to evaluate the performance of forecast, alert, and mitigation measures in the United States prior to the modernization of the NWS systems. One of them is the 1993 Upper Mississippi flood, the most expensive flood in United States history. The other is the 1997 Red River flood in North Dakota. Examples of operational systems in other countries can be found in Valdés and others (1995b) and in Valdés and Fattorelli (1999).

Upper Missouri-Mississippi Flood, 1993

The 1993 floods in the Midwest were one of the major disasters that have occurred in the United States, and the greatest due to floods. The floods left 38 people dead, 74,000 persons without housing, and $12 billion to $16 billion dollars in damage. The agricultural sector sustained more than half of those damages. Damages to housing were due both to the flood itself and to the high level of underground water and the backwater in the drainage networks.

Costs directly related to the emergency were estimated at approximately $6 billion. Other costs, for example, loss of profits, have not been quantified (Interagency Floodplain Management Review Committee 1995). Of the approximately 1,400 banks in the flooded area, 800 were inundated or destroyed. Many were saturated and failed several weeks after keeping the river contained. The city most affected was Des Moines, where the flooding of the water treatment plant left 250,000 residents without a safe water source for 22 days. An estimate of the losses covered by the NFIP was $50 million, approximately less than 1 percent of total losses.

In January 1994 a group known as the Interagency Floodplain Management Review Committee (ITFPMRC) was formed to analyze these problems. The committee's report, "Sharing the Challenge," contained the following recommendations (ITFPMRC 1994):

- Create legislation that clearly defines floodplain management responsibilities.
- Activate the Water Resources Council (WRC) to coordinate federal and federal-state-tribal activities in water resources.
- Modify the principal federal water resources planning document, "Principles and Guidelines," to ensure full consideration of nonstructural measures.
- Increase the efficiency and effectiveness of the NFIP. It is estimated that during the Mississippi flood only 10 percent of the affected housing had insurance provided by the NFIP.

Among additional recommendations the committee proposed to increase the waiting period to be eligible for the insurance benefits from 5 days to 30 days, to more proactively disseminate the program, and to provide small ex-post flood assistance to owners who were eligible for coverage but had not acquired it.

Red River Flood, 1997

The Red River induced an important flood in April 1997 in Minnesota and North Dakota. This flood caused considerable damage, particularly in the cities of Grand Forks, North Dakota, and East Grand Forks, Minnesota, where the flood level surpassed by more than 1 meter the previous maximum flood (1979). Damages were estimated at $4 billion; of these $3.6 billion were in the two aforementioned cities and their vicinity. These damages were partially attributed to errors in the generation, dissemination, and use of the forecasts provided by the National Weather Service (*USA Today* 1997, Pielke 1999).

As is its practice, after the event the NWS did an analysis of the flood characteristics and the performance of the forecast systems (NWS 1998). The report points out the successes as well as the areas in forecast generation and dissemination that can be improved. One of the recommendations is the implementation of the AHPS system in the region.

Pielke (1999) conducted an independent evaluation of the flood. In February 1997 the NWS had produced an "Outlook" presenting two possible scenarios of precipitation and temperature. The Red River elevations forecasted by these scenarios in the locality of East Grand Forks were 47.5 and 49 feet respectively (the maximum value was 21 feet above the flood level). This Outlook was complemented with daily forecasts in the weeks prior to the flood, but the maximum elevation value was forecasted only hours before it occurred. Pielke mentions that a major mistake in disseminating the forecast to users was that the estimated nature of the Outlook was not emphasized.

In his analysis Pielke points out that a survey of decisionmakers on the use of the Outlook offered multiple variants. Some of the decisionmakers believed the maximum elevation to be reached was 49 feet with no uncertainty. Others believed that the total variability was between 47.5 feet and 49 feet. Still others recognized the uncertainty in the forecast but when asked to indicate the variability said it was between +/-1 foot to +/-6 feet.

Pielke made several recommendations, two of which follow. First, the NWS should have better knowledge of the uncertainty of the forecasts and explore ways to better communicate uncertainty. Second, the decisionmaking responsibility should be at the local level. The NWS should not be put in the position of determining the level of risk that a community should face.

Impact of the Climate Change

An analysis of flood risks in a society also should take into account the possibility of climate change, whether natural or anthropogenic. The impact of climate change should be measured not only by the increase or reduction of the average value of the hydroclimatic variable (precipitation, temperature, flow) but also by the increase or reduction of its variability.

A study of the precipitation registries in the United States from 1900 to 1994 indicates that in the majority of the seasons average and extreme precipitation increased (Karl and Knight 1998, Karl and others 1995). Similar findings in Argentina are presented in the last report of the Intergovernmental Panel for Climate Change (IPCC 1999).

With respect to streamflows Lins and Slack (1999) conducted a similar study, but the results were not conclusive. The authors mention that there is no good physical reason to explain the divergence between precipitation and streamflow patterns other than sampling bias. This bias can be due to the difference in the area coverage of the streamflows study with the area studied by Karl and Knight. Pielke and Downton (1999) argue that the trends in extreme hydrologic floods are not as large as the increase in the vulnerability of society to these extreme events.

Final Comments

Floods and other natural phenomena present dangers for society in extreme situations that are not completely avoidable. However, planning for risk conditions and the use of forecast and early alert mechanisms can have a considerable impact on the prevention and mitigation of economic damages and of loss of lives due to natural disasters. Past experience with floods in the United States has shown the need to plan and to carry out mitigation works, both structural and nonstructural, at the basin level, not at the locality level. This planning, however, should be coordinated with the regions and communities to make mitigation efforts coherent. One of the problems in addressing natural risks in the United States has been the fragmentation of the responsibilities to prevent, combat, and mitigate their destructive effects.

Sustainable development with respect to floods should be based on the participation of all stakeholders in the decisionmaking process, in fiscal responsibility, in sharing the costs of the mitigation measures, and in balancing structural and nonstructural measures. Not taking action in advance to regulate development of the floodplain results in inexpensive nonstructural measures being replaced by expensive structural measures. Acting proactively rather than reactively is the key for the sustainable development of water resources.

References

American Rivers. 1997. "Real Choices: Reforming America's Flood Policies." Washington, D.C.

Federal Emergency Management Agency. 1981. "Flood Hazard Mitigation: Handbook of Common Procedures." Washington, D.C..

Fread, D. L., and others. 1999. "Recent Experience with Ensemble Streamflow Prediction in the Des Moines River Basin." In "Proceedings from the 14th Conference in Hydrology." American Meteorological Society. Dallas, Tex. 10-15.

Interagency Floodplain Management Review Committee. 1994. "Sharing the Challenge: Floodplain Management into the

21st Century." U.S. Government Printing Office. Washington, D.C.

James, D., and R. R. Lee. 1971. *Economics of Water Resources Planning*. New York: McGraw-Hill.

Karl, T. R., and R. W. Knight. 1998. "Secular Trend of Precipitation Amount, Frequency and Intensity in the United States." *Bulletin of American Meteorological Society* (79):231-41.

Karl, T. R., R. W. Knight, and N. Plummer. 1995. "Trends in High-Frequency Climate Variability in the Twentieth Century." *Nature* (377): 217-20.

Kunreuther, H. C., and G. F. White. 1995. "The Role of the National Flood Insurance Program in Reducing Losses and Promoting Wide Use of Floodplains." In *Coping with the Flood: The Next Phase. Water Resources Update* (95): 31-35.

Lins, H., and J. R. Slack. 1999. "Streamflow Trends in the United States." *Geophy. Res. Lett. 26*: 227-30.

National Research Council. 1995. "Flood Risk Management and the American River Basin: An Evaluation." Washington, D.C.

National Research Council. 1999. "New Directions in Water Resources Planning for the U.S. Army Corps of Engineers." Washington, D.C.

National Weather Service. 1998. "Service Assessment and Hydraulic Analysis." Washington, D.C.

Pielke, R. A., Jr. 1999. "Who Decides? Forecasts and Responsibilities in the 1997 Red River Flood." *Applied Behavioral Science Review* 7 (2):83-101.

Pielke, R. A., Jr., and M. W. Downton. 1999. "U.S. Trends in Streamflow and Precipitation: Using Societal Impact Data to Address Apparent Paradox." *Bulletin of American Meteorological Society* (80) 1435-36.

U.S. Army Corps of Engineers Hydrologic Engineering Center. 1988. "Floodway Determination Using Computer Program HEC-2."

U.S. Army Corps of Engineers Sacramento District. 1991. "American River Watershed Investigation, California: Feasibility Report." USACE Sacramento District and The Reclamation Board, State of California.

U.S. Water Resources Council. 1972. "Regulation of Flood Hazard Areas to Reduce Flood Losses." Vols. I and II. Washington, D.C.

U.S. Water Resources Council. 1982. "Economic and Environmental Principles and Guidelines for Water and Related Land Resources Implementation Studies." Washington, D.C.

Valdés, J. B., and J. B. Marco. 1995. "Effectiveness of Flood Control Infrastructure: Reservoirs." In "Proceedings of the U.S.-Italy Workshop of the Hydrometeorology, Impacts and Management of Floods." National Science Foundation and National Research Council (Italy). Perugia, Italy.

Valdés, J. B., and others. 1995. "Water Resources Extremes and Sustainable Development." In "Proceedings of the 1995 International Symposium on Sustainable Development," Taipei, Taiwan. Texas A&M University and the Ministry for the Environment of Taiwan. Office of International Programs, Texas A&M University, College Station, Tex. ROC, 94-112.

Valdés, J. B., and S. Fattorelli. 1990. "Operational Systems for Hydrologic Forecasting: A Revision and Application to the Paraná, Paraguay and Uruguay River Basins. Report to the Subunit for Coordination of Emergencies" (in Spanish). Ministry of Interior, Buenos Aires, Argentina.

World Bank. 1993. *Water Resources Management. A World Bank Policy Paper*. Washington, D.C.

Wurbs, R. A. 1983. "Economic Feasibility of Flood Control Improvements." *ASCE Journal of Water Resources Planning and Management* 109 (1): 29-47.

Chapter 7

Cultural Heritage and Natural Disasters: Incentives for Risk Management and Mitigation

June Taboroff

Cultural heritage, encompassing the archaeological and historical built environment and movable heritage, is at risk from natural disasters, especially in low-income countries. Fires, earthquakes, flooding, tsunami, land and mud slides, winds, and tropical storms are among the major causes of loss and damage. These disasters result in the loss of irreplaceable artistic and cultural assets and are costly. The harm to cultural heritage further increases in the absence of adequate risk estimation, evaluation, and minimization measures. Just as the loss of family photographs and treasured art objects is one of the most painful personal blows resulting from a natural disaster, so is the loss of significant cultural heritage landmarks a sore impoverishment for communities.

Major disasters—that is, high consequence/low probability events—occur with relentless disregard to cultural assets. Less serious events that might occur either over longer periods (sea level rise or climate change) and with greater frequency (periodic flooding, siltation, or desertification), than high probability/lower consequence situations, can also be highly damaging,

The last decades have witnessed a series of costly disasters that have struck cultural centers: the 1997 earthquake in Assisi, which destroyed priceless Giotto frescoes; the 1996 earthquakes in Yunnan Province in China, which reduced to rubble parts of the World Heritage city of Lijang; the fire in Madagascar, which destroyed the national archive; the 1997 floods in eastern Germany; and the 1998 Central American hurricanes.

The historic record relates many tales of natural disasters: floods, earthquakes, fires, and storms. Perhaps the most famous natural disaster of all time was the eruption of Mount Vesuvius and the destruction of Pompeii, Herculaneum, and other nearby towns. The mythical story of Atlantis symbolizes the loss of a whole civilization due to a powerful and mysterious natural occurrence.

Although there is a long tradition of devastating natural disasters that have destroyed irreplaceable cultural resources, awareness of the need to reduce risk is low, and memory is short of costs incurred because of lack of preparedness. In the developing world evidence points to a pattern of higher vulnerability to these natural disasters, a weak record of implementation of protective measures to control or limit damage, exacerbated negative impacts, and lengthy recovery time.

Why? Effective risk management of cultural assets is rare because of inadequate knowledge of the assets, failure to calculate the true cost of loss and damage, and the difficulty of putting a value on the nonmarket nature of many cultural heritage values. Arguments deployed in Venice by elected officials are typical: "…. there is no point in spending $3 billion on a project now when the next really bad flood could be 167 years away." Moreover, like other types of environmental risk management, the risks are highly location dependent, which seems to reduce the likelihood of concerted national or international efforts.

The following comments will consider the types and degree of risk to cultural heritage; systems and tools for reducing and mitigating risk; principles of risk preparedness for cultural heritage; existing programs to avert risk; incentives to manage risks; and proposals for improving risk management for cultural heritage.

Venice: An Example

In the past in Venice devastating floods, like that of 1966, occurred once every 800 years. Scientific evidence now suggests that their frequency is likely to quadruple to once every 200 years. This increase is due to the influence of sea level rise, subsidence, and changing weather patterns. After the 1966 flood a huge effort was undertaken, despite political squabbling and the familiar shortcomings of the Italian bureaucracy, to repair sea walls, churches, and palazzi, and the artistic heritage left to decay by years of negligence. A consortium proposed a system of large mobile gates, Operation Moses, to defend Venice from high waters by shutting off the lagoon from the sea. One argument says that the floodgates would " provide Venice with the ultimate long-term insurance policy complementing other more conventional measures."

Yet decisionmakers remain uncertain about what steps to take. The current mayor of Venice has insisted that the issue of high water be kept in perspective: "The problem of acqua alta does not resolve the city's other problems," namely his administration's efforts to revive and modernize his decaying city while preserving its artistic legacy. As one journalist wrote, "While scientists continue to argue, a tide of other troubles risks swamping Venice, tourism for one. More than 10 million tourists visit Venice every year, including 7 million day trippers. As their numbers rise relentlessly, the Venetians are continuing to desert their city." In the context of urban environmental problems, deciding on a plan to protect cultural heritage from natural disasters seems elusive.

Types of Natural Hazards

The main types of natural hazard that affect cultural assets are fire, flooding, earthquakes and related disasters, tsunami, land and mud slides and avalanches, winds and tropical storms, and sea level rise. Examples of types of damage to historic buildings and their contents, historic districts, and archaeological sites and cultural landscapes follow.

Fire

Fire causes severe damage directly and indirectly to property and cultural heritage. The main types of damage that result from fire are:
- Damage to buildings and their contents: full or partial destruction of objects and building elements by burning
- Damage from heat smoke and combustion by-products to structures, interior finishes, and objects
- Water damage resulting from the effects of fire fighting
- Damage to historic districts: damage to structures and objects as above; destruction of municipal infrastructure systems
- Damage to archaeological sites and cultural landscapes: damage to structures and objects located within sites and landscapes as above, destruction of natural habitat, increased risk of secondary damage from floods and mud slides.

Flooding

Severe direct and indirect damage to property and cultural heritage can be caused by flooding. Floods are varied in form: slow rising rivers; rapidly rising rivers, as in the 1997 floods in East Germany; and breakdown of river system controls or dams.

Damage may range from soiling basements and lower floors and their contents, and long-term increase in residual moisture to destruction of structures and buildings from the tremendous force of flood waters. Forms of damage to buildings and their contents include:
- Collapse or movement of a building due to force of water flow

- Soil erosion near buildings or foundation settlement
- Detachment of connected elements such as stairs
- Inundation of building services sited in basement areas
- Contamination of water with sewerage systems
- Damage to objects from water and humidity.

Damage to historic districts includes:
- Damage to constituent structures and objects
- Full or partial destruction of municipal services
- Loss or damage to municipal infrastructure.

Damage to cultural landscapes and archaeological sites consists of loss or destruction of landscape elements and defining features, alteration of landscape functioning, and deposition of debris.

Earthquakes and Related Disasters

Earthquakes can cause damage both directly and indirectly to property and cultural heritage, resulting in various types of damage.

Damage to buildings and their contents consists of structural collapse and damage related to lateral forces transmitted to buildings. Historic districts, in addition to damage to component structures and objects, may also suffer damage to their infrastructure and transport systems. Archaeological sites and cultural landscapes may suffer the types of damage noted for individual monuments and buildings as well as damage to landscape features, increased risk of secondary damage from fire and flooding, and loss of habitat.

Tsunami

Tsunamis (tidal waves) are of high importance in coastal regions, particularly in the Pacific basin. Damages are similar to high force flooding.

Land and Mud Slides and Flows, and Avalanches

In mountainous or hilly regions, land and mud slides and avalanches are hazards of importance. They are often related to other hazards: mud slides occur during flooding, particularly in eroded areas. This winter's avalanches in the French, Swiss, and Italian Alps are a warning of the potential to destroy property and life.

Winds and Tropical Storms

Storms associated with high winds and precipitation are hazards typical of coastal areas in tropical and subtropical climates. These storms are devastating and indiscriminate in their paths. The recent storms in Honduras exemplify the impacts of these disasters on human settlements and their cultural assets.

Sea Level Rise and Coastal Change

Many coastal zones are located in geologically dynamic areas where sea levels and coastal profiles are changing, Historically, change in sea level has been an important cause of damage to cultural sites. Witness the underwater ruins off the Turkish coast. Today measuring sea level change has become more reliable, but short of elaborate systems of dikes or other sea barriers, little can be done to prevent the incursion of water onto land. Similarly, changes in river courses over time have had an impact on cultural sites. Sites that once were at river's edge now may be some kilometers from the river bed; or sites that were once some distance from rivers now may be inundated.

Elements of Disaster Planning and Mitigation

Although the specifics are different, disaster planning and mitigation will need to take into account many of the same sorts of factors. Three basic questions are critical:
- What can go wrong?
- What are the range and magnitude of the adverse impacts?
- How likely are the adverse impacts?

In summary form, information needed for the major types of natural disasters are as follows:

For flooding:
   Historical record of past floods
   Probability of flooding occurring

Probability of height and volume of flood waters
Sensitivity of cultural heritage to flooding

For tsunamis:
Probability of tsunamis occurring in the region
Probability of tsunamis height and run-up (zoning maps show areas that would be submerged at various run–up heights)
Sensitivity of cultural heritage to tsunami waves

For land and mud slides and avalanches:
Historical record of past landslides and avalanches
Assessment of slope stability
Extraneous factors (water saturation, construction works)
Mapping of cultural heritage sites

For tropical storms:
Probability assessment for the intensity and frequency of storms (velocity, duration, direction)
Topographic features that may protect or expose heritage features
Possible effects of other structural, vegetative, or landscape features
Adequacy of roofs and supporting structures to withstand wind forces

Analysis of Risk from Natural Disasters:
Risk Profile

Risk analysis concerns three components: hazard, control mechanism, and receptor. The magnitude of hazard is related to the nature and quantity of materials and/or process that constitute the risk source, that is, water flows, wind strength, earthquake strength. Controls might be physical (dikes, dams, seismic reinforcement) or management based (procedures and training). Receptor (or target) can be a historic town, museum, archaeological site. Because much has been written on this subject, the present paper will not examine analysis at length.

The combination of the three factors will determine how significant a risk exists by considering what is the probability of the adverse event and what would be the consequences. Risks are site dependent.

Important contributory factors that affect outcomes for cultural heritage are: the type and volume of objects on site (ceramics, glass, paper); location of above ground or underground storage tanks and other infrastructure; leak detection mechanisms; maintenance arrangements; staff training and awareness; and presence of residents.

Evaluating Risk for Cultural Heritage

Two factors are at work in evaluating risk of damage to cultural heritage: the probability that events will cause or lead to degradation, and the severity of the degradation. Among the standard approaches for evaluation is a ranking matrix for severity and probability.

Typically, severity will be evaluated on a scale of 1 to 5 in which 1 represents fatality, property damage, or business interruption over $50 million; 2 = severe injury involving hospitalization and evacuation of the public, property, or business interruption greater than $1m and less than $50 m.; 3 = property damage greater than $50,000 but less than $1 m; 4 = minor injury, contamination restricted to site, damage greater than $1,000 but less than $50,000; and 5 = minor injury, fire that is controlled by hand held fire extinguishers.

Probability is also judged on a scale of 1 to 5 in which 1 represents once per year – high ; 2 = once per 10 years – moderate; 3 = once per 100 years – medium; 4 = once per 1,000 years – low; and 5 = once per 1,000,000 years – very low.

Risk Mapping

Risk mapping, which provides a geographical component to risk evaluation, adds another set of information to enable better prediction. Such mapping is being tried in Italy, partially as a response to several decades of severe earthquakes. The U.S. National Park Service has also instituted a system of risk mapping for cultural and natural resources under its control.

Principles of Risk Preparedness and Mitigation for Cultural Heritage

Cultural heritage management has benefited from advances in environmental planning and a change in orientation from the focus on individual monuments to heritage in its wider physical and social context. These lessons in turn help define a series of principles for heritage risk management in which advance planning stands as a determinant of effective protection. The nine principles can be defined as follows:

1. Disaster planning for a cultural heritage site should be conceived for the whole site including its buildings, structures and contents, and landscapes.
2. This planning should integrate relevant heritage considerations within a site's overall disaster preparedness and mitigation strategy.
3. Preparedness requirements should be met in heritage sites by means that will have least negative impact on heritage values.
4. Documentation of heritage sites, their significant attributes and any history of disaster response is the basis for appropriate disaster planning.
5. Maintenance programs for historic sites should take into account a cultural heritage at risk perspective.
6. Property occupants and users should be directly involved in the development of emergency response plans.
7. During emergencies, securing heritage features should be a high priority.
8. Following a disaster, every effort should be made to ensure the retention and repair of structures or features that have suffered damage or loss.
9. Conservation principles should be integrated where appropriate in all phases of disaster planning and mitigation.

Risk Management for Cultural Heritage

Risk management is the process of implementing decisions about accepting or controlling risk, based usually on cost-benefit analysis. Risks may be controlled through the application of technology, procedures, or alternative practices. In the field of cultural heritage, the formative experience of World War II showed the need for emergency planning for museums and other places of high cultural value.

To identify and minimize potential damage and liabilities, significant gains in reducing risk can be achieved by using the following systems, preferably in a coordinated manner: national inventories of historic sites; Object ID; and an emergency works and advice service. At a site-specific level, individual disaster plans can be detailed. Although standards for inventory and Object ID will be set at the national level, much of this preparatory work can be delegated to the local level.

National Inventories

National inventories of historic places are the keystone of heritage management for the simple reason that knowing what one's resources are is a prerequisite for effective safeguarding. It is a hallmark of the developing world that inventories are incomplete, dusty, hard to access, and unrelated to overall spatial planning.

Two recent advances enhance the effectiveness of national inventories. The first is the definition of "core data standards" for archaeological and historic sites under the auspices of the Council of Europe. The core data approach encourages a more efficient and uniform system of recording information. The second advance is the advent of inexpensive computer technology and diffusion of Geographic Information Systems (GIS). GIS has opened the possibility of large and speedy gains in national inventories. The GIS data base combines spatial attributes and thematic map layers with information such as administrative boundaries, cadastre information, historic maps, site inventories. Maps can be layered with additional features and information sets as needed. After years of stagnation fine work has been carried out with the help of international aid in Jordan, Tunisia, and the West Bank–Gaza, the latter by a nongovernmental organization (NGO), Riwaq.

Such inventories have proven highly useful for disaster mitigation. A GIS database can provide precise locational information depicting historic features and extent of damage (for example, from floods). In a recent flood episode in the Chesapeake and Ohio Canal National Park in the United States, the standard operational procedure to assemble a disaster response team composed of park officials and an interagency task force was modified by adding mapping professionals. Among the data collected were peak flood data, which helps to analyze patterns of flood impacts over time; flood damage monitoring; and direct aid to the most vulnerable areas. A Geographic Information System (GIS) can aid disaster response to identify resources, create accurate maps showing both natural and cultural resources, and establish databases to enhance maintenance of facilities.

Object ID

Object ID is an international documentation standard for the information needed to identify art and antiques—the movable heritage. It responds to the failure of the current practice of recording objects to enable owners, dealers, customs officials, and police to identify objects confidently and quickly and was initially prompted by the dramatic costs of loss of art works through illicit trade and theft. Its applicability for disaster mitigation is also high. Today illicit trade in antiquities, theft of art works, and loss of art through disasters particularly impoverishes the developing world. Spearheaded by the Getty Information Institute, Object ID is the result of intensive consultations with key groups involved in the art trade: museums and cultural institutions. art galleries and auctioneers. appraisers. customs officials. police. insurance companies. and international agencies. The contents of the standard were identified by a combination of background research, interviews, and surveys of major institutions.

Object ID is based on the concept of core data standards, that is, the minimum basic information required for identification. The inclusion of the category "distinguishing features" is an important factor in the usefulness of the tool for the purposes of recognition. Object ID was designed to meet the needs of the recorder as well as the retriever: information is easy to input, and it is easy for a lost object to be found. It complements existing object inventories of museums and other collections. Launched in 1997, it is still to gain general currency.

Emergency Works and Advice Services

Some countries have put into effect emergency works and advice services for disasters. In the United Kingdom, English Heritage recently set up an Emergency Works and Advice Scheme. It is designed to help owners deal with sudden catastrophes and unforeseeable circumstances and to prevent dramatic deterioration in a building or monument: "to buy time" for it until a permanent solution can be put into place. It includes advice and a site visit, and covers work that is necessary immediately to protect the overall stability or integrity of an historic building or to preserve specific features. The proposed work must be the minimum necessary, using the most cost-effective means to achieve the objective. Regional teams are responsible for the delivery of this system.

Individual Disaster Plans

At the individual site level, disaster plans are essential. Most major museums and some historic cities have such plans in place. The plan may include appointment of a disaster team including volunteers; evacuation of material; removal of debris and cleaning; evaluation of structural damage; securing of funding to return site to pre-disaster condition; and training of staff to deal with dangers and other aspects of disaster response. Risk reduction through adherence to building codes, fire proofing, fire alarms, resistant glass, and seismic strengthening are key elements in any preventive effort.

Initiatives to Reduce Risk from Disasters

A number of initiatives have tried to improve current practice. Among the most relevant are the following:

Operation Blue Shield

Borrowing the emblem of the 1954 Hague Convention, the Blue Shield initiative to improve risk preparedness for cultural heritage was begun by the International Council on Monuments and Sites (ICOMOS) in 1992. In 1996 an international committee of the Blue Shield was created for coordinating emergency response efforts on behalf of ICOMOS, ICOM, ICA, and IFLA. The committee identified five key areas: funding, emergency response, training and guidelines, documentation, and awareness. But the very areas that they defined have proven to be stumbling blocks for Blue Shield: lack of adequate funding, ineffective coordination with international and national agencies responsible for disasters, and inability to respond in a timely manner to disasters. Blue Shield has yet to deliver tangible results.

The Getty Conservation Institute Disaster Preparedness, Mitigation and Response Activities

In 1990 the Getty Conservation Institute (GCI) began a collaborative project in Skopje (in the former Yugoslavia) to develop a methodology for seismic strengthening of Byzantine churches and other historic structures. In the same year in California GCI initiated a study with similar aim for adobe structures. Also in this year it organized an international conference in St. Petersburg, Conservation and Disaster Recovery: International Cooperation at the Library of the USSR Academy of Sciences," which reviewed the post-1988 fire. The CGI has had no recent activities.

Appropriations for Disaster Relief

In the U.S. natural disasters in the 1990s prompted the Congress to approve supplemental appropriations for disaster relief. In 1994 the Northridge Earthquake caused significant damage in the Los Angeles area. Congress responded by earmarking $10 million for historic preservation activities from a total appropriation of $550 million from the President's Discretionary Fund for Unanticipated Needs. In the previous year flood relief funds also allocated monies for preservation actions (some $5 million out of $6 billion). In the later case flood relief was used to fund nonconstruction activities such as on-site inspection by teams of preservation professionals to inspect buildings and pro-

vide technical advice. Printing and dissemination of a technical booklet, "Treatment of Flood Damaged Older and Historic Properties," was also funded.

Regional Workshops

A regional workshop on Integrating Cultural Heritage into National Disaster Planning, Mitigation, and Relief was held in Macedonia in 1997. Sponsored by the University of York, the Getty Grant Program, the Ministry of Culture of the Republic of Macedonia, and U.S. and Macedonia ICOMOS, this meeting had as its aim the development of national disaster plans. A case study on the World Heritage Site at Orhid was prepared, focusing on risks from fire and earthquake. A network of experts was initiated, but there has been virtually no follow-up on the conference.

English Heritage Emergency Works and Advice Scheme

As noted above, this scheme is designed to help owners deal with sudden catastrophes and unforeseeable circumstances and to prevent deterioration in a building or monument until a permanent solution can be put into place. It is built upon the regional conservation capacity of English Heritage.

Incentives for Mitigation and More Effective Risk Management

Incentives are bound to two factors: knowledge and delivery systems. Knowledge in this sense takes the form of both know-how or technical knowledge, for example, on what works needs to be undertaken, and information problems. Technical knowledge of best practice for earthquakes or water damage is unevenly accessible so that inappropriate techniques may be used that may cause additional damage. As in the case of other forms of knowledge, knowledge is less widely available in poorer countries and among the poor. Other incentives can be activated through the legal system and devolution of some responsibilities to the private and voluntary sector.

Knowledge of the value of cultural heritage and the cost of its loss is weak, particularly in poor countries. In some cases the financial implications from adverse events to the heritage may be difficult to assess. Nevertheless, the huge costs of repair or replacement have not been used effectively by those responsible for cultural heritage to persuade decisionmakers of the cost effectiveness of preventive planning and systems. Recent work on the economics of heritage conservation will be useful for understanding the total economic value of heritage.

An interesting effort to improve information problems is the Treasury of St. Francis of Assisi exhibition on view at the Metropolitan Museum of Art. As the *Financial Times* review notes, "If any good could be said to have come from the calamitous earthquakes that ravaged the Upper Church of the Basilica of St. Francis in Assisi in 1997, it is through the pleasure afforded by the 70 spectacular and revered icons, relics and religious works of art....that have been dispatched on an international tour in its wake." The exhibit, funded by a private Sienese bank, has raised awareness of the gravity of the Umbrian disaster.

Delivery of mitigation systems is also a problem. Comprehensive national inventories of historic sites, recording systems for movable cultural property, such as Object ID, and emergency regional expert teams are three simple ways to reduce damage, yet are not widespread.

There are however, a number of incentives that can be employed to improve the management of risk. These include legal requirements and activating the private and voluntary sector.

Legal Requirements

Legal compliance can be a powerful tool in improving disaster management for heritage. This may include compliance to specific building codes, earthquake resistant measures, and use of fire retardants. The consequences of breaching legislation can be extremely serious, and in addition to any fines for breach of legislation, repair or replacement costs (if applicable) or clean-up works can also be levied.

Indemnities are also a tool. In the case of art objects that are lent to foreign institutions, a system of indemnities is in place that operates at a national level. This represents a sort of insurance against loss due to natural disasters and acts of god.

Private Sector Role in Reducing Losses

In many countries private sector insurance and reinsurance plays an important role in sharing risks and reducing economic losses caused by disasters. They help cushion the blow for historic properties. Citizen groups can organize into neighborhood groups to respond to natural disasters, perhaps focused around historic religious structures.

The Poor, Cultural Heritage, and Protection

The poor are particularly vulnerable to loss of their cultural assets when natural disasters strike. In historic cities where cultural sites are dense, whether in Quito or Tblisi, low income households are often proportionally over-represented and thus are more likely to suffer when disaster hits. They are also less likely to be able to mobilize the resources needed to repair damaged cultural sites.

Natural disasters often aggravate already vulnerable situations. Chronic lack of maintenance of cultural heritage and inadequate infrastructure services deepen damage from disasters. In the historic center of Tblisi, Georgia, buildings already weakened by water damage from leaking pipes and inadequate maintenance were dealt a death blow by earthquakes that brought down historic buildings on their inhabitants' heads. Thus, a large number of relatively minor events such as groundwater contamination, lack of down pipes, and poor overall maintenance, when coupled with earthquake damage, have destroyed many historic buildings.

Recommendations for Adoption of Natural Disaster Risk Management

Cultural heritage is highly vulnerable in natural disasters, and current mechanisms to manage risks do not meet the growing, and overlooked, needs of mitigation and management. A careful program of support will result in significant cost savings to national and local governments, the insurance industry, individuals, and international relief agencies. Priority actions to be implemented include:

- Integrate measures for cultural heritage protection in global disaster management efforts.
- Support the creation of comprehensive national inventories of historic places.
- Institute the use of Object ID.
- Identify higher risk sites for priority action.
- In vulnerable areas draw up emergency preparedness plans, especially for museums.
- Allocate resources for planning and implementation of management systems.

Although disasters are disastrous, perversely they are often a catalyst and an opportunity for improvement. Cities such as Dubrovnik have seized on the opportunities presented by damaging natural disasters, in their case an earthquake, to draft legislation to enable new fiscal measures and to rehabilitate historic districts.

References

The Kobe/Kyoto Declaration on Risk Preparedness for Cultural Heritage. Resolution of the International Symposium on Risk Preparedness for Cultural Properties. Kobe/Tokyo, Japan. Adopted January 1997.

National Park Service Western, Pacific Northwest, and Rocky Mountain Regional Offices, Management of Disaster Mitigation and Response Programs for Historic Sites. Symposium held at the University of California, Berkeley, June 1995.

Stovel, H. 1998. "Risk Preparedness: A Management Manual for World Cultural Heritage." ICCROM, UNESCO, ICOMOS, WHC.

World Bank. 1997. *Environmental Assessment Sourcebook Update.* Environmental Hazard and Risk Assessment. Washington, D.C.

Chapter 8

Single-Family Housing: The Window of Opportunity for Mitigation Following Natural Disaster

Ronald S. Parker

The mission of the World Bank is to reduce poverty and to improve living standards through sustainable growth and investment in people. Unfortunately, progress in these areas can be short-lived if disaster strikes a borrower country, leaving development project beneficiaries worse off than before. Disasters strike the poor especially hard, and it takes them longer than the rest of society to recover.

Most natural disasters are recurrent rather than single events. The same types of disaster strike the same nations repeatedly. For example, during the last century Guatemala had 48 earthquakes greater than 6.0 on the Richter scale. So just as the poorer members of society are getting back on their feet, they often get knocked down again. Indeed, recurrent natural disaster is one of the causes of poverty in developing countries because it forces significant diversion of resources from sustainable development.

When the devastation caused by storms or earthquakes of similar magnitude in developed and developing countries is compared, the injury and death rates can be as much as 100 times higher in the poorer developing countries. Despite similar seismic characteristics and overall disaster vulnerability, the average annual death toll from natural disasters in Japan is under 100, while in Peru it is nearly 3,000. The 1989 earthquake in California produced only 67 casualties. In a country with mud homes and no building codes the same earthquake's death toll, no doubt, would have been in the thousands. Clearly, the quality of the built environment is a significant determinant of disaster-

related casualties and damage, and the more robust the economy, the shorter the recovery period. Lack of mitigation itself is an indicator of underdevelopment, one that the World Bank can help overcome.

Both the recurrent nature of disaster and the fact that technological remedies have existed for decades make disaster relief a field in which *mitigation* must be an integral part of a strategy of both recuperation and pre-disaster planning. Mitigation refers to policies and actions intended to reduce the impact of disaster the next time it occurs. While disasters are not fully preventable—earthquake-resistant buildings have fallen on their sides while staying intact—they can be mitigated so that fewer lives and less of the constructed environment are lost.

Disasters Are Windows of Educational Opportunity to Produce Responsible Behavior

As the Bank becomes more responsive to client needs and more focused on poverty, it will find itself working on single-family housing in the post-disaster context much more than it has it has in the past. Fortunately it has had a number of recent successes, such as the Argentina Flood Rehabilitation Project, which highlight important lessons. A quick response to housing losses following natural disaster is important. However, recent experience shows that it is equally important to identify the particular vulnerabilities of the local built environment and determine how to reduce them in ways that lead to durable solutions. For private single-family housing, durable solutions involve using locally available materials, culturally appropriate styles, and traditional building techniques. Any deviation in this respect is highly counter-developmental. If, following the reconstruction effort, families cannot provide themselves and their grown children with additional housing (as families grow and children marry), they will be obliged by circumstance to revert to dangerous traditional styles. Post-disaster reconstruction is no time to experiment with new materials, radical designs, or elaborate techniques beyond the skills of local masons and carpenters. Such things allow the window of educational opportunity to close without leaving behind sustainable improvement.

In reconstructing private housing following a major flood or earthquake, mitigation usually has a strong educational component. Educational messages focus on how to build safer housing. Such messages often are conveyed in community meetings, through the schools, and the media, and often directly to specialized groups involved in the building trades. Considering how long engineers have known why buildings fall down during earthquakes and storms, it is worth considering why almost none of that knowledge has been communicated to the poor in developing countries. Following 20 some field visits during a Harvard-sponsored study of reconstruction efforts, I became aware of a common failing of this approach. To protect victims from a worst-case scenario and/or to protect householders from substandard construction (in the event that builders do not follow instructions perfectly), most mitigation projects promote too many changes to traditional styles. Communication professionals know that any presentation with more than three main messages is ineffective. The development community needs to learn this lesson if disaster mitigation efforts aimed at private individuals are to attain their objectives.

During the recovery from each emergency, measures are almost always needed to reduce the risk of similar future disasters. Options to be considered should always include financial incentives, land use and management practices, a review of land tenure patterns, upgraded building codes, training for construction

craftsmen, and other nonstructural measures to lessen vulnerability. Although public officials generally have a basic understanding of what is required to deal with these challenges, their efforts invariably miss the people and neighborhoods that need them most. Extremely poor areas, both urban and rural, and informal settlements are the locations in which the bulk of the disaster-related homeless are likely to be found, but they are often the least likely to receive timely and effective help. These areas, where building codes are not enforced, require special treatment.

Natural disasters are hardly extraordinary events. They are part of everyday life in many countries—because of insufficient investment in prevention, the frequency with which they strike, and the manner in which they interact. For example, cyclones are followed by floods and landslides. During three decades the city of Tumaco, Colombia, experienced devastating earthquakes, floods, and fire. Private housing and public infrastructure had to be reconstructed repeatedly, and indirect costs multiplied. Public agencies could rely on the national government for help, and the wealthy relied on family and the banks. However, the poor had little recourse other than nongovernmental organization (NGO) support for a lucky few.

The implications of unlearned lessons from past reconstruction efforts interact as destructively as the various types of natural disaster, leading to endless repetitions of the same failed intervention strategies:

- The size of the population that needs to be reached with the mitigation message is enormous.
- Victims' *collective* potential to learn effectively is limited; they usually have little or no schooling and limited attention span.
- Victims' need for an educational mitigation message is extremely time sensitive.
- Each family is on a different reconstruction schedule.
- An overly complex educational message is almost always sent.
- Research into disaster-resistant construction tends not to be helpful because it focuses on identifying many small ways in which traditional buildings can be improved. Research should focus on what are the three most important modifications that can be made.

After making great efforts over long periods to invest in housing for their families, citizens in disaster-stricken countries can lose the use of expensively constructed structures in an instant. Cumulatively, over 20 years natural catastrophes worldwide are responsible for nearly 1 billion people losing their homes. On average, estimating average family size at five, this comes to 10 million homeless a year. Averages hide a lumpy reality: some years are significantly worse, while others are quite a bit better. In 1998 more than 14 million people lost their homes in a single event when two rivers in China flooded at the same time.

Not only did these families lose their residences, which were uninsured. They also lost consumer goods that they had saved diligently to pay for. Recovering from the crisis of a lost home is accompanied by the urgent need to purchase multiple items needed for daily living. This urgency often occurs while local economies are reeling, traditional sources of income are diminished, and regular employment opportunities lost. For these reasons reconstruction can stretch out for 7 to 10 years. Families who see themselves as being financially five years away from rebuilding are interested in only one educational message. They ask themselves, "Can we provide ourselves with a safer home?" Reconstruction projects promoting mitigation need to send the message during the first months after disaster that safer housing is within everyone's reach. Once that idea is out, it can be reinforced with classes, model buildings, and posters. But once the fear engendered by the disaster event is gone, if people have not heard that safer possibilities are available to them, the window of educational opportunity has closed until the next disaster.

The Bank Can Help Borrowing Countries Get Back on Their Feet Quickly and Inexpensively by Learning to "Satisfice"

The most immediate need following a rapid-onset disaster is likely to be shelter. During the preparation of most emergency loans, however, task managers confront an intensive debate. The first question is whether the World Bank should finance a private good. The

second question is to what extent disaster recipients of a replacement dwelling should be required to contribute to their own relief in the form of up-front contributions followed by repayments over time, that is, a loan. A review of past emergency loan projects shows problems with cost recovery from beneficiaries who have lost furniture, clothing, kitchen utensils, food, and employment, and need to replace them in short order. The Bank can still be responsive to its clients' urgent needs in times of crisis by providing more modest solutions and by recognizing that lending for single family housing is justified because such reconstruction solutions break a repetitive cycle of disaster and costly recovery.

Since disasters are recurrent—and worse, since the link between the lack of disaster mitigation and under-development is clear—consideration of disaster vulnerability has to be an integral part of the project preparation process. In reconstruction, however, the key to success is to strive for "satisfice" objectives. In other words organizationally, we need to recognize when an intervention will lead to reconstructed building that is good enough. We need to learn how to be comfortable leaving behind a house that is significantly more disaster-resistant than what was there before, even if it looks ugly. The poor are often pushed onto dangerous areas, but poor families' decisions not to construct technically perfect homes wherever they live should be respected. Safer *is* better. In vulnerability reduction the best is the enemy of the good.

A United States Agency for International Development (USAID)-funded reconstruction effort in Madagascar following Cyclone Kamisy took a satisfice approach in low-income urban areas. Large zones consisting of wood frame houses and corrugated iron roofs were devastated. Many homes had been flattened. The project opted to promote

1. Modifying the angle of roofs to defeat the "wing effect," whereby high winds cause the roof to become airborne
2. Using special large-headed screw nails to attach the corrugated roofing to the homes' wood frames
3. Using cyclone straps (metal straps that reinforce wood joints) to create an unbroken chain of reinforcement from the ground up.

The project provided carpenters to work with the victims during the rebuilding process and sold building materials at a subsidized price, using the re-flow to purchase more materials. Staff strongly encouraged the recycling of wood and other building materials from the damaged homes. In a few months the devastated areas were rebuilt. They looked much like they had before, with many of the homes being no better than shacks—as they had been before. The difference was that for a very low cost the project had rebuilt homes that were greatly more cyclone resistant than the pre-disaster housing stock.

Had there been no targeted intervention, reconstruction still would have used recycled materials financed by the victims themselves. However, the rebuilt buildings would have been weaker than they had been before the last disaster; and the next time a storm blew, there would have been little left of the homes that could be reused. This might have created a more expensive problem at a time the country might have been less able to afford a response. For example, it might still have been paying for reconstruction from the first storm. Spending as little as an additional 10 percent on mitigation can stop recurrent losses.

World Bank task managers have shied away from working on housing in countries where housing was desperately needed. One reason is that the design of a one-room home is often criticized within the Bank as though it needed to be constructed with the same rigor as the Jamuna suspension bridge (which spans two highly unstable river banks in Bangladesh on one of the world's largest rivers). Significant risks are associated with respecting beneficiaries' willingness-to-pay and beneficiaries' decisions about tolerable levels of risk. But it is better to run these risks than to saddle the poor with a house and a debt beyond their capacity to repay, effectively depriving them of access to credit, or to provide an even more elegant housing solutions to elites, leaving lower income families homeless or in cardboard shacks for years. An over-emphasis on the perfection of construction details slows the rebuilding process and leads to unproductive conflicts with homeowners. The result is that a smaller percentage of the population winds up with homes that are truly safer.

One important role for the Bank's Disaster Management Facility is to encourage discussion and consensus-building on the issues that come up following each major disaster. Only when the Bank understands the trade-offs involved in working with single-family housing and the poorer members of society in the post-disaster context, and makes rational policy decisions, will task managers be able to respond effectively and expeditiously to borrowers' priorities.

Replacement housing should respect local construction styles, increasing disaster resistance to acceptable levels while sticking to prevalent construction patterns. Mitigation-related increases in construction costs should be kept under 10 percent. Reconstructing safer housing with techniques and materials that are beyond local skill levels, and costs that greatly exceed what is traditionally spent for housing in the victim country, ensures that improvements will not be replicated as families expand a core unit and construct new units for expanding families. Such reconstruction practices probably lead to poor (household) loan repayment, which eventually shuts the low-income victim group out of the credit market for years, if not forever.

The Best Technical Solution May Not Be Climatically Sound

In housing mitigation the optimal technical solution for earthquake or windstorm single-family house reconstruction is rarely appropriate for the climate. For example, solid aluminum houses could be anchored, braced, and strapped to resist storms. Because they are light-weight, they would resist earthquakes, but they would be ovens in the sun and would be chilly inside when the outside temperature was cool. Low-income families may be willing to risk a remote recurrence of a disaster event to be comfortable within an earthen structure that resists extremes of heat or cold. Therefore, an improvement that simply ensures that an inexpensive earthen or clapboard house will not injure or kill its occupants may be sufficient.

The poor make very rational housing choices for themselves—far better than outsiders can make for them. In health projects borrowers accept serious risks when they undertake AIDS education. Farmers' failure to follow agricultural projects' directions can be equally dire, yet Bank-financed schemes routinely accept the risks of less than total compliance with project recommendations. Requiring people to do what is in their own best interests is paternalistic and tyrannical. Mitigation efforts are rarely capable of moving vast regions from vulnerability to an ideal state; they usually achieve only significant improvements. Forcing people to comply with rules destroys the educational opportunity.

Conclusions

There is no cookbook for designing post-disaster interventions. Each country, culture, and disaster present opportunities and constraints. Nevertheless, given other competing priorities, every appropriate response in a developing country must give serious consideration to the risk horizon of the individual and the relative importance of disaster for each family. How feasible is useful mitigation action? What other risks need to be considered? Where does natural hazards risk fit among health risks, agricultural risks, and sociopolitical risks? We have to recognize the context of worries and consider remedies that are in appropriate proportion to the potential risk.

- One resource we should not waste is the attention of the individual or potential victim. This attention is a finite commodity that should not be misdirected.
- There is also the matter of the optimal distribution of responsibility over the various levels involved in reconstruction: individual, community, regional, and national government. To date most Bank activity has focused on the government level. It is the individual homeowner who makes the critical decisions during reconstruction. To be effective, responsibility for decisionmaking needs to penetrate downward. Bank policy should help borrowers move toward distributing responsibility for natural hazards mitigation over all levels. In other words the Bank needs to shift more attention to the private sector and individuals. Natural hazards typically are low in frequency but high in consequences—and the poor know this better than policymakers.

Natural hazard mitigation is central to sustainable development. Natural hazards are a constant although infrequent characteristic of the environment. To sustain means to survive in a given environment. If sustainability is not to be time-bound by the return period of potentially catastrophic natural events, a disaster policy that helps the poorest victims rapidly get their lives moving again after an event must be a fundamental component of socially and economically sustainable development.

Chapter 9

Women and Children Facing Disaster

William A. Anderson

Many countries throughout the world face significant risk from natural hazards. However, countries and communities differ significantly in their degree of vulnerability to natural disasters. This is also true of groups within any particular country or community. There is, then, significant inequality in disaster vulnerability, even when the physical dimensions of particular threats are similar (Parker and Thompson 1991). Developing countries are the most vulnerable to natural hazards because they have fewer financial and other requisite resources, such as knowledge, institutional arrangements, and technology, to counteract them. Finally, within both developing and industrialized societies, the most vulnerable are the poor, particularly poor women and children.

In developing countries disasters seriously deplete scarce resources, causing these countries to slide deeper into poverty. When disaster strikes, development plans are set aside, and vital resources, from both internal sources and external donors, are redirected to meet emergency recovery and reconstruction needs. Thus, if sustainable social and economic development goals are to remain within reach, effective disaster management is imperative in at-risk, low-income countries. Furthermore, for disaster management efforts—including mitigation and preparedness actions—to succeed, the needs of women and children, who make up such a large portion of the poor in developing societies, must be taken into account. It follows that the status of women and children with regard to disaster risks has a major impact on development.

This chapter discusses some of the issues regarding the special exposure of women and children to disasters. It examines what the exposure means from a policy and programmatic standpoint. Only relatively recently have researchers turned their attention to the impact of gender and age on disaster vulnerability (Wiest, Mocellin, and Motsisi 1994). There is a real need for more systematic research on this important topic. New knowledge from additional research would advance sound disaster management and development policy.

Vulnerability of Women and Children in Developing Countries

Research suggests that in general women and children are at greater risk to natural disasters than men, especially in developing countries (Fothergill 1996)). One important explanation for this is social inequality. Women and children comprise a larger portion of the poor in developing countries, even in many developed countries, such as the United States. Thus, women and children have less capacity to take effective preventive actions and to recover from disasters once they occur. Research has shown that in some earthquake and famine disasters morbidity and mortality rates have been highest among women and children (Morrow and Phillips 1999). Findings from a study on the 1991 Bangladesh cyclone during which a reported 130,000 persons died point to the same problem.

Sixty-three percent of the deaths were in the under-ten age group, whereas this age group represented only 35 percent of the pre-cyclone population. Similarly, 42 percent more females died than males, a pattern which is similar to the 1970 cyclone.... The difference between male and female rates is more pronounced in very young and elderly groups. Among children under 5 years of age, the death rate for females was 15 percent higher than their male counterparts (Chowdhury and others 1993, p. 301).

Much more research is needed to fully understand the extent to which gender plays a role in differential casualty rates.

Evidence also exists that women have more difficulty rebounding from the effects of disaster (Morrow and Enarson 1996). This slower recovery has been attributed to the fact that they tend to have less access to resources provided during emergency and recovery periods (Khondker 1996). In addition, they are subjected to gender discrimination and sometimes become the victims of increased domestic violence brought on by the stress of disaster circumstances (Wiest and others 1994).

Other societal factors used to explain women's greater vulnerability to disasters are their caregiving roles and their lack of mobility (Fothergill 1996). In most societies the care for dependent family members, including children and aged parents, falls in the hands of women. This responsibility sometimes reduces their opportunity to take certain self-protective actions open to men, such as migrating in the face of disasters such as drought. Similarly, it has been noted that while men often have the option to pursue new job opportunities in other communities after a disaster, women often do not take such actions because they are bound by obligations to other family members. These obligations may be particularly problematic in female-headed households, a pattern that characterizes a large percentage of poor families in both developing and industrialized countries.

Like poor women, poor children in developing societies are highly vulnerable to natural disasters. As de-

pendents, poor children share lives of poverty with their parents and experience inadequate housing, nutrition, and education, and a lack of protection from natural disasters. Because of their age and dependency, where there is no safety net, children may be even more vulnerable to disasters than adults. In addition to casualties, when disasters strike, children also suffer greater hardship from inadequate food, shelter, and health services, and experience significant psychological stress. What happens to parents and other caregivers, such as death, injury, and loss of resources, compounds the hardship that children experience following disaster. Such losses can lead to homelessness, a life on the street without adult guidance and support, and the long-term disruption of their education. Wiest and colleagues note:

> During emergencies, families are often separated. Some children become orphaned, others abandoned or physically separated from their families. The emotional and physical security provided by the home, as well as the guidance given to adolescents is often lacking (Wiest and others 1994, pp. 30-31).

An estimated 114,000 school-aged children were made homeless by the August 17, 1999 Turkey earthquake, a figure that dramatically indicates the disruptive impact that disasters can have on the often already fragile lives of children (World Bank 1999).

Comparative Vulnerability of Women and Children

Like their low-income country counterparts, many women and children in developed countries are exposed to risks from natural disaster. Although perhaps not to the extent of those in developing countries, women in industrialized nations can also experience inequities related to disaster management practices. Research has shown that women in the United States are underrepresented in key decisionmaking bodies and in the emergency management profession, and have more difficulty obtaining disaster loans. Poor minority women are particularly disadvantaged in this regard (Morrow and Enarson 1996).

Many of the natural hazards that create risks for developing countries are, of course, also faced by industrialized countries. For example, Japan and the United States are exposed to such hazards as earthquakes, floods, and wind storms. However, because they are so highly developed, they are much better able to develop a full range of disaster countermeasures, including measures and techniques to identify hazards, protect buildings, regulate land use, design and manage emergency response systems, and transfer risks through formal insurance programs. This greater development partially explains why deaths from even major events in the U.S. have been far lower than those caused by comparable events in developing societies. For instance, deaths from the 1989 Loma Prieta earthquake and the 1994 Northridge earthquake, both in California, numbered under 100 in each case,

The vast majority of casualties caused by natural disasters occur in the world's poor countries. The dollar losses in developed countries can be quite high due to the exposure of their vast resources. Nevertheless, because of their relative wealth the losses do not have the staggering impact that far smaller total losses have in poor countries. This differential translates into lower risks even for the poor in developed countries. Developed countries' greater resources usually mean that help is on the way after a disaster, even if it is sometimes perceived as slow in coming and even when women are not in the decisionmaking chain and experience certain inequities. The point is that even though industrialized countries may lose more total wealth to disasters than low-income countries, industrialized countries will still have far more resources to share with their citizens, including poor women and children.

Disparate Resources for Research and Programs

The research enterprise itself is an example of a resource that is available to developed countries to reduce the vulnerability of its citizens to natural disasters. Such research does not exist at the same level in at-risk developing societies. For example, in recent years a critical mass of disaster researchers have emerged in major academic institutions and other sectors in the U.S. to more systematically investigate issues related to gender and disaster. As a result, a significant amount of the research that is being carried out on this topic is by U.S.-based researchers.

This research effort has the potential to reshape disaster policy and programs in the U.S. so that they are more sensitive to the special needs of women and children. Such researchers are working to influence policies through their research and publications, interactions with policymakers, and interactions with advocates and other stakeholders. An example of the recent mobilization around these issues that involves U.S. as well as some experts from other countries is the creation of the Gender and Disaster Network. This is an internet-based educational effort by both women and men interested in the relationship between gender and disaster that grew out of the 1997 session of the Annual Hazards Workshop held by the Natural Hazards Research and Applications Center at the University of Colorado (Morrow and Phillips 1999). The annual workshop and other efforts by the center, such as its newsletter and scholarly publications, have been fertile ground for the development of new insights and innovations that impact research and policy, especially in the U.S. As noted in its website, the goals of the network include

- Documenting and analyzing women's and men's experience before, during, and after disasters
- Putting gender relations in a broad political, economic, historical, and cultural context
- Building and sustaining an active international community of scholars and activists.

These efforts reflect the fact that developed countries can mobilize more resources to tackle disaster problems, including those related to gender, than developing countries. Such resources include funds that can be devoted to research as well as to wide access to new technologies such as the internet. Such disparities can be reduced when industrialized countries share resources and cooperate with at-risk poorer countries.

As in the case of women, developed countries have measures in place that also make children far less vulnerable to disaster than in poor countries facing similar natural hazards. The 1933 Long Beach, California earthquake, for example, resulted in the passage of the Field Act in California, which set the first minimum construction standards for schools to make them more earthquake resistant (Olson 1998). Both Japan and the U.S. have children's preparedness programs to increase children's awareness of a variety of natural hazards and how to cope with them. In the U.S. children's hazard awareness and preparedness programs have been developed at the local, state, and federal levels. Salt Lake City, Utah recently approved a $200 million bond measure to seismically upgrade all 38 of its schools. The Federal Emergency Management Agency (FEMA) supports the development of preparedness programs throughout the U.S. The National Science Foundation (NSF) supports efforts of academic institutions to develop hazard education programs for children in elementary through high school in connection with research programs at the institutions.

Research is also supported in the U.S. on ways to make facilities used by children safer. Both NSF and FEMA have supported research on seismic mitigation for school buildings. In the private sector the Institute for Business and Home Safety (IBHS), a nonprofit organization sponsored by the insurance industry, recently launched Protecting Our Kids from Disasters, a national program to reduce disaster risk for children in thousands of U.S. childcare centers through nonstructural safety measures. Despite such efforts major problems regarding children's safety in the face of natural disaster remain to be solved in industrialized countries. Nevertheless, such countries have far more resources than developing economies with which to protect vulnerable children.

Addressing the Greater Vulnerability of Women and Children

The vulnerability of women and children to disasters and its even greater manifestation in poor countries have both research and policy implications. Many have called for further research in this area because our present knowledge is so thin. After reviewing the extant literature, one researcher noted:

> Taking stock of our research in this area allows us to identify what remains unknown or underresearched. Several smaller, exploratory studies discussed here raise new issues that have not been systematically researched. Domestic violence, intensified in a disaster, is one such issue that needs further investigation. In addition, the areas of preparedness, recovery, and reconstruction contain gender differences, yet the data are minimal and the gaps are large. Furthermore, the relationship between childcare responsibilities, location in the disaster, and chances of survival deserves greater analysis, as such a connection would have great practical and methodological implications. (Fothergill 1996, p. 49)

In addition to the suggestions above, systematic quantitative analyses of casualties caused by disasters throughout the world disaggregated by gender, age, and socioeconomic status are needed to develop a more comprehensive understanding of the relative vulnerability of women and children. Research, including both carefully designed case studies and surveys, is also needed to better understand the similarities and differences between the risk exposure of women and children in developing and industrialized countries. In addition research is needed on the transferability of best practices and technology for reducing the vulnerability of women and children from originating industrialized countries to developing countries. The evidence suggests that so far only modest transfers have occurred (Alexander 1997).

Activists, advocates, and researchers have called for policy and programmatic changes to improve the protection of women and children in the face of disaster threats. Such recommendations include

- Integrating women in community-based mitigation and planning activities (Enarson 1999)
- Involving agencies that offer shelter and services

to battered women and their children in the community disaster planning process (Morrow and Phillips 1999)

- Designating women as focal points for interaction with local and national disaster officials (Domeisen 1997).

Perhaps some policies to reduce the disaster-related vulnerability of women and children in developing countries and elsewhere would work best if they were integrated with other efforts aimed at protecting and improving the quality of life of citizens. For example, in some cases, rather than developing special programs that are difficult to sell to stakeholders, governments, NGOs, and private sector groups can most effectively address the vulnerability of women and children when they also contemplate related actions, such as improving housing and educational facilities in at-risk communities.

Mechanisms developed in other sectors, such as microfinance and insurance, that have the potential to increase the capacity of poor women and children to meet the challenges posed by living in a hazardous environment also deserve full examination. This investigation would involve both research and the development of pilot and demonstration projects. Such mechanisms are discussed in other chapters in this volume.

Conclusion

Vulnerability to disaster is a function of both physical and social factors. The former includes exposure to such risks as earthquakes and floods. The latter involves social arrangements and expectations related to such statuses as gender and age. Part of the vulnerability of women and children is socially constructed, involving existing barriers to the full participation of women in society and the failure to devote time and resources to more fully protect children, despite the fact that children represent a society's most valuable social capital and its future.

However, women and children should not be seen merely as potential victims of disaster (Enarson 1998).

Although often less visible, women do carry out important disaster-related functions, including preparedness and response activities that often reflect their traditional gender role of caregiver (Fothergill 1996). Yet women represent an under-utilized resource in both developed and developing societies. They have the potential to make greater contributions to their own safety as well as that of others. Attention needs to be given to developing ways in which women can participate more fully in disaster prevention, preparedness, response, and recovery efforts.

Children, too, are more than potential victims of disaster. They represent the gateway to creating a culture of prevention in society. They can be taught the value of prevention and encouraged to play a proactive role in disaster reduction efforts, including conservation and ecological activities that increase protection from floods and other natural disasters.

The international community can help developing countries meet the far greater challenge they face regarding the exposure of women and children to disaster risks by giving more attention to gender issues. One of a growing number of positive signs in this respect is that the World Bank is investigating gender in relation to the experiences of Honduras and Nicaragua following Hurricane Mitch, which struck in 1998.

The international community also can help developing countries by initiating cooperative capacity building efforts aimed at the problem. Efforts focusing on prevention and preparedness are especially needed. Some of these types of activities have been implemented in the past few years. In collaboration with partner organizations, the nonprofit organization GeoHazards International recently completed demonstration projects for increasing school safety in Ecuador and Nepal (Tucker 1999). These projects involved training local builders in earthquake-resistant design and construction practices, and raising hazard awareness among government officials, teachers, children, and parents. Such capacity building activity is needed on a wide scale in developing countries. In helping to reduce the impacts of disasters on women and children, it would also help lift a major barrier to social and economic development in poor countries.

References

Alexander, D. 1997. "The Study of Natural Disasters, 1977-1997." *Disasters* 21 (4): 284-304.

Chowdhury, A., and others. 1993. "The Bangladesh Cyclone of 1991: Why So Many People Died. *Disasters* 17 (4): 291-304.

Domeisen, N. 1997. "The Role of Women in Protecting Communities from Disasters." *Natural Hazards Observer* 21 (5): 5-6.

Enarson, E. 1998. "Through Women's Eyes: A Gendered Research Agenda for Disaster Social Science." *Disasters* 22 (2): 157-73.

Enarson, E. 1999. "Women and Housing Issues in Two U.S. Disasters: Case Studies from Hurricane Andrew and the Red River Valley Flood." *International Journal of Mass Emergencies and Disasters* 17 (1): 39-63.

Fothergill, A. 1996. "Gender, Risk, and Disasters." *International Journal of Emergencies and Disasters* 14 (1): 33-56.

Khondker, H. 1996. "Women and Floods in Bangladesh." *International Journal of Mass Emergencies and Disasters* 14 (3) 281-92.

Morrow, B., and E. Enarson. 1996. "Hurricane Andrew through Women's Eyes: Issues and Recommendations. *International Journal of Mass Emergencies and Disasters* 14 (1): 5-22.

Morrow, B., and B. Phillips. 1999. "What's Gender 'Got to Do with It'?" *International Journal of Mass Emergencies and Disasters* 17 (1): 5-13.

Olson, R. 1998. "Fits and Starts: 20th Century Seismic Safety Policy in the U.S." *In The EERI Golden Anniversary Volume: 1948-1998*. Oakland: Earthquake Engineering Research Institute. 23-27.

Parker, J., and M. Thompson. 1991. "Floods and Tropical Storms." In *The Challenge of African Disasters*. New York: World Health Organization and United Nations Institute for Training and Research. 38-56.

Tucker, B. "Improving School Seismic Safety." Presentation at the Second International Earthquakes and Megacities Workshop, December 1-3, 1999, Manila, Philippines. Organized by the Earthquakes and Megacities Initiative, Menlo Park, CA.

Wiest, E., J. S. P. Mocellin, and D. T. Motsisi. 1994. "The Needs of Women in Disasters and Emergencies." University of Manitoba, Winnipeg.

World Bank. 1999. "Turkey: Marmara Earthquake Assessment." Turkey Country Office, World Bank, Washington, D.C.

Chapter 10

Climate Change from a Development Perspective

Maarten K. van Aalst and Ian Burton

This chapter is drawn from "Come Hell or High Water–Integrating Climate Change Vulnerability and Adaptation into Bank Work."[1] It presents the report's general discussion about climate change vulnerability and adaptation from a development perspective, and summarizes its main conclusions.

Adaptation to Climate and Climate Change

Climate change has been recognized as an issue of sufficient importance by the international community that a Convention, the United Nations Framework Convention on Climate Change (UNFCCC, 1992), has been negotiated, adopted, and ratified. Under the UNFCCC, particularly in the Kyoto Protocol, the developed country Parties have agreed to reduce their greenhouse gas emissions by substantial amounts (5 percent between 2008 and 2012 against the 1990 baseline). The Protocol also contains provisions with respect to adaptation to climate change in the development context. At the same time the problem of how best to manage climate change remains charged with uncertainty and divergent views and interpretations. These circumstances constitute an important context for the consideration of appropriate responses by development agencies like the World Bank.

The steps that might be taken to better understand the impact of development activities on vulnerability in developing countries depend on how the problem is defined and constructed. The climate change prob-

lem has been formulated in the UNFCCC and elsewhere primarily as a pollution issue. That is, the primary cause of the problem is seen to be the emission of greenhouse gases as a result of human activities. Therefore, the primary response required is the reduction of emissions. This is the main intent of the Kyoto Protocol.

This construction relegates adaptation to a minor role. For many developing countries, however, adaptation is the larger and more important part of the question. They contribute proportionally very little to the global emissions of greenhouse gases and place greater emphasis on their vulnerability to climate change. Among the options that developing countries have to consider are the actions that they can take to reduce that vulnerability in human-designed and managed systems as well as natural ecosystems. Thus, concerns about development, vulnerability, and equity become mapped onto what was first construed as a pollution problem.

Adaptation is not something new. Economic and social activities in all countries are already designed and managed in ways that take into account the present climate and its variability. A logical place to begin is to assess the success of present adaptation to present climate, including its variability. Improving present levels and types of adaptation to reduce present vulnerability is an essential first step towards taking account of climate change. A general principle of adaptation science is that the stronger the adaptation capacity, the lower the vulnerability to climate both in the present and the future, regardless of the specific environmental changes that may arise. Adaptation to climate (as distinct from climate change) is an ongoing, everyday process.

Insofar as the UNFCCC applies to adaptation, it is limited to adaptation to climate change and does not extend to adaptation to normal climate. From the point of view of the UNFCCC and the Global Environment Facility (GEF) it is important, indeed necessary in terms of funding, to distinguish between adaptation to climate and adaptation to climate change. Financial support for vulnerability reduction in developing countries that would come through these channels would be applicable only to adaptation to climate change, not to normal climate.

On the other hand from the perspective of development agencies, developing countries, and especially the people directly affected, such a distinction could have a distorting effect. For farmers or coastal dwellers it matters little how much of the damage from a drought or coastal erosion can be attributed to climate and how much to climate change. The objective is to reduce losses from climatic events and conditions, including their variability and extremes.

Development activities that are economically justified on their own terms, regardless of climate change, may, if appropriately designed, also help to reduce vulnerability to climate change. The amount of additional benefits would depend on the extent and rate of climate change. A challenge for development policymakers and project managers therefore is to identify and appropriately modify those projects and related activities that provide "no regrets" adaptations to climate change or win-win results.

In the longer term the distinction between "normal" climate and climate change will be hard to sustain. By "normal climate" is meant the climate as it is or would be under natural conditions without alteration by human activities. Recognizing that under natural conditions climate does change significantly although at a slower rate, the practice is to measure climate in terms of the observations made over the prior three decades. Such statistics describe what are known as the climate "normals." At the end of each decade the earliest of the three decades in the "normal" statistics is dropped and

the latest decade is added. Thus, the climate "normals" themselves change slowly from decade to decade.

The selection of the baseline data for the onset of climate change is therefore an additional consideration. It is probably true to say that the climate normals now in use (1961-1990) already show some of the effects of climate change, but this cannot be asserted unequivocally. According to the Intergovernmental Panel on Climate Change (IPCC), there is already "a discernible human influence" on climate.[2] This means that when the switch is made to the next set of "normals" (1971-2000), the influence of some anthropogenic climate change will be contained within the "baseline" climate conditions. The task of separating normal climate from climate change in the 1990s is a question that cannot be fully resolved by climate science or climate statistics. This suggests that the definition of climate change-induced damages will continue to be a matter for informed expert judgment case by case, unless some credible and acceptable deciding rule can be agreed. The question of how best to ensure that consistency and equity are applied to such decisions requires continued attention.

Scope of Adaptation

All countries every day experience economic loss from normal weather events and climatic conditions. Similarly, in all countries adaptation measures are in place and routinely are applied to reduce damage. Houses are designed to be cool when the weather is hot and to be warm in the winter. Bridges are built high and strong enough to withstand most floods. Crops are chosen to suit the prevailing temperature conditions and may be planted earlier or later according to the timing of seasonal rainfall.

Normal climate is a pervasive factor in social and economic development. It is so universally present and so deeply ingrained that when times are good, it is barely noticed. Climate is indispensable and taken for granted. Human beings and their cultures are adapted to the distinct climate of the places in which they live. This is most obviously understood in sectors such as agriculture, in which the choices of crops and the modes of cultivation have been finely tailored over decades, even centuries, to the prevailing climate. The same is true for other economic sectors that are obviously weather dependent and weather sensitive such as forestry, water resources, recreation, and tourism.

What is less widely understood is that climate norms including climate variability and extreme events are taken into account in all human-built infrastructure. Climate is a factor in the design of houses, industrial and commercial buildings, roads, bridges, drainage systems, water supply and sanitation systems, irrigation and hydroelectric power installations, docks, harbors, and transmission and communications towers and lines. In fact, everything that is built has to be designed and managed taking climate variables into account. Often this is done through formal procedures such as building codes; standards for wind resistance, heating, and ventilation; and water levels. In more traditional societies the designs sometimes are not the result of formal analysis and regulation but have been developed over long periods of trial and error.

The significance of climate does not end with weather-dependent sectors such as agriculture and weather-sensitive infrastructure. It also extends to finance, banking, trade, and other commercial activities, and to human health. The public health protection system has in-built safeguards against disease vectors including viruses, bacteria, insects, and parasites. Similarly, the practices of insurance, credit, and commodity futures are attuned to climate norms and known variability.

There are two sides to the story of climate damage and adaptation to normal climate. Viewed from the longer time perspective of human history, the process of adapting to climate has been extremely successful. Viable human societies and productive economies have been established in a wide variety of climates encompassing an extremely wide range of climatic conditions. Successful societies have been established in open savannah woodlands, semiarid grassland, tropical forests, mountains, and in warm and cool temperate regions extending even into the sub-Arctic.

In addition peoples of diverse cultural groups from Inuit to Tuareg have been able to migrate between different climatic regions and adapt their cultures and livelihoods accordingly. From a probable origin in East Africa the human species has successfully occupied most of the land surface of the planet. Modern Africans, Chinese, and Europeans among others have migrated to other continents and have adapted to new climates. This experience supports the notions that, in principle at least, considerable human adaptive capacity exists and that without a lot of public intervention adaptation will take place spontaneously.

Adaptation is nevertheless a painful process and can be costly. It takes time, and it has not always succeeded. Failed attempts at adaptation leave little record, to which evidence of collapsed societies in archaeological investigations is silent testimony. Rarely, if ever, is climate implicated as the sole factor in social collapse. On the other hand it is often a contributing factor to which it is difficult to assign a specific weight.

Against the long-term record of generally successful adaptation the immediate perspective is less encouraging. The capacity to adapt to climate change is not evenly distributed across countries, peoples, or economic sectors. However, it is known to be less in the least-developed countries and among the poor and disadvantaged in all developing countries. The determinants of adaptive capacity include the availability of financial resources (wealth) and technology, and a body of trained persons to use them effectively. Access to information and the existence of legal, social, and organizational arrangements are also crucial.

Conversely, poverty, lack of skills, and undeveloped social institutions inhibit the capacity to adapt. An implication is that successful economic development; alleviation of poverty; access to technology; education and training, and the strengthening of legal, social, and organizational arrangements are important means to reduce vulnerability to climate change. Since there is no single best or stable answer to the question of what adaptation measures are needed, when, where, and by how much, reducing vulnerability by adaptation necessarily involves incremental learning from experience. Therefore, institutions that encourage flexible response, like markets, are to be encouraged.

Beyond these broad generalities not a lot is known about the specific vulnerability of countries, development projects, or economic sectors. Research to date has focused on the impacts of climate change in physical and biological terms. This research has been summarized and assessed in IPCC reports, but it gives little indication of the magnitude of the new economic risks that developing countries now face. It is generally thought that the poorest developing countries, small island states, and countries in semiarid regions of now uncertain rainfall are likely to be most vulnerable, but no systematic test or measure of aggregate vulnerability has been developed.

Adaptation Science

If serious attention is to be devoted to assisting developing countries to adapt to climate change, it is important to recognize the range of potentially relevant expertise. The body of knowledge crosses a wide spectrum of policy, management, and decisionmaking and is fragmented into disciplinary expertise and professional specialization. This holds true in developed countries as much as in developing countries. With the advent of climate change all the standards and criteria in these fields should be revisited and revised as appropriate. An important role for development agencies like the World Bank is to provide access to the knowledge base on which such standards and criteria can be reassessed.

The changes needed go beyond the careful adjustment of design standards and criteria on project by project or sector by sector. Such an approach is sufficient for the direct effects of climate change on each sector, the "first- order" impacts. A difficulty with such impacts is that they also carry over into second, third, and nth order effects which are interrelated in complex and often unforeseen ways. For example, rising sea level can damage or destroy coastal marshes and wetlands that are breeding grounds for some species of fish. Thus, locally available food supplies from the sea may be reduced at the same time that less rainfall and higher temperatures on land are reducing agricultural productivity. This combination of threat to food supplies and consequent drop in nutrition standards may impact the health of a population that is simultaneously being exposed to new diseases through the spread of

hitherto-absent disease vectors. In such circumstances expanding communities may occupy more hazardous lands along the coast, in flood plains, and on steep slopes thus increasing their vulnerability to tropical storms.

An integrated adaptation response is required, which might involve new coastal zone protection, the creation of new breeding grounds for fish, the expansion of irrigation agriculture, the implementation of new public health measures, and the avoidance of creating risks of larger disasters from extreme events by land use planning and building codes. Taken in a selective way in the absence of an integrated assessment, such measures could well be ineffective or counter productive. The assessment of vulnerability to climate change is not a simple matter. Development agencies could help create a capacity for developing a more integrated cross-sectoral assessment of climate change impacts and adaptation options linked to overall development strategies.

What is involved here is the creation of a new body of integrated knowledge and practice that may be called "adaptation science." This is a task awaiting all countries in which significant impacts are expected. In developed countries the task is already on the research agenda, although it has not yet reached the level of application except in a very few cases. The revision of standards and criteria across sectors in developing countries will have to be undertaken as the impacts of climate change are increasingly felt.

How rapidly these revisions should be done depends to some extent on the rate and magnitude of climate change in a specific place. It also depends on the capacity of the country, sector, and management unit to carry out the necessary studies and to take effective adaptation measures. For societies or economic sectors that have deployable financial resources, strong technical and managerial skills, and the necessary administrative, political, and legal structures in place, adaptation science and its application can probably proceed rapidly enough, albeit at some social cost that is presently unknown.

Where these resources and capacities are weak or lacking, as in many developing countries, adaptation will be more difficult, and the impacts of climate change are likely to be correspondingly greater. Development agencies can play a significant role to help developing countries strengthen and expand their own adaptation science capability through the use of training programs, technical assistance, and knowledge management.

The urgency with which this should be addressed varies greatly from country to country. It would be helpful to have a systematic screening process designed to identify situations of greater short-run vulnerability. A two-step process is suggested through which a preliminary screening would be used to identify more urgent situations. These could then be the subject of more detailed risk assessment and supported by capacity building activities.

Management Criteria

Two main criteria underlie the wide array of management decisions on adaptation, guided as they are by social policies. The first is economic efficiency. Because weather constantly varies and climate varies over time, decisions about climate risk always involve choices about the level of expenditure and the benefits to be gained. Underinvestment in climate adaptation might result in significant losses that could have been avoided for a small marginal increase in adaptation expenditures. Similarly, overinvestment in climate adaptation is a waste of resources that might have been better spent elsewhere. Under strong constraints on financial resources this risk is probably low.

The second criterion is disaster avoidance. In theory the risk of catastrophic losses can be taken into account in a conventional economic analysis by reducing future anticipated losses to present annual value. However, at an appropriate discount rate there is, it may be argued, a social value above and beyond this level that would accept higher costs in return for the avoidance or prevention of disasters. The degree to which people are or wish to be risk averse probably is not always well reflected in project design.

The application of the criteria of economic efficiency and disaster avoidance in the adoption of adaptation measures is prejudiced now in developing countries by the frequent lack of a quantitative risk assessment approach in investment decisions. This applies now under conditions of current or normal climate and can lead to unanticipated costs. Unless action is taken now to strengthen the use of risk assessment techniques in the assessment of adaptation measures, more serious consequences can be expected as climate change advances. In development activities extra attention should be given to the risk of weather extremes such as floods, droughts, hurricanes, and forest fires in the light of climate change. The risk analyses based solely on past records are unlikely to provide an adequate guide to future investments. At the same time experience in dealing with extreme events can strengthen adaptive capacity for adapting to longer-term climate change.

A Problem in Risk Assessment

Although anthropogenic climate change is not yet an established fact proven according to the strict canons of scientific proof, it is known that the observed increases in concentrations of greenhouse gases, especially carbon dioxide, are due to human activities. It is also known that unless the pattern of human development is changed quite rapidly and quite radically, the concentrations will double over preindustrial levels by the middle of the 21st century and will increase three or four or more times in the next century or so. That such a change in the chemical composition of the atmosphere poses risk of significant climate change is not in doubt.

While the potential consequences are uncertain, should something like the worst-case scenario ever happen, the potential consequences are very large. The case of climate change is a classical example of an uncertain risk with uncertain (and possibly very high) consequences. Recognition of this situation has led to widespread international acceptance of the "precautionary principle."

While the precautionary principle has been advocated with respect to the reduction of greenhouse gas emissions, it also applies to adaptation. Since the signing of the Kyoto Protocol, debates has evolved steadily toward more recognition of the need for precautionary adaptation to climate change. This evolution has occurred for two main reasons. First it has become increasingly clear that reduction of emissions will take time and will not be accomplished rapidly enough to prevent significant climate change. Since some climate change is now happening and more is inevitable, it is only common sense to extend the "precautionary principle" to strengthen adaptation capacity. Second, the marked increase in losses due to extreme weather events over the past two decades is making it clear that present levels of adaptation to climate variability fall well short of what is possible.

Research to date on vulnerability to climate change has been driven to a considerable extent by the availability of outputs of General Circulation Models (GCMs), which project climate conditions out to "two times carbon dioxide equivalent equilibrium" at some time around the middle of the next century (2050). Thus, the estimates of physical, biological, and, less frequently, economic damage are based on model studies that impose an uncertain future climate on the present-day economy, or on unknown future socioeconomic conditions.

For purposes of development planning and consideration of the vulnerability of development activities, a more pragmatic, effective approach would appear to be to focus on the present and near term future, especially where the first impacts of climate change are likely to be felt. Adaptation actions designed to reduce the vulnerability of some future unknown economy to some future unknown climate are less likely to be on the mark than adaptation actions to reduce present and near term risks. At least the benefits of adaptation to currently well-defined risks are more certain to be realized. Other things being equal, the more that climate changes, the more that benefits will flow from economically justified adaptation to present climate variability and extremes. The implications for development activities are that the prospect of such win-win situations should be allowed to influence the design and choice of near term investments. This holds true when adaptation to current climate variability is consistent with the kind of changes expected under climate change. For example, adaptation to floods in the short term might prove less attractive should floods cease to be a problem and drought become a more prevailing risk.

In practice such simple trade-off relationships are not likely. Destabilization of the climate system and intensification of the hydrological cycle are likely to increase the incidence of both floods and droughts.

For discussion it may be helpful to adopt a rather arbitrary distinction between slow incremental changes in the climate system, and climate variability, especially the most extreme events that are potential causes of disaster. Small-scale incremental changes are likely to be of greater significance in cases in which the relationship between human activities and the weather is already stretched. Examples include situations in which quantity of water use presses closely on available supplies, as in many semiarid zones, or crops are being grown at or close to their limits of heat tolerance.

It is suggested that these two situations (close to the margin of tolerance for incremental change and disastrous extremes) are the first in which the impacts of climate change will be clearly seen. Consequently, it is here that vulnerability assessment and adaptation efforts should focus for the time being.

Implications of Climate Change Vulnerability and Adaptation for the World Bank

The report, "Come Hell or High Water: Integrating Climate Change Vulnerability and Adaptation into Bank Work," examines the vulnerability of World Bank projects to climate change, the impacts of Bank activities on national vulnerability in client countries, and steps that could be taken to assess and address vulnerability to climate change in the Bank's client countries. It also discusses the implications of the provisions on adaptation in the United Nations Framework Convention on Climate Change (UNFCCC), and the Bank's role as an implementing agency for the Global Environment Facility (GEF). This section summarizes the report's main conclusions.

Risks

World Bank projects and client countries are at significant risk from climate change and variability, and this risk will increase in the future. The magnitude and extent of the risk cannot be precisely stated, and it is important that additional steps be taken that will improve understanding of vulnerability, available adaptation options, and the adaptive capacity to implement them.

Priorities

At the present time and in the near term the impacts most likely to be felt are from extreme weather events and from less extreme variations in climate in which development activities are close to the margin of tolerance. Thus, the most cost effective approaches to climate change vulnerability, which deserve priority attention among other development needs, are to

1. Reduce vulnerability to extreme events in the World Bank's development projects (investment loans, including emergency loans)
2. Invest in risk reduction in situations whose present development activities are close to the limits of tolerance for climate variability
3. Enhance the capacity to adapt to future climate changes, including surprises.

An essential first step is to assess current adaptation practices to present climate and its variability in a sustainable development context.

Addressing Extreme Events

Extreme weather events potentially associated with climate change now cause disasters, which in turn can cause severe setbacks to economic development. Adaptation to extreme events now can be good preparation for longer-term climate change.[3] The stronger the adaptation capacity, the lower the vulnerability, both now and in the future. Unfortunately, emergency loans for disaster recovery and rehabilitation tend to focus on the restoration of conditions to the predisaster state. They thus miss the opportunity to reduce vulnerability to future events, including increased risk from climate change.

Vulnerability Assessments

Vulnerability varies substantially by sector and region within countries, and also by socioeconomic group.

The poor and otherwise disadvantaged are at greater risk and will become more so unless the distributional effects of losses are taken into account. Better understanding is also needed of this aspect of vulnerability and the means to reduce it.

Degree and type of risk vary substantially among sectors. For example, large capital infrastructure projects with high initial costs and a long physical life are at higher risk. Projects that affect the long-term development path of a sector or region (for example, land zoning) can have an equally if not more powerful impact on overall vulnerability.

Although no standardized and comparable indices of vulnerability are available either at an aggregate level or for sectors, it is possible to identify in broad terms countries that are more vulnerable, as well as sectors and regions within countries that require urgent attention to climate risks. Such assessment has not yet been incorporated in Bank work. Project preparations do not take into account existing risks of climate and climate variability nor the need to reassess those risks where they are likely to increase due to climate change.

Vulnerability in World Bank Projects

To the extent that climate change risks are adequately captured in standard economic analysis, existing World Bank practices leave ample room to address the climate change issue, recognizing that expenditures on climate change adaptation will always have to compete for scarce resources with other urgent needs. On the other hand, project evaluation typically concentrates on financial and economic risks and neglects natural environmental hazards, including those likely to be associated with climate change.

In project preparation considerations of vulnerability are rarely extended beyond the time horizon of the economic analysis of a project. In many cases the expected physical life of a project is significantly longer, and the project itself as well as the dependencies it creates may be vulnerable to climate change. Unless a more sustainable development perspective is adopted, Bank projects can actually increase human vulnerability to climate change and variability.

The World Bank's Country Assistance Strategies (CASs) do not take into account climate change and variability. They also tend to overlook the risks of current climate and natural hazards. The inclusion of a climate and natural hazard risk assessment parallel to the economic risk assessment would influence project design, and over time the mix and character of the investment portfolio. This is turn would contribute to the reduction of disaster losses and adaptation to climate change.

Capacity Building

The World Bank can play an effective role in reducing the vulnerability of its client countries and its own investment portfolio by expanding its own capacity to assess and address vulnerability and adaptation. Additionally, the Bank can assist in capacity building for vulnerability assessment and adaptation work in its client countries.

Avoiding a Two-track Response

The theoretical distinction between normal climate and climate change is an important consideration for financial assistance under the UNFCCC but matters little from a development perspective. There is a danger of the creation of a two-track system in which adaptation to climate change could become isolated from normal development activities. The World Bank is in a good position to use its influence to help ensure that climate change adaptation is carried out as an integral part of development. This exigency lends additional rationale for a focus on extreme events and situations close to the margin of tolerance.

Notes

1. Ian Burton and Maarten K. van Aalst, "Come Hell or High Water—Integrating Climate Change Vulnerability and Adaptation into Bank Work," World Bank Environment Department Papers 72, Washington, D.C., 1999.

Those interested in the issues discussed here, in particular in the analysis of the implications of climate change vulnerability and adaptation for the World Bank, are strongly encouraged to read the complete report. Copies can be requested from Grace Aguilar, Global Climate Change Team, World Bank Environment Department, 1818 H St., N.W., Washington, D.C. 20433, USA, gaguilar@worldbank.org; or from the authors at ian.burton@ec.gc.ca and aalst@phys.uu.nl.

2. IPCC, "Climate Change 1995: The Science of Climate Change. Contribution of Working Group I to the Second Assessment Report," Cambridge University Press, Cambridge, U.K. 1996.

3. In the community of disaster specialists this would be referred to as "mitigation." In the context of climate change, however, mitigation refers to reductions of greenhouse gas emissions and carbon sequestration to minimize anthropogenic climate change. Adaptation refers to reducing vulnerability to climate change and its impacts.

Fallen freeway due to Kobe
earthquake, Japan, 1995.

PART III

RISK TRANSFER AND FINANCE

Chapter 11

Risk and Insurance by the Poor in Developing Nations

J. G. M. (Hans) Hoogeveen

Abstract

Households in developing nations face enormous fluctuations in income.[1] Such income variability does not have to be of major concern to a utility maximizing household that is interested in consumption stability, unless income shocks get transferred to consumption. In this case shocks may pose a threat to survival, and even temporary shocks may cause permanent consequences for welfare.

To avoid the worst outcomes, households facing limited formal insurance and credit arrangements use various mechanisms to smooth consumption. They can take measures in advance and reduce uncertainty over income realizations, or they can rely on adjustments after the fact. These include the accumulation and running down of assets, or the pooling of income risk using informal insurance and credit arrangements.

This paper reviews the literature on the means that households have to smooth their consumption. It presents theoretical background on the different means of protection and reviews empirical evidence on the functioning of these mechanisms. The paper suggests policy interventions that may enhance the capacity of households to deal with income risk, but warns against applying any of these suggestions without deep knowledge of local circumstances.

A distinctive feature of developing countries is the importance of risk in daily life. Risk is immediately apparent for those who are dependent on income from rain-fed agriculture. Weather variations; the incidence of disease, pests, and fire; and numerous other factors cause yields to fluctuate unpredictably. Variations in the price of marketed output can cause farm profits to vary, while illness at the moment of planting may seriously affect the household income for that year.

Risks are not limited to farming. Landless laborers are vulnerable to fluctuations in income following illness, accident, or unemployment. The poor especially are vulnerable to relative price shifts brought along by rapidly accelerating inflation or adjustments in the economy. No one can be shielded from risks such as theft, natural disaster, or political and financial crises.

Not in all cases are risks as dramatic as a major drought, volcanic eruption, earthquake, or the Asian financial collapse. In Zimbabwe, for instance, the government is caught in a vicious cycle of high public debt and large interest payments. The accompanying high level of inflation gradually erodes household per capita consumption, to the extent that a study by the Zimbabwe's statistical bureau finds that the prevalence of household poverty increased from 40 percent to 63 percent between 1991 and 1996 (CSO 1998). Death of adult family members erodes the productive capacity of many households, and with the increasing occurrence of HIV/AIDS, even that of whole economies.

Risk not only affects the individual or the household but also has an important bearing on society through the distribution of wealth. This result is easily illustrated with an example. If *n* rural households with equal wealth, say four heads of cattle, play a game of chance in which half the households experiences an increase in its wealth by 50 percent (that is, for each two beasts one calf is born), and the other half experiences a decrease in wealth by 50 percent (of each two beasts, one dies or gets stolen). After two years, one out of every four households would have been lucky twice and possess nine heads of cattle (more than a doubling). Another group of households of equal size would have been unlucky two times in a row. Their wealth would have declined to one beast, not even enough to pull a plough. The remaining households would be somewhere between these two extremes.

The previous example illustrates two points: (1) of the many causes of poverty, chance or risk is one of them, and (2) risk at the individual level contributes to inequality in society. Both are worth avoiding.: the first because the presence of poverty is cause for grave concern in itself; the second because more and more empirical evidence shows that greater inequality leads to reduced growth and henceforward to relatively less means for poverty alleviation.

Both possibilities are not independent of each other. Their relation follows from the realization that commonplace worries such as the consequences of a bad harvest on a family's ability to afford school fees for children or the implications of a wage earner's illness for the ability to provide a healthy diet are hazards with potentially long-lasting consequences. Workers who lose their jobs for a prolonged period lose their skills. Evidence from the Asian financial crisis has shown that one of the ways to cope with the crisis is by cutting expenditures, including those for child education. But once taken out of school, children might never return. In efforts to deal somehow with price increases, one may decide to reduce food intake, thus risking that young children become stunted physically and cognitively. If people have to sell productive assets to assure short term survival or to foot medical bills, temporary shocks may have permanent consequences for the potential to earn income in the future.[2] In the aggregate this leads to both increased inequality and reduced growth.

To avoid the worst outcomes, people facing limited formal insurance arrangements use various mechanisms to protect their levels of consumption. In smoothing consumption they can make use of arrange-

ments ex ante to reduce uncertainty over income realizations, such as through diversification of economic activities. They can also make ex post adjustments that allow them to smooth consumption contingent on realized outcomes, such as borrowing and lending or drawing down of assets. Or they can collaborate with others and pool risks using informal arrangements including mutual reciprocity, remittances, state contingent credit transactions, and sharecropping.

This chapter presents a review of the literature on the topic of risk and insurance in developing economics and takes household actions as the point of departure. In section two a theoretical exposé on the Pareto efficient allocation of risk is provided, clarifying why fully efficient risk pooling is rarely achieved and examining the use of intertemporal consumption smoothing through saving and credit markets as a substitute for full risk-pooling. Section three reviews the mechanisms poor households use to smooth consumption in the absence of formal insurance arrangements. The distinction is made between ex ante adjustments that control the distribution of risky variables and ex post mechanisms that stabilize household utility contingent on a realized state. Section four is an overview of the literature on the role and scope of informal institutional mechanisms in protecting the poor by pooling idiosyncratic risks. Section five takes a closer look at the informal insurance institutions that are found in practice. Based on information from section five, section six looks at interventions aimed at increasing household security.

Assuring Smooth Consumption

Income variability does not have to be of concern to a utility-maximizing household interested in consumption stability. As long as the latter can be assured ex post (through insurance, credit transactions or the accumulation and decumulation of buffer stocks), considerations regarding consumption smoothing will not influence decisions regarding the generation of income. To provide some background to this observation, this section starts with an illustration of a simple model of full insurance. It will be shown that full insurance can deal with cross-sectional income variability but not with variation in income over time. To deal with the latter, intertemporal transactions are required, such as credit transactions or savings. Each of these mechanisms will be considered in turn. The presentation follows Alderman and Paxson (1992), Ray (1998), and Bardhan and Udry (1999).

Consider a village economy in which all income risk is shared. "Village" should be interpreted as a metaphor for any group, ranging from the family to the international capital market, within which incomes can be pooled. Let there be N households (indexed i) in the village and T periods, indexed t. There can be S states of nature (indexed s), which are commonly known to everybody in the village, and the probability of state s happening is π_s. In state s each household receives an income $y_{is} > 0$, and c_{ist} represents the consumption of household i if state s occurs in period t. Suppose that each household has a separable utility function of the form

$$U_i = \sum_{t=1}^{T}\left(\frac{1}{1+\delta}\right)^t \sum_{s=1}^{S}\pi_s u_i(c_{ist}) \qquad (1)$$

where u( ) is a strictly concave utility function (hence these households care about risk: they are risk averse) with $\lim_{x\to 0} u'(x) = +\infty$ and where δ is the rate of time preference. A Pareto efficient allocation of risk within the village can be found by solving the welfare program represented by the equations (2) and (3) in which the weighted sum of the utilities of each of the N households is maximized and in which the welfare weight of household i is λ_i such that $0 < \lambda_i < 1$ and $\Sigma \lambda_i = 1$.

$$\underset{c_{it}}{Max} \sum_{i=1}^{N}\lambda_i U_i \qquad (2)$$

subject to

$$\sum_{i=1}^{N} c_{ist} = \sum_{i=1}^{N} y_{ist} \qquad (3)$$

where the latter is the village resource constraint, stating that total village consumption in any state at any

period has to be equal to total village income: no saving takes place in the village. Assume that y_{ist} consists of several different independent components: an individual specific fixed effect or expected household income (assumed to be constant over time), μ_i, a time varying village specific shock v_{st}, and an idiosyncratic shock e_{ist}

$$y_{ist} = \mu_i + v_{st} + \varepsilon_{ist} \qquad (4)$$

The term v_{st} captures the effect of factors that affect the incomes of all people in the village, while the idiosyncratic component ε_{ist} is not correlated across individuals within the village. The expected values of v_{st} and ε_{ist} are zero.

Clearly, consumption has to be positive to survive, so we add another constraint

$$c_{ist} \geq 0 \qquad \forall i,s,t \qquad (5)$$

but given the shape of the utility function—at low levels of consumption, marginal utility tends to infinity—this constraint will always hold so long as there is any income in the village, which is what was assumed. The first-order conditions corresponding to c_{ist} and c_{jst} for households i and j respectively imply

$$\frac{u'(c_{ist})}{u'(c_{jst})} = \frac{\lambda_j}{\lambda_i} \qquad \forall \ i,j,s,t \qquad (6)$$

This equality holds for all N households in the village in any state at any point in time. For expositional ease let the household weights λ_i be identical so that $\lambda_i = \lambda_j = 1/N$. It follows then from (6) that marginal utilities and therefore the consumption levels of all households in the village are identical.

Clearly, any solution that follows from equations (2) and (3) has to be Pareto efficient for the simple reason that if this were not the case, utility could be increased further for some households without reducing it for any other, leading to an increase in total utility. By the second welfare theorem, this Pareto efficient allocation can also be attained as the equilibrium of a complete set of competitive markets after a suitable redistribution of initial endowments. So if we are ready to assume the existence of a complete set of markets (that is, for each combination of s and t there is only one good), this welfare optimum can be attained in a decentralized way. It follows that household consumption need not be affected by idiosyncratic shocks to household income ε_{ist}, but it is affected by shocks in village income, ν_{st}. With full insurance households have no incentive to diversify their income sources for risk mitigation, and households can specialize in the activity they do best. The only risk faced by the household is that faced by the village as a whole.

For such complete insurance to exist, solutions have to be found to the problems of asymmetric information and contract enforcement. Again consider equation (6). The full insurance model implies that a household that receives an idiosyncratic shock that permanently increases its income nonetheless will continue to receive only its previously fixed portion of total village income. Likewise, the community will maintain for life the consumption of a household that became permanently poor. Clearly, the λ-weights can be adjusted accordingly, but this leaves unchallenged the fact that this mutual insurance is history independent. In other words after transferring real resources from household i to household j for a number or successive periods, mutual insurance will not refrain from doing so if household j continues to be struck by bad luck.

Obviously, this results in huge incentives to renege on risk-sharing contracts, and unless contracts can be strictly enforced, full insurance typically will not be feasible. The model also suggests that risk is exogenous and that the insured party cannot influence the outcomes. But only rarely will this be the case. Thus, fully insured individuals will have less of an incentive to avoid bad outcomes (moral hazard), or only the worst risks will like to participate in the insurance (adverse selection).

Monitoring can solve these asymmetric information problems. In addition nonmarket institutions may have an advantage over formal institutions such as banks or insurance companies, for instance, because the participants in an informal insurance interact in a variety of contexts so they have greater ability to monitor each other. This can explain why many nonmarket institutions function in environments in which formal insti-

tutions fail. But in cases in which a local insurance would have enough information to overcome the moral hazard, covariance between outcomes makes many risks uninsurable at the local level. A national or international insurer could overcome the covariance problem, but would lack the local information to overcome the moral hazard. In section five we return to the issue of under which conditions informal institutions can function.

In the presence of these information and enforcement obstacles, a complete set of markets typically will not exist. In the presence of these information and enforcement obstacles, a complete set of markets typically will not exist. The conditions for the second welfare theorem are not fulfilled and Pareto efficiency is not assured, so that at least some idiosyncratic income variation will remain uninsured.[3] Moreover, cross-sectional risk pooling does not insulate the household from community-wide shocks. As described above, complete risk sharing can protect households from only the effects of idiosyncratic shocks to income. Even if risk sharing arrangements function efficiently within the village, they will produce little shielding of consumption from income shocks if the largest part of the total income risk is covariate.

The complementary ex post mechanism for protecting consumption from the effects of covariate fluctuations in income is consumption smoothing over time using credit transactions or savings. Let us first focus on credit transactions. Consider a household that fully participates in cross-sectional risk pooling—thus insulating itself from a least a portion of its idiosyncratic shocks—and that intends to insulate its consumption against any remaining covariate and idiosyncratic income fluctuations through a credit market assumed to exist outside the village. At this credit market households can store their stock of assets (or savings), or they can borrow as much as they wish at exogenously determined rates, r, which are identical to the rate of return on the stock of assets. Assets can thus be positive or negative, in which case they represent borrowings. Denote by $\bar{y}$ disposable, but stochastic, household income after the maximum feasible income pooling took place at the village level. The utility function is the same as in (1) but has been slightly rewritten to emphasize that the decision problem the household faces is an intertemporal one

$$U_t = E_t \sum_{t=1}^{T} \left(\frac{1}{1+\delta} \right)^t u(c_t) \tag{1a}$$

subject to the sequence of constraints

$$a_{t+1} = (1+r_t)a_t + \bar{y}_t - c_t \tag{7}$$

where the subscript i is dropped and the expectations operator E is the probability-weighted average of possible outcomes and a_t is the stock of assets.

Ponzi schemes, in which the household has access to infinite resources by borrowing money and repaying the interest and the principal by borrowing even more money, are not allowed. In other words the household is required to leave no debt, so that

$$a_{T+1} \geq 0 \tag{8}$$

must hold.

One approach used to arrive at a consumption function in such an intertemporal setting is dynamic programming. Applying this to the decision represented by the equations (1a) and (7) enables the derivation of the stochastic Euler equation[4]

$$u'(c_t) = \frac{1+r}{1+\delta} E_t \left(u'(c_{t+1}) \right) \tag{9}$$

This equation states that in discounted utility terms a forward-looking household will not want marginal consumption to be worth more in one period than another (adjusted for a time factor). If the rate of time preference δ equals the rate or return r on assets, it shows that in the optimum the household is indifferent whether it consumes its last dollar in the current period, or saves it and consumes it in the next period. Thanks to the presence of a credit market, households are able to smooth consumption optimally over time and to have complete certainty about the level of consumption at all dates. If the household faces a bad income draw and is out of assets, it borrows money to repay later. If the household's available resources (income plus accumulated assets) exceed what is required

for optimal consumption, it passes the excess on to the next period.

So if $\delta = r$ (9) simplifies to

$$u'(c_t) = E_t u'(c_{t+1}) \tag{10}$$

If the additional assumption is made that marginal utility is linear, (10) becomes

$$c_t = E_t c_{t+1} \tag{11}$$

implying that the household makes consumption plans such that the current level of consumption is equal to the expected future level of consumption. Since (8) implies that lenders do not permit the household to disappear with unpaid debts and as it cannot be optimal for a household to leave the scene with unused resources, it follows that $\alpha_{T+1} = 0$. It follows that the discounted value of consumption from period one to time T equals the value of the households assets at time one plus the discounted value of its income stream from the first period to T. If this is combined with the fact that consumption is equal to expected future consumption (11) and T goes to infinity, the household consumes the annuity value of its current assets plus the present value of expected stream of future income. This is the permanent income hypothesis advanced by Friedman (1957).

An important consequence of (7) is that household consumption diverges between villages that are identical at t=0 but that experience different shocks over time. This is the crucial difference between consumption smoothing through insurance and via credit. If resources are pooled between villages, then households in a village that experienced negative village-wide shocks three times in a row consume just as much as households in a village that remained shock-free. But if households insure only one another within the village—as (7) suggests—and credit is used for consumption smoothing between the villages, then borrowing reduces the level of current assets α_t in the village that experienced the negative shocks. This arrangement curtails the annuity value of current assets plus the present value of expected stream of future income. It follows that consumption in the unlucky village will be permanently lower than that in the village unaffected by shocks. Clearly, it would be more efficient if the two villages agree beforehand to pool their resources (because of the concavity of the utility function; see also section five). However, doing so might be infeasible, for instance, because the villages are located far from one another. Because of its dependence on the past, the use of credit is a second-best solution to the presence of idiosyncratic risk.

In reality households do not have access to the kind of credit market just described. Savings and lending rates diverge, and in many places formal credit markets are absent (lending rates are infinite), especially if credit is sought for consumptive purposes by poor households. Credit markets also have a comparable set of informational problems as those for insurance. Since credit involves an intertemporal allocation decision, loan transactions are inherently risky and subject to the same informational and enforcement problems. Monitoring is costly, and the fixed costs involved imply that the unit costs of borrowing and lending decline as loan sizes increase, making small loans to the poor unattractive. Raising interest rates on small loans does not overcome this problem since it eventually leads to adverse selection (Stiglitz and Weiss 1981), in which only lenders with very risky projects are prepared to borrow. In addition in the case of a covariate event, many households will seek credit at the same time, leading to increases in local interest rates.

An important consequence of the absence of credit markets is that households no longer can have negative asset holdings so that household assets always have to be larger or equal to zero

$$a_t \geq 0 \tag{12}$$

The asset constraint ensures that consumption can, at maximum, be current income plus the value of the stock of assets. Now the household can be confronted with two situations:

1. The asset constraint makes itself felt. The household will consume all its income and assets and would like to borrow but cannot.

2. The asset constraint does not limit household decisions, and current income plus assets are sufficient for the stochastic Euler equation (9) to hold. The marginal utility of current consumption is equated to expected future marginal utility and the household would not wish to borrow money even if it could.

These two cases can be joined in a single expression, in which the second part is the stochastic Euler equation presented as equation (9)

$$u'(c_t) = \max\{u'(\bar{y}_t + a_t); E_t u'(c_{t+1})\} \tag{13}$$

With borrowing constraints it is no longer assured that consumption is shielded from variations in income. This follows immediately from (13). If a household has few assets and income is low, the household will consume all current resources. If income is low for a number of periods and all assets have been depleted, then all income variability from village-wide and uninsured personal shocks will be translated into consumption.

Recapitulating, to shield consumption from fluctuations in income, households have three options, each of which can be explored. The household may pool risk with others through insurance. This possibility works in a cross-section. If insurance is less than perfect or risks mainly covariate, the household may want to smooth consumption intertemporally through credit markets by borrowing resources in times of income shortfall and repaying them in more favorable times. Or the household can accumulate liquid assets in good seasons and dispose them in adverse times. Each of these possibilities can be explored, but it is unlikely that even in combination they will lead to complete consumption smoothing.

It follows that if consumption cannot be shielded from income variability, the separability between income and consumption decisions breaks down. For consumption smoothing reasons, households may have an interest to reduce the variability of income, even at the expense of lower mean income. Income decisions no longer will be based on profit maximization. Rather, risk mitigation tends to start to play a role in the decision process. Clearly, this is costly, but the reduction in utility from the lower level of expected consumption should outweigh the utility cost of fluctuating consumption. Otherwise, households would not attempt such measures.

To get an indication of the money-metric amount households are prepared to give up to avoid fluctuations in consumption, Newbery and Stiglitz (1981) show how this amount can be approximated by the formula

$$\frac{\rho}{c} \approx \frac{1}{2} R \sigma^2 \tag{14}$$

in which *r* indicates the risk premium, *R* the relative rate of risk aversion, and σ the coefficient of variation of consumption. It follows that, to attain a stable consumption, a mutually, but imperfectly, insured household, without buffer stocks and with no access to credit markets, with a mild level of relative risk aversion of between one and two and a coefficient of variation of income of about 50 percent,[5] is prepared to give up between 12.5 percent and 25 percent of its average income. This is a very large amount, especially for households that are already poor and for which the marginal utility of extra consumption is high. In the absence of insurance and credit markets, these households thus have a large incentive to accumulate a stock of assets. If they do so, simulations carried out by Deaton (1989) show that such households may still achieve a high degree of consumption stability. Nonetheless, a buffer stock strategy will not lead to complete insurance, primarily because assets stocks will become depleted after a series of adverse events, but also because assets may decay (stores of food), be stolen, or have values positively correlated with the manifestation of the risk.

Self-Insurance Options

In the previous section four ways were distinguished to shield consumption from income variability: insurance transactions, credit transactions, accumulation and decumulation of buffer stocks, and adaptations in the riskiness of the income process. A common element of the first two mechanisms is their susceptibility to information and enforcement problems. The latter two mechanisms are not affected by this as they are carried out by the household itself and not in interaction with others. This section focuses on the latter two mechanisms, which we label self-insurance.

Self-insurance comprises options for dealing with income risk that are carried out by the household itself and that are, for that reason, not affected by information and enforcement problems. In seeking self-insurance, households may explore (1) *risk management* or (2) *risk coping* strategies, or a combination of the two. Alderman and Paxson (1992) introduced this terminology and classify the former as aiming to reduce the variability of income and the latter as aiming to cushion the effect of income risk on consumption intertemporally. They include under risk-coping savings behavior as well as credit and insurance transactions. The treatment of these latter two transactions is postponed to the next section. This section will focus first on risk management and then on buffer stocks.

In the absence of means to smooth consumption ex post, households may attempt to self-insure by reducing the variability of income. Ample suggestions exist on how this can be done, each exploring some kind of income-source diversification.[6] For farmers if rains or soil type are heterogeneous, spreading plots spatially may help to ensure a stable yield. If the length and pattern of the rainy season are variable, differences in planting dates may reduce income risk. In homogeneous areas diversification can be attained by growing crops with different characteristics. And if the covariance in agricultural outcomes is high, farm income may be complemented with off-farm income (from several sources).

Since spreading risk comes at the cost of specialization, lower income variability is attained at the cost of lower expected income. Just and Candler (1985) provide evidence for such a tradeoff between income variability and expected income. They show in Nigeria how crop diversification and mixed cropping can reduce the variability of agricultural income. Indeed, they find that the reduction of income variability comes at a cost, as the safest outcomes have the lowest returns.[7,8]

How much expected income households are prepared to sacrifice for greater safety depends on the degree of risk aversion. This follows immediately from the formula presented as equation (14), which approximates the risk premium. Households with a higher level of risk aversion pay a higher premium. A number of studies attempt to show that deviations from profit-maximizing behavior result from risk aversion (Moscardi and de Janvry (1977), Antle (1987), and Hazell (1982)). That risk aversion matters for crop choice does not imply that all deviations from profit maximizing behavior can (or should) be attributed to risk aversion. The deviations in allocation decisions from profit maximizing behavior that these studies attribute to risk aversion might also be attributed to factor market imperfections and imperfect information about production techniques.

The assumption made thus far of the absence of means to smooth consumption ex post is clearly absurd since in reality such possibilities do exist. Even the poorest household can save in times of relative prosperity awaiting worse periods. The other extreme is to suggest that sufficient possibilities to smooth consumption ex post exist. In that case the level of risk aversion should not matter for income choice, and even a highly risk-averse individual will take income-generation decisions as if she is risk neutral. The reason can be inferred by comparing Deaton's model, in which credit markets are absent (equation (13)) with one in which these markets function, as is the case for the permanent income hypothesis (equation (10)).[9]

Liquidity-constrained households must accumulate assets to protect consumption from variability in income. Since asset accumulation takes place at the expense of current consumption, it follows that households sacrifice consumption now for greater safety later. Suppose that the same level of safety can be attained by changing the income process. If the net present cost in utility terms of a reduction in expected income, which accompanies this choice for a safer income process, is equal to the net present reduction in utility terms following the postponement of consumption required to accumulate assets, then the household should be indifferent between both options. In

that sense risk management and the accumulation of buffer stocks operate as substitutes.[10]

The reverse argument also holds. With sufficient buffer stocks available, the household need not be worried about income variability being transferred to consumption. The household can take income decisions as if risk is of no concern, that is, it can follow an income-maximizing rule. This argument suggests that wealthier households may be in a position to benefit from higher yielding, but more variable, income opportunities. If liquidity constraints are related to wealth, for instance, because wealth is maintained in the form of liquid buffer stocks or because wealthy households have better access to the credit market, as seems likely, then poor households will be less willing to bear risk, even if they have risk preferences identical to those of wealthier households.

Rosenzweig and Binswanger (1993) find evidence for the suggestion that in some villages in India wealthier households allocate their productive assets to riskier activity portfolios than do poorer households. They find that increasing the coefficient of variation of rainfall timing by one standard deviation would, for a household in the bottom wealth quartile, reduce farm profits by 35 percent. For a household of median wealth profits would be reduced by 15 percent, while the increased riskiness would have a negligible effect on the profitability of the richest farmers.

Dercon (1996) obtains similar results. In Tanzania he shows that sweet potatoes are a low-risk crop yielding a low return that is favored by the nonwealthy. Households in the wealthiest quintile devote a little less than 2 percent on average of their land to sweet potatoes, as opposed to 9 percent by households in the poorest quintile. Dercon (1998) finally argues that imperfect credit markets force households to use their savings for investment. Profitable activities often require lumpy investments, limiting entry by poorer households, resulting in increasing welfare differences. In Tanzania cattle are a profitable but lumpy investment and a liquid asset for consumption smoothing. He finds evidence that richer households own substantial cattle herds, while poorer households specialize in low-return, low-risk activities.

So, there is reason to suspect a tradeoff between risk and return so that improved ex post insurance possibilities should lead to higher average incomes. But not in all cases have empirical results been this straightforward. A study of the Sahel by Reardon, Delgado, and Matlon (1992) associates both higher and more stable incomes and food consumption with income diversification. Collier and others (1986) find a similar relationship for Tanzania: richer households are characterized by more noncropping income. Dercon and Krishnan (1996) shed more light on this issue. Using survey data from rural Ethiopia and rural Tanzania, they analyze the different income portfolios of households and suggest that the most attractive off-farm employment opportunities have the highest entry barriers. Entry is determined by investment in particular skills or by access to capital, something which can only be afforded by the wealthier.

Let us turn to buffer stocks. Implicit in studying the use of buffer stocks is the suggestion that households have a long-term perspective in the sense that they are prepared to forego current consumption in exchange for benefits at an unspecified future time when income may be temporarily low.[11] The intertemporal condition that should hold is the Euler equation (9). If the permanent income hypothesis that follows from it (under certain additional conditions) as summarized as equation (11) is valid, it follows that consumption will change little in the case of a positive transitory income shock that leaves the present value of the expected stream of future income unchanged. In response to such a shock the household will accumulate assets, to be depleted later when a negative shock arises. If the income shock causes a large change in the household's expectation regarding its future income stream, the income shock will be seen as permanent and consumption will respond.

To test whether the permanent income hypothesis is realistic, one has to be able to distinguish between permanent and transitory shocks. In practice this is difficult but Paxson (1992) in her study on Thai rice farmers found such a way. She identifies rainfall variation as an exogenous transitory component of income

and confronts this with household savings to find that the marginal propensity to save transitory income is high. Farmers save three-quarters to four-fifths of transitory income changes. These figures are not significantly different from one, which the coefficient should be in the case of complete consumption smoothing. There is more evidence to suggest that consumption smoothing is real and significant (Musgrove 1979, Bhalla 1979 and 1980, Wolpin 1982), although Deaton (1997) argues that these latter estimates are less than convincing.

How smoothing is carried out in practice is illustrated by Kinsey, Burger, and Gunning (1998). They show that households resettled in 1982-83 in a Zimbabwean land-reform program were able to accumulate considerable assets. These were used in turn to smooth consumption during the droughts of 1992 and 1995, of which the one in 1992 was the worst in living memory. Even during these very adverse circumstances few households were in danger of running down their assets (primarily financial assets, food stocks, and livestock) completely. Walker and Jodha (1982) also report the responses of drought-hit rural households in India. They show that in some areas assets were depleted by up to 60 percent and debts increased by up to 192 percent, but total consumption expenditure per household fell only 8 percent to 12 percent compared to a normal year. In these cases buffer stock assets, accumulated in more prosperous times, were able to ensure a fall in consumption that was small relative to the fall in income.

This finding is consistent with Webb and Reardon's observation (cited in Alderman and Paxson) that in Burkina Faso and Ethiopia famine conditions were observed after only two successive droughts. Apparently, consumption levels could be maintained during the first year of the drought thanks to the use of buffer stocks, but when buffer stocks started to get depleted, consumption had to be adjusted to the available income and low level of buffer stocks. At the same time, after the drought, consumption is likely to remain low for several years because assets have been depleted and debts need repaying. All this empirical evidence illustrates Deaton's (1989) simulation results that sufficient savings have the potential to protect consumption from income variability.

Although the evidence suggests that buffering takes place, in a developing country context good savings instruments are scarce. A good buffer instrument can be bought and sold without incurring high transaction costs, yields a positive return, is easy to store without too much risk of theft, and has a value that is preferably negatively correlated with income shocks. In many places inflation is rampant and real interest rates on savings accounts are negative so that monetary savings are not very attractive. Moreover, fluctuations in the prices of food are an important risk against which financial savings are not indexed. Saving by accumulating food stocks is an alternative, but due to storage losses, such an option is expensive. Other assets such as land or housing are not available due to the lack of title deeds. Livestock, gold, jewelry, carpets, or cloth then present an alternative, especially if such markets are integrated and prices uncorrelated with the income process. Simulation exercises along the lines of Deaton (1989) by Dercon (1992a) show that if there is a large positive covariance between asset values and income, an asset strategy to smooth consumption becomes less effective. If prices drop sufficiently, the use of the asset as buffer stock may even be dampened, in which case buffer stocks can be used only to insure against idiosyncratic shocks. Finally, note that even ideal assets may be unattractive as buffer stock if familial claims and obligations are hard to resist.

The empirical literature, which tests whether buffer stocks contribute to consumption smoothing, has focused primarily on livestock. For India, Rosenzweig and Wolpin (1993) provide convincing evidence that livestock sales and purchases are an integral part of farm households' consumption smoothing strategy. They find that bullock sales increase significantly when weather outcomes are poor and incomes low, and that purchases of bullocks increase when rainfall is ample and incomes above average. For West Africa, Fafchamps, Udry, and Czukas (1998) find less convincing results. Yes, livestock is accumulated when there is a windfall income gain, and disinvestment takes place in years with adverse weather shocks.

However, during the Sahelian drought livestock sales compensate only a surprisingly low 20 percent to at most 30 percent of (drought-related) income shortfalls due to village-level shocks. A reason might be that livestock markets are less integrated and that prices plummeted. Fafchamps and Gavian (1996) show, for instance, that in neighboring Niger, the spatial integration of livestock markets is poor, so that the price of livestock is likely to plummet during drought. For Zimbabwe, Kinsey, Burger, and Gunning (1998) show that livestock are the prime means to smooth consumption in drought years. Nonetheless, they also report that, despite having sufficient assets for consumption smoothing, at the peak of the 1992 drought households sharply reduced both the frequency and the quantity of meals.

That households adapt their consumption downward during a covariate crisis is consistent with a buffer stock strategy if price fluctuations are taken into account. It can easily be shown that by including prices in the budget constraint (7) and allowing the interest rate to vary, the stochastic Euler equation changes to

$$u'(c_t) = \frac{1+r_t}{1+\delta} * \frac{p_{c,t}}{p_{c,t+1}} * \frac{p_{a,t+1}}{p_{a,t}} Eu'(c_{t+1}) \tag{16}$$

where p_c is the price for consumption, and p_a the price of the buffer asset. Due to the scarcity of food during a shock and the large supply of buffer assets, both price ratios rise in a drought year as compared to the level attained in normal years especially if markets are thin.[12] After the drought, buffer stock assets such as bullocks are likely to be scarce (hence valuable) so that it is worth waiting. If borrowing is possible, more households will try to do so, driving up interest rates. The increase in the right hand side of the equation can then only be matched by reducing current consumption relative to the level that would have be attained in a normal year. Hence, in the face of price fluctuations a buffer stock strategy may very well fail to maintain consumption, yet be the result of an optimal intertemporal substitution strategy.

Another reason to cut back current consumption has already been mentioned: the sale of assets reduces future income and is implicit in the budget constraint presented as equation (7). Johda (1978) illustrates this when he suggests that, when faced with extreme food shortages, the primary concern of rural families is not the protection of current consumption. Families are primarily concerned with the protection of productive assets, which are disposed of as a last resort, since their loss is likely to affect their households' long-term prospects of recovery from a crisis.

Pyle and Gabbar (1990) make the same case. They label the three stages of household coping. Initially, households pursue strategies that do not endanger future production but conserve their assets, including collecting wild foods, consuming food stores, and recalling of loans. If the bad conditions prevail, less favored measures have to be followed, which affect the household's potential for future income generation. They include severe rationing of consumption, sale of productive assets, and, in farming, consuming seeds. When the bad conditions prevail and all these strategies are insufficient, households may starve or survive without much to fall back on, leaving them extremely vulnerable.

Whether due to changes in relative prices or fear of depleting productive assets, household consumption is generally adapted downward following temporary income shortfalls. Agarwal (1990) describes how drought conditions reduce consumption and shift the types of foods eaten from fine to coarse grains to animal feed. As scarcity of milk, meat, fruits, and vegetables worsens, food is stretched longer by cooking fewer meals a day or going hungry for several days. The decline in food consumption is accompanied by the decline in other consumption such as clothing and religious ceremonies and the postponement of marriages. Education expenses also may fall. For example, Jacoby and Skoufias (1997) report that in India investment in children's education decreases in response to income shocks. Behrman (1988) finds that because households in rural South India are not able to smooth consumption, the health of children, especially that of girls, suffers during seasons before the major harvest.

Finally, Udry (1995) shows that Nigerian farmers hold buffer stocks, and he distinguishes different assets: grain stocks, cash savings and livestock. His results show that grain stocks and cash savings are used

to buffer consumption from income, but that livestock savings are unaffected by transitory shocks. Udry concludes that livestock are held primarily for productive purposes because livestock are subject to diminishing returns while the return to grain storage is constant. Therefore, households prefer to buffer through grain stocks, because selling livestock become increasingly expensive in terms of foregone return, although it is possible that the crisis was never grave enough to warrant the use of livestock. Using the ICRISAT data set from India, Lim and Townsend (1994) find a comparable result. They use measures of changes in all farm assets to find that livestock and consumer durables are not playing a role in smoothing income and that crop inventory does play a relatively large role.

The consensus from the literature is that households are able to smooth consumption by using a buffer stock strategy, but that such a strategy easily unwinds in the face of a covariate crisis for several reasons. Due to changes in prices and in the face of thin markets, (1) reducing current consumption becomes an optimal intertemporal substitution strategy. (2) It also helps protect households' capacity to earn income in the future if productive assets have to be run down. (3) However, in a succession of shocks, all means for buffering may become depleted. Buffer stock strategies are costly in utility terms because the downward adaptations in consumption affect current welfare. They also may have permanent consequences for the ability to generate income and henceforward for consumption. This effect is exacerbated if the rate of time preference exceeds the rate of return on keeping buffer stocks (making the postponement of current consumption expensive in utility terms), or if the rate of return on productive investments elsewhere in the economy is higher than that on buffer stocks kept by the household.

Empirical Evidence on Insurance
and Credit Transactions

The difficulty in finding suitable assets for consumption smoothing, the utility cost of dealing with shocks through self-insurance, the presence of idiosyncratic risk, and the efficiency gains that can be attained by diversifying risk over households opens scope to explore ways to smooth consumption through insurance transactions. If the mechanisms are formal and market oriented, they require a legal framework to guarantee contract enforcement and bring along high costs to deal with adverse selection and moral hazard. In the absence of formal financial institutions, informal, nonmarket institutions organized among individuals who tend to know one another well can fill the holes left by market failures, particularly if they can exploit the advantage in monitoring and enforcement capacity (Besley 1995). This section will address several such mechanisms, including funeral insurance, marriage, and certain interlinkages observed in agricultural contracts. Many of the mechanisms with an insurance function appear as credit mechanisms, such as the rotating savings and credit associations or reciprocal gift relationships. These also will be treated.

Section two concludes that if risks have an idiosyncratic component, risk-averse households could group together and share these risks. If idiosyncratic risks are fully pooled as suggested in equation (6), then household consumption should track village income and nothing else. Townsend (1994) tests this hypothesis but rejects the strongest form of complete risk sharing for households in three of the ICRISAT Indian villages. Nonetheless, controlling for village-level risks, he finds that consumption is not much influenced by own income, sickness, unemployment, or other idiosyncratic shocks, leading him to conclude that risk pooling is less than perfect, but nonetheless considerable. Ravallion and Chaudhuri (1997) confirm the comovement in consumption among households in Townsend's villages, but also provide evidence that raises doubts about his interpretation of near-complete risk sharing. Deaton (1992) examines a similar hypothesis of efficient risk pooling within villages in Cote d'Ivoire. He finds little evidence of risk pooling, although Grimard (1997) does find somewhat stronger evidence of partial risk pooling, but within ethnic groups. Finally, Jalan and Ravallion (1999) find evidence of partial insurance for a panel of sampled households in rural China. Interestingly, they distin-

guish the level of insurance by wealth group and find that the poorest decile is much less insured than the wealthiest. For the poorest wealth decile, 40 percent of an income shock is passed on to current consumption, as opposed to approximately 10 percent for the richest third.

Given the presence of (partial) informal insurance against idiosyncratic risk, it is relevant to know how households organize this. Self-insurance has already been discussed. Another way is through interlinked transactions. Interlinking is the simultaneous fixing of transactions between two parties over several markets, with the terms of one transaction contingent on the terms of another. For example, in sharecropping contracts, the lessee (of land or fishing equipment) pays the lessor a predetermined share of the harvest instead of a fixed sum. These institutions contribute to risk sharing—at low outcomes, rents are low, while they are high when the lessee can afford it: at high outcomes—although sometimes at a considerable cost.

Another form of interlinkage is between credit and marketing, in which a borrower uses the lender as exclusive wholesaler for his output. It often takes several periods before a significant loan is made, enabling the borrower to assess the lender's capacity and willingness to repay. This strategy reduces information problems and improves the farmer's opportunities to borrow. Interlinkage may thus induce Pareto improving changes in the allocation of resources (Hoff and others 1993). Nonetheless, in many instances interlinkage is associated with large costs and distortions. The miserable employment conditions many permanent farm workers have to put up with in exchange for some security of employment are a telling example (Drèze and Sen 1989). The distortions associated with a 50 percent share are similar to those associated with a 50 percent marginal tax rate (Stiglitz and Hoff 1999). These examples illustrate that informal insurance arrangements may provide solutions to the problem of risk in areas in which formal insurance and credit markets are absent, but these solutions may be second best.

Often the distinction between credit and insurance becomes blurred, and many informal insurance arrangements appear as credit schemes (Besley 1995).

In fact few pure forms of insurance appear to exist. Funeral societies, commonly found in Asian and African villages, probably provide the closest approximation to pure insurance.

Rotating savings and credit associations (ROSCAs) are at the other end of the spectrum. ROSCAs are savings cum credit arrangements in which participants make regular payments to a common pool, which is periodically allotted to each of the participants. The sequence according to which the fund is received may be determined at the beginning of the period, may be purely random, or may be based on the intensity of the participants' needs. In the first two instances the ROSCA enhances the accumulation of indivisible items by the household, since the pot of funds can be given to one member who can invest before she would have been able to do were she left to accumulate on her own (Besley 1995). In the latter case, the ROSCA may serve a risk-sharing function if the pot is allotted to individuals who experienced shocks to their health or incomes. In many instances, however, those who receive the pot early have to pay some sort of interest, so the ROSCA serves more as a credit mechanism than as a means of insurance.

An interesting illustration of mixing credit and insurance is advanced by Platteau and Abraham (1987). They discuss a system of reciprocal credit employed by fishermen in a South Indian village. These fishermen live close to the margin of subsistence and are engaged in an activity with highly fluctuating, idiosyncratic proceeds. Their *insurance* is effectuated through frequent, very small *credit* transactions within the village, subject to the implicit understanding of mutual assistance irrespective of whether debts have been cleared. The latter is the insurance element. Udry (1990) reports something comparable for northern Nigeria. Here, too, credit markets are actively used to deal with income shocks. Repayment is contingent on the experience of production and consumption shocks by both borrower and lender.

Many of these transactions appear distant from the credit or insurance as Westerners know it, so distant that Platteau (1997) introduces a separate term for them: balanced reciprocity. He defines this as a gift that must be returned at some future time, although neither the exact date at which the countergift will be made nor its exact form are known in advance. Nor do people necessarily insist on receiving strict equivalents of what they have contributed. The main risks covered under balanced reciprocity are illness of productive family members or livestock, crop damage by wild animals or fire, and other relatively idiosyncratic risks such as fishing yields.

Platteau's illustration is the functioning of informal sea rescue organizations that exist in small fishing communities in Senegal. In these organizations captains commit themselves to helping to rescue fishermen in trouble at sea and to contributing towards repairing or replacing damaged equipment. Such contributions are made in the expectation of future reciprocity. Reciprocal exchanges are common forms of mutual support in traditional societies. They comprise gift giving, reciprocal interest-free credit, shared meals, communal access to land, sharing bullocks and work-sharing arrangements (Scott 1976). In the literature of political economy they have been labeled the economy of affection (Hyden 1981). Interesting in Platteau's example is that participants who have repeatedly contributed without having benefited are allowed to withdraw from the network while their past money contributions are being returned. This practice distinguishes rescue groups from insurance arrangements, while the absence of interest payments distinguishes them from credit arrangements.

A key feature of informal risk pooling mechanisms found in practice is that information regarding the outcomes of the activity, fishing or farming flows freely and that enforcement mechanisms (social pressure, punishment, or the threat of future exclusion) can put pressure on recalcitrant participants. These characteristics confine informal insurance arrangements primarily to small villages, which, ironically, are often geographically less dispersed and hence subject to covariate geographical risks.

Families may provide similar features of freely flowing information and social pressure, while they need not be confined to the same agroclimatic zone. Caldwell and others (1986) report that a principal reason why rural households in nine Indian villages were able to prevent severe reductions in consumption levels during drought was their ability to secure resources from relatives. Rosenzweig (1988) finds further support for the idea that South Indian households mitigate income risks and facilitate consumption smoothing by fostering geographically dispersed kinship ties through the marriage of daughters to locationally distant households. Using information for the same villages, Rosenzweig and Stark (1989) find that households facing greater volatility in farm profits are also more likely to have a household member employed in steady wage employment. Lucas and Stark (1985) show that rural households in Botswana living in drought-prone areas received, for given wealth, more remittances from migrant family members than families living in nondrought areas.

Although these traditional mechanisms are often ingenious ways of insuring against idiosyncratic risks, at bad times many of these arrangements break down (Drèze and Sen 1989). Vaughan (1987) observes that community-based insurance collapsed during a famine in Malawi. Pyle and Gabbar (1989) report the same for Sudan. Kinsey, Burger, and Gunning (1998) show that informal credit transactions ceased to exist during a particularly bad drought in Zimbabwe. Probable exceptions are interlinked transactions, which allow poor households to share risks with wealthy households, whose accumulated assets put them in a better position to deal with such risks. A disadvantage of interlinked transactions between the wealthy and poor is that the divergence in wealth implies that the poor can are easily be driven down to their reservation utility level.

To conclude, myriad context-specific mechanisms enable households to insure themselves, partially, against idiosyncratic risks. Several features of these mechanisms stand out: they are initiated by people who know one another well; many comprise a mixture of credit and insurance elements; and in times of real hardship they tend to break down.

A Closer Look at Informal Insurance

Section two shows that mutual insurance is a first-best response to the presence of idiosyncratic risk but

that covariant risks cannot be covered. The latter is less of a disadvantage for formal insurance arrangements, as they are able to cover a wide variety of risks over many households. Thus, what constitutes a covariant risk is mostly a matter of scale and formal insurance has the potential to cover, without the threat of bankruptcy, most risks faced by people in developing countries. Formal insurance requires written, legally binding contracts that stipulate the transfer payments contingent on certain events. Formal insurance thus also requires a government to record and enforce written contracts and a literate population to make such contracts. In addition insurors must create incentives to avoid the problems of moral hazard and adverse selection. In practice this means that part of the risk remains uninsured, leaving scope for informal insurance. However, like formal insurance, informal insurance has to deal with informational problems. On top of that come enforcement problems and the fact that covariant risks cannot be covered. This section will look more in depth at the organization of informal insurances.

Let us begin by slightly extending the model developed in section two. Assume that there are no physical assets that can be passed on to the next period and that the village consists of two households with identical concave utility functions, each facing the prospect of earning a high y_h or a low income y_j in the next period. The probability that household A receives income y_i and B receives income y_j is denoted by π_{ij}. Assume that there are symmetric probabilities so that $\pi_{ij} = \pi_{ji} > 0$. There are four pairs of potential outcomes (y_l, y_l), (y_l, y_h), (y_h, y_l), (y_h, y_h). Clearly, if (y_l, y_l) or (y_h, y_h) happens, the risk is covariate, and there is no scope for insurance. For cases that have scope for insurance (one household earns y_l and the other y_h) it follows from the concavity of the utility function that $U(y_l) + U(y_h) < U((y_l + y_h)/2)$ so that there is room for a Pareto improvement if both households commit themselves to insurance with some transfer τ_{ij} from the household with a high income to the one with a low income.

Table 1 shows the four possibilities. Since the probabilities are symmetric, A and B can be interchanged. In the upper left corner a situation is depicted in which no insurance takes place. The lower right corner pre-

Table 1 Pay-off matrix when insurance is an option

A B	$U(y_l)$ $U(y_h)$	$U(y_l + \tau_{ij})$ $U(y_h - \tau_{ij})$
A B	$U(y_h - \tau_{j\,i})$ $U(y_l + \tau_{j\,i})$	$U((y_h + y_l)\,/\,2)$ $U((y_h + y_l)\,/\,2)$

sents the case in which there is complete mutual insurance. The other two cells present some intermediate form of insurance in which the transfer is insufficient to provide complete insurance i.e. $\tau_{ij} < y_h - (y_h + y_l)/2$.

What table 1 represents is in fact a prisoner dilemma, in which the lower right corner presents the optimal outcome, the upper left cell the worst, and the other two cells some intermediate insurance. Thus, will B share her income with A once the incomes are known? The answer is no, for the obvious reason that B attains a higher level of utility by consuming all income herself: $U(y_h) > U(y_h - \tau_{i\varphi}) > U((y_i + y_j)/2)$. Both A and B know that no matter what is agreed ex ante, the household that obtains the highest income will renege. Insurance becomes impossible, and the Nash equilibrium is the upper left corner.

What this demonstrates is the enforcement problem. There are three ways out of this dilemma, two of which are illustrated by Greif (1993) with examples from merchants in medieval Europe. One is through the introduction of punishment, either by a third party or by the other parties that participate in the insurance. If punishment is serious enough, that is, if $U(y_h - \delta) < U((y_h + y_l)/2)$, where δ indicates the punishment, then mutual insurance can be ensured. This formulation explains why formal insurance is possible in the case of contract enforcement by the government and why informal insurance requires a socially close-knit group. Udry (1990) reports that the simplest and most direct penalty for default carried out by lenders in northern Nigeria is the exclusion of the defaulter from future opportunities to borrow from the lender. If there are more than one lender, such a sanction will be of little consequence, unless the sanction is enforced by all lenders. The threat of collective

punishment is credible within a tight social group and has been described for those living within certain villages (Udry) or for minority groups (Greif; Fafchamps 1998).[13]

A second possibility (not illustrated by Greif) is advance payment. The enforcement problem does not occur if each member in the insurance pays an insurance premium before the event takes place. In this case, the mutual insurance becomes more of a transaction in which, in the face of uncertainty, each individual purchases the expected value. Like credit, advance payment comprises an intertemporal transaction. But unlike credit, advance payment for insurance is not a second-best solution to risk, because the premium paid is independent of the history of the insured party. The mechanism is relied on by formal insurance mechanisms and is generally absent in most informal mechanisms, which explains why the enforcement problem is more prominent in these kind of arrangements. The only exception appears to be funeral insurance, which is found across the globe.

But one need not rely on punishment or advance payment. A third possibility in the absence of outside enforcement is an incentive-compatible insurance scheme in which it is more attractive to continue to participate than it is to default. The solution to the enforcement problem lies in the repeated interaction by the participants. Coate and Ravallion (1993) explore this possibility and the following paragraph draws upon their work.[14]

In an infinite game (or a game whose end is uncertain) a feasible insurance scheme is one in which the difference between each household's expected utility under continued participation and the status quo with zero transfers is always greater than the gain from current default. Hence, insurance is feasible if for each period the utility of reneging on the insurance plus the discounted expected utility (EU) that will be obtained if one is excluded from future insurance is less than or equal to the utility obtained while sticking to the contract now and in the future. This case would yield (the disposable, but stochastic, household income obtained after the maximum feasible income pooling within the village. See section two)

$$U(y_0 - d) + \sum_{n=1}^{\infty} \frac{1}{(1+\delta)^n} EU(y_n) \leq U(\bar{y}_0) + \sum_{n=1}^{\infty} \frac{1}{(1+\delta)^n} EU(\bar{y}_n) \quad (17)$$

After rearranging, equation (17) can be written as

$$U(y_0 - d) - U(\bar{y}_0) \leq \frac{(EU(\bar{y}_n) - EU(y_n))}{\delta} \quad (18)$$

where the left side of the equation indicates the utility gain from reneging on the contract (attractive only when income is high) and the right side the present value of the gain in expected utility from a situation with insurance relative to a situation without insurance.

From observing equation (18) it follows that

1. At low levels of income (when the utility cost of transferring τ_{ij} is high) an insurance arrangement is more likely to be reneged upon. This explains why informal insurance tends to break down in extremely adverse circumstances.

2. Enforcement is more difficult if the discount rate is higher. Such might be the case if individuals are impatient, if they perceive a low probability that interactions among them will continue, or if the frequency of the shocks is low (hence the interval between different events long). These points explain why it is difficult to informally insure low frequency events and why it is easier to find mutual insurance in coastal fishing villages rather than in agricultural villages.[15]

3. The discount rate will rise if the insurance system is perceived as unstable. This rise makes the perceived instability of the scheme self-fulfilling, and the scheme may break down simply because this is expected. This point illustrates how multiple equilibria are possible, implying that the same type of insurance might function well in one place, but fail in another.

4. Enforcement will be more difficult if the level of risk aversion is lower. If risk aversion decreases with wealth, it means that wealthy people have less of an incentive to participate in mutual insurance networks. If there is a permanent improvement in the lot of one of the members in the insurance, that individual has a disincentive

to contribute to the scheme. Drèze, Lanjouw, and Sharma (1998) suggest that mutual solidarity in the village of Palanpur, India, declined between 1957 and 1993 "because economic circumstances of different households have become less similar" (p. 541).[16]

5. If mutual insurance interacts with self-insurance or access to credit, the utility loss from being excluded from future insurance is reduced. Wealthy households, with many assets, therefore have a greater disincentive to participate in a mutual insurance, while the introduction of good buffer assets may contribute to a tendency for insurance schemes to fall apart.

Apart from the enforcement problem, insurance schemes have to deal with the fact that insured parties have less of an incentive to avoid a bad outcome: moral hazard. To illustrate, consider a household that can choose between two levels of activity. One requires a high level of effort costing the household W in utility terms and yielding with probability π a high return, y_h and with probability $(1-\pi)$ the low return y_l. The other requires less effort and yields a low return, y_l. It is assumed π is positive so that $\pi y_h + (1-\pi) y_l > y_l$. The household will opt for the higher level of effort if

$$\pi U(y_h) + (1-\pi) U(y_l) - W > U(y_l) \quad (19)$$

which is assumed. If the household could insure itself by sharing risk with many households, it could expect a constant income, equal to $(\pi y_h + (1-\pi) y_l)/2$. Insurance is attractive because $U((\pi y_h + (1-\pi) y_l)/2) - W > \pi U(y_h) + (1-\pi) U(y_l) - W$, which follows from the concavity of the utility function. But as soon as an insurance has been agreed on and the household is assured of the certain income[17] $\pi y_h + (1-\pi) y_l$, it loses the incentive to incur the cost W. Furthermore, since all households will react in the same way, the insurance breaks down.

A de facto solution is to offer incomplete insurance so as to provide a built-in incentive to maintain effort at the desired level. This works if

$$\pi U(y_h^*) + (1-\pi) U(y_l^*) - W \oplus \pi U(y_h) + (1-\pi) U(y_l) - W \quad (20)$$

where an asterisk indicates income after insurance, and if the constraint

$$\pi (y^*_h) + (1 - \pi) (y^*_l) \oplus \pi (y_h) + (1 - \pi) (y_l) \qquad (21)$$

holds, implying that the total amount of resources in the economy remains constant and at the high level. Inequality (20) will hold if the insured income has a smaller spread than the uninsured income. On the other hand a guaranteed constant amount, or an amount too close to a constant amount, should also not be offered, because it increases the incentive to put in a low level of effort. Insurance is thus partial, and individual consumption will move with individual income, a finding that is consistent with most of the empirical research of mutual insurance at the village level presented in section four.

The presence of moral hazard by causing insurance to be partial implies that real-life insurance policies rarely will be first best. Nonetheless, in close knit villages, in which unfavorable behavior can be avoided through monitoring, complete mutual insurance is, at least theoretically, a possibility. This also holds for villages that are composed of members who feel some altruism toward one another. In this instance the incentive constraints are somewhat loosened, because each household (or member of the family) internalizes the undesirable implications of his own shirking behavior on the members of the village. Hence, it is not surprising to find that many insurance arrangements are among members of extended families, those of the same kin groups, or those who closely collaborate. The flip side of this argument is that most members in these groups tend to live close to one another, hence are subject to covariate risks.

In the face of incomplete contract enforcement a final possibility is not to pool income but to rely on credit. There are several reasons why one would find credit arrangements where insurance arrangements are expected. Although not first best, a credit contract has several advantages over mutual insurance. Because of the presence of moral hazard, the latter, as we have seen, usually is not a first-best solution or is absent if the enforcement problem is effective.

1. The enforcement problem is less severe. In a mutual, the household with a low income has to make sure that income is transferred to it in the period in which it experiences the low income. In a lending agreement there is also such problem, because the lender has to ensure repayment, but to do so, an infinite number of periods are available.[18] Finally, if loans are made under the condition of repayment, if the situation is reversed (as for the state contingent loans described by Udry), and if there are many periods, the system becomes self enforceable in the Coate and Ravallion sense. It is more attractive to lend (at least something) when income is high and marginal utility of extra income low than to refuse to give a loan and be excluded from future borrowing when income is low and its marginal utility high.

2. If one has a psychological disposition to believe that the outcomes of exogenous events, or luck, are "owned" by the household, a credit arrangement with positive real interest will more acceptable than an equal split of the windfall. Credit then allows a lucky household to capitalize on its luck and increase its household permanent income. This is obviously not possible under insurance, in which the permanent income of both households remains unchanged after the event. Credit thus implies for two households with equal wealth and identical expected incomes in period zero, that immediately after the first income draw, permanent income starts to differ.

   But if one is more inclined to a situation in which shocks do not affect permanent income, credit arrangement are sufficiently flexible to allow for this possibility. For instance, if level of interest is contingent on the realization of shocks, it may even lead to complete insurance. Udry (1990) describes such a situation.

3. Very wealthy households may no longer be interested in insurance because their risk aversion is low. Such households might nonetheless be prepared to provide loans.

4. A verbal promise to insure one another may be hard to effectuate if its precise content is open for dispute. as is likely given the incentives to renege after the manifestation of the event and the limited reliability of human memory. This issue holds less in the case of the physical transfer of goods for which the precise content of the transaction deal is easy to identify (for example, a bag of maize) and which can also be easily verified by outsiders.

5. As long as moral hazard or the enforcement constraint remain issues, a credit (cum insurance) contract may be superior. This can easily be seen from (20), where due to the presence of moral hazard, only partial insurance is feasible. In (20) a lucky household is prepared to continue to participate in the insurance because it is allowed to consume part of its windfall in the present.

Another option is to ensure that the future consumption of the household will be higher by promising the household a larger share of the future pooled income. In effect this is a credit transaction, because the contribution of the household to the pool is "repaid" by a larger share in the future. Clearly, this state of affairs is not permanent, since today's high outcome household may be tomorrow's low outcome household. The advantage of this system is that the household has a built-in incentive to avoid moral hazard. After all, it will have to bear the full consequences of a bad outcome. Therefore, a credit-like insurance scheme has the potential to attain a smoother consumption pattern than a mutual insurance scheme in which it will always be problematic to establish beyond doubt whether a bad outcome could have been avoided by the household.

This differentiation might explain why credit-like insurance relations as described by Udry (1990) and Plateau and Abraham (1987) are observed so much in practice. It helps explain Plateau's (1997) finding that fishermen can opt out of their mutual insurance if they want to and get their money back. What appears as a mutual should be considered a credit scheme. Such a credit system can work only if those affected by bad luck are not allowed to pull out. Unfortunately, Plateau does not give information on this.[19]

In conclusion, formal insurance remains preferable as it can deal with enforcement problems and more types of risk. But it suffers from informational problems so that always scope will remain for informal insurance. Through their very nature, informal insurances tend to be partial as well. Thus, especially if enforcement and moral hazard problems are large, credit cum insurance transactions become important. It follows that by not being a perfect mutual, differences in wealth may occur between households identical except for the history of events that affected them. So also even when insurance is present, households can end up in different wealth positions, exactly as was described in the introduction.

Policy Interventions

Section two shows how the utility cost of unsmoothed consumption increases with the square of the amplitude of the fluctuation in consumption (equation 14).[20] It follows that small fluctuations are not very costly, but large fluctuations are.

Does this imply that one should intervene during large income crises? Not necessarily. The previous sections have shown in detail that temporarily low income does not automatically lead to low consumption, but rather that adaptations will take place—sale of assets, borrowing, transfers from other households, diversification of income sources, and changes in consumption patterns. Hence, there is little basis for an automatic reflex calling for interference as soon as an income crisis arises on the ground, on the assumption that the income crisis will lead to consumption stress. Furthermore, even if consumption is reduced, there is no consensus on the long-term consequences. Changes in intra-household allocation may protect the vulnerable. For example, nutritional needs may be reduced by doing fewer physical tasks, operating more ergonomically, or reducing the rate of energy expenditure per unit of body mass at rest, all without permanent consequences.[21]

However, suppose that there are permanent consequences of the type reported by Hoddinot and Kinsey (1999), who found that the 1992 drought in Zimbabwe permanently stunted children. Is this sufficient ground for action? Clearly, becoming smaller through childhood hunger or infection or both is unacceptable even if it is too mild to perceptibly increase the risks to death or functioning. However, it is not self evident that moderate stunting leads to increased death risk, reduced resistance to infection, or worsened cognitive performance. Therefore, it is unclear whether there is an unambiguous link between temporarily low consumption and permanent harmful consequences (Lipton and Payne 1994). On the other hand if resources are already low, as is likely for the poor or those who experience a series of shocks, then even small income shocks may push households below the line of what should be considered an adequate level of consumption.[22] Whether this point is reached is an empirical matter that must be evaluated case by case.

It has been pointed out that in the face of covariate risks, self and mutual insurance possibilities are prone to failure in reaching their objective of smoothed consumption. It is therefore tempting to conclude that interventions should be aimed at covariate risks. However, such conclusions would be premature. The degree to which the poor are insured relative to the better off has not been established. Nevertheless, it is quite conceivable that the poor are in a worse position either because they are excluded from informal insurance networks or because they possess fewer options (assets, human capital) for self-insurance. Jalan and Ravallion (1999) (see section four) provide evidence suggestive of this. If that is the case, action directed toward dealing with idiosyncratic risks is just as well justified.

If one decides to act, it is a given that the first best way to deal with consumption fluctuations is through fully operational insurance markets. Insurance markets require for their operation a transparent and accessible legal framework that guarantees contract enforcement. Thus, enhancing rules and regulations would help, particularly if at the same time measures are taken to shield the often illiterate populace from abuse, corruption, or the risk of default by the insurance company.

This is not a trivial issue. Although the literature stresses informational and enforcement problems, organizational problems abound, as exemplified by insurance. Advance payments can solve the enforcement problem; therefore, it is legitimate to ask why so few advance payment insurance schemes are observed in situations in which one could expect great demand for insurance. There are several possible answers, including the fixed costs to set up an insurance scheme, but there is also the fact that the insurer has to be trusted to pay out during a crisis.

Or consider credit. Drèze, Lanjouw, and Sharma (1998) describe how bank managers of one particular bank in the village of Palanpur, India, have an incentive not to recover loans, because not doing so allows them to roll over non-repaid debt at a hefty "administrative" fee. Those at another bank set up specifically to reach the poor paid little attention to these requirements because they felt it was extremely difficult to ascertain whether the applicants were genuinely below the poverty line. In addition, the bank manager had few dealings with poor borrowers, whom he considered to be particularly prone to default.

However, not all lending institutions are corrupt. The authors also discuss the case of the seed store in the same village that gives out small wheat loans, manages to recover most of these loans, and reaches the poor. Its institutional set-up ensures transparency, gives managers incentives that are in line with the objectives of the institution, and makes loan repayment by those who have the means to repay difficult to avoid.

Another institutional innovation that recognizes the fundamental informational problems in rural financial markets and that recently has gained much attention is microfinance programs, such as group lending schemes. These schemes make a borrower's neighbor co-signer to a loan, mitigating problems created by informational asymmetries between lender and borrower. Neighbors now have incentives to monitor each other and to exclude risk borrowers from participation, promoting repayments even in the absence of collateral requirements (Morduch 1999). Attractive as the group lending schemes may appear, two qualifying remarks have to be made. First, group lending schemes enhance the possibilities for credit but this is nearly exclusively intended for productive purposes, and less for consumption smoothing. Next, a group lending scheme is not a first best solution. The cost involved in group lending is that an agent with a large diversified portfolio such as a bank is in a better position to bear the risk of default than the cosigners of the loan (Stiglitz 1993).

However, the absence of formal insurance possibilities does not necessarily imply that the most effective intervention would be to set up an insurance program. Hoff and Stiglitz (1997) show, for instance, how the wrong policy—subsidizing interest rates (because the poor pay such high rates of interest in the informal credit market—may lead to the perverse effect of even higher informal interest rates. In the case they describe, the root of the problem is the costs moneylenders have to expend to screen borrowers and to obtain repayment. The reasoning behind their paper is that lower opportunity costs for credit induces new entry into the market for money lending. This reduces the monopoly power of the existing money lenders and induces them to increase their lending. At the same time new entry increases the enforcement costs of lending because borrowers get an incentive not to repay their old loan but to approach the new lender instead. The lender has to recover these costs through higher interest rates or greater enforcement costs.

The proper way to address the issue of high informal interest rates in this case would be to improve the infrastructure for screening and repayment. It follows that for a proper judgment of what is required, deep knowledge of the local situation is needed. A similar conclusion follows from the numerical simulations carried out by Coate and Ravallion (1993), which suggest that small changes in the environment easily disrupt existing informal insurance arrangements. They show the sensitivity of informal arrangements to small changes in initial conditions and how an active informal insurance arrangement may vanish entirely with a seemingly small drop in a household's risk aversion or an increase in its discount rate.

The status quo is not desirable in all cases. In certain situations, for instance, if an alternative in the form of market insurance is present, one might want to do away with existing informal insurance arrangements. Arnott and Stiglitz (1991) analyze such a case

in which informal insurance crowds out formal insurance. Their reasoning is that because of the presence of moral hazard, fully insured individuals exert too little effort to avoid disaster. In response the competitively determined market insurance rations the amount of insurance that can be obtained at the equilibrium price, so that insured households would like to obtain additional insurance at the market price. Since this is not possible, they enter into informal insurance arrangements. But because they do so, they have less incentive to avoid accidents, and the accident frequency will change. In response the market insurance will contract further, creating additional room for informal insurance. In this case, nonmarket insurance crowds out market insurance, and welfare is lowered, but this need not be true in all situations. If the partners in the nonmarket insurance monitor one another so that they take greater care than they would otherwise, the moral hazard problem is reduced, the market insurance can expand, and welfare is increased. What seems obvious at first sight–there is a nonmarket insurance with a clearly identifiable function so it deserves protection—is less so if analyzed properly. In this case the analysis suggests that informal insurance contributes positively to welfare only if it is instrumental in dealing with the moral hazard problem.

Apart from enhancing insurance possibilities, interventions can also aim at enhancing self-insurance, whether risk management or risk coping. A favorable economic environment automatically increases the possibilities for income-source diversification by the household. If a crisis hits nonetheless, income smoothing possibilities may be offered by the authorities. Options include direct (cash or good) transfers, food/cash for work projects, or food subsidies.[23] Each of these programs has great potential, provided that targeting is well done, they are operated efficiently, they can be expanded reasonably quickly after a shock, and the budgets for their provisions can be quickly increased at times of crises.[24] The functioning of asset markets may be improved as well. Equation (16) has shown that if asset prices fluctuate, they become less valuable as buffer stock. In Zimbabwe, for instance, rural households use livestock for buffering purposes. During drought, beasts flood the market, and the price of livestock tends to fall dramatically because the domestic market in unable to absorb the supply of meat. Expanding the market through enhanced export possibilities would reduce these price fluctuations.

Increased savings services by banks might also be attractive. Although the interest elasticity of savings tends to be relatively low, evidence from Japan suggests that so long as returns are positive (implying not too high an inflation rate) and transaction costs low, postal savings accounts can mobilize enormous amounts of savings. It follows from the same equation that in addition to reducing the fluctuations in asset prices, stabilizing food prices would help, especially for the poor who spend a large share of their total income on food.

As always, such suggestions have to be approached with extreme care as they could easily lead to perverse effects. Not all households are net food consumers, and net sellers of food will lose out if stabilizing food prices leads to a lower price on average. And suppose a government decides to stabilize prices by putting food in storage when prices are low and taking it out when prices are high. If such government storage is successful in reducing price volatility, it will displace private storage as it reduces the incentive to store (the price fluctuation). This crowding-out will, in turn, increase the cost of the stabilization program, and if public storage is more expensive than private, result in inefficient resource allocation (Stiglitz 1993).

Sachs (1999) provide compelling examples of areas in which government intervention might enhance the possibilities for risk management by the household. He points out that the risks the poor face are often different from those that affect the rich. The poor tend to live in different ecological zones, face different health conditions, and be forced to overcome agronomic limitations that are very different from those of the rich countries. Commercial scientific research is directed primarily at the rich country's interest, given that these areas have the most purchasing power and that having to sell the beneficial product at a price that makes it affordable to the poor entails risk. This leads to an underprovision of research of malaria vaccines[25] or of hardier plants. The availability of such goods clearly would help households to reduce the

risks they face (risk management). Public authorities might want to interfere in these markets to promote the provision of these goods.

Another area is in the development of new financial products. In developing countries the insurance industry is usually underdeveloped, because it cannot access the global reinsurance market. This difficulty persists, despite the fact that the risks they potentially have on offer, such as drought insurance, are a desirable diversification for international insurors. As a consequence offering insurance against locally covariant risks is not an option for local insurance companies, despite the fact that suitable instruments can be conceived of. Rainfall insurance in which the insured pays a premium each year and receives a prespecified amount if the trigger event takes place, is an example.[26] Since covariant risks are generally the most dangerous risks against which many households would be prepared to purchase insurance, this is a situation of unfulfilled demand.

New financial instruments have the potential to solve the supply side problems. An example of such an instrument are the so-called catastrophe bonds. These are nothing but regular bonds issued with embedded contingent options that provide the right to withhold some or all of the principal and accrued interest in the event of a defined trigger event. The bonds need not rely on measures of actual loss, so that moral hazard is avoided so long as the trigger is an objective measure of the intensity of an event and the indemnity is paid according to the intensity of the trigger event.

Another instrument is contingent credit. Under a contingent credit arrangement the lender charges a fee, which is paid so long as the trigger event does not occur. If an event does occur, the borrower can rapidly draw down the funds (Kreimer and others 1999). If the latter instrument allows the providers of consumer credit to deal with the risk of massive non-repayment in the case of a catastrophe, it has the potential to improve the security situation of individual households by making more consumer credit available to them.

In conclusion, interventions specifically aimed at enhancing household security are possible but require a deep knowledge of the local circumstances. Policies that work in one environment may work very differently in another. Finally, in approaching interventions, it is always useful to consider (1) to what extent it improves the environment in which households operate, or (2) if a service is provided, why the service could not be provided satisfactorily before. These may vary from badly functioning institutions to the presence of externalities due to which too little of the service could be offered.[27]

Conclusion

The theoretical literature on addressing risk is very clear. Provided that satisfactory solutions for the informational and enforcement problems are found, formal insurance is first best. In the absence of well functioning formal insurance markets, informal (credit-cum) insurance or self-insurance possibilities may be explored. In this regard households have three options:

1. They may pool risk with others through informal insurance. A great variety of context-specific mechanisms exist that enable households to insure themselves against idiosyncratic risks. Informal insurance works, provided it can deal with informational and enforcement problems and risks are not covariate. Due to the presence of these problems informal insurance tends to be partial and to take place among people who can easily monitor one another. It follows from not being a perfect mutual that differences in wealth may occur between otherwise identical households because of differences in history.

2. If insurance is partial or risks primarily covariate, then households may want to smooth consumption through (in)formal credit markets or credit cum insurance arrangements. Credit allows a lucky household to capitalize on its luck and increase its permanent income. The use of credit thus implies for two households of equal wealth and with identical expected incomes in period zero that after the realization of the first income draw, permanent income, hence consumption, starts to differ.

3. A household can accumulate liquid assets in good seasons and dispose of them during adverse times. A buffer stock strategy can be quite successful in dealing with idiosyncratic risks but easily unwinds in the face of covariate crises. Because of this, buffer stock strategies are costly in utility terms. This cost is exacerbated if the rate of time preference exceeds the rate of return on keeping buffer stocks. If households have to dispose of productive assets, a buffer strategy can easily have long-term consequences for the capacity to generate future income.

Each of these three possibilities can be explored, but it is unlikely that, even in combination, they will completely smooth consumption. This partial effect gives households an incentive to reduce the variability of income and to take income decisions not solely to maximize profit but also to mitigate risk. Since safe outcomes have lower returns, it follows that the presence of partial insurance reduces aggregate income. The poor, who tend to be less insured because they have fewer assets, are also the ones who have the greatest incentive to opt for safe but low-return income possibilities. Partial insurance thus contributes to a two-class society in which the wealthy have both higher incomes and better capacity to protect their consumption levels.

If a crisis occurs (after risk management strategies have failed) and insurance strategies are incapable of maintaining household consumption at its original level, then consumption has to be reduced. If this happens to poor households or if the reduction in consumption is large, reduced consumption easily leads to great human suffering that may have permanent consequences for the potential to generate future income. This may result because productive assets have to be sold, reduced consumption affects one's labor and cognitive abilities, or children have been taken out of school. A series of small shocks, rather than one large one, also may lead to undesirable inequality in society.

As mentioned earlier, interventions aimed at enhancing household security are possible but require thorough knowledge of the local circumstances. In approaching an intervention, it is useful to always consider:

1. The extent to which it improves the environment in which households operate. Enhanced market integration, for instance, through investments in infrastructure will reduce covariances in risks and in incomes and asset values and enable households to diversify their sources of income.

2. What externalities prevented previous satisfactory provision of insurance heretofore. In some cases it is preferable for a government to intervene directly because it is able to spread the risk over more economic agents. Or it may be advantageous to create the conditions that enable private agents to offer financial or risk management services. In other cases outside agencies may have no particular advantages over local insurance mechanisms, or local institutions may need to be strengthened.

Notes

1. The author is affiliated with the Vrije Universiteit Amsterdam and the Tinbergen Institute Amsterdam. Comments and suggestions received from Jan-Willem Gunning and Peter Lanjouw are greatly appreciated. All errors are the author's.

2. Such responses have also been labelled perverse coping because they incur permanent losses.

3. In section five this point is elaborated in greater detail.

4. A formal derivation can be found in Obstfeld and Rogoff (1996).

5. For households engaged in rain-fed agriculture, this is a realistic level of *income* variation. Dercon (1992b) reports a coefficient of variation of crop income of 67 percent in the Sahelian zone and 52 percent in the Sudanian zone. Hoogeveen (1999) reports a coefficient of variation of total household income for rural households in Zimbabwe between 60 percent and 71 percent. He calculates that the lowest level of income variation attainable at the village level through mutual insurance is 46 percent. Simulation exercises suggest that this level of income variation transfers into a coefficient of variation for *consumption* of about 20 percent if the possibilities of buffer stocks are explored efficiently. The latter strategy bears a cost however, and Hoogeveen estimates that the total money-metric utility cost of risk is approximately 10 percent to15 percent of average household consumption.

6. For a recent review of the literature on diversification see Ellis (1998).

7. This does not mean that in farming monocropping is the kind of specialization that yields the highest expected income. Blarel and others (1992) report that farm cropping systems such as mixed cropping and field fragmentation take advantage of complementarities among crops, variations in soil types, and differences in micro climate, so that risk spreading is possible with little loss in total income.

8. The relationship is not always monotonic. Dercon and Krishnan (1996) and Dercon (1998) show that in the presence of entry barriers, the safer outcomes also may be the ones with the highest returns.

9. Eswaran and Kotwal (1990) present a similar reasoning.

10. This substitutability is true only from a household utility perspective. At the aggregate level, at which, through the law of big numbers, idiosyncratic risks cancel out, buffer stocks are preferred to risk management as the latter leads to lower expected aggregate income.

11. The notion that farmers have a long-term perspective was not always considered evident. Bauer and Paish (1952), for instance, write that " small producers are unlikely to have the self-restraint and foresight to set aside in good times sufficient reserves to cushion the effect of worse ones, or, even if they have, they may be debarred from doing so by social custom and obligations" (p.766). But ever since Schultz launched his thesis about the rational but inefficient peasant farmer, this notion has been left. Empirical evidence to defend this notion abounds.

12. In Zimbabwe it is not uncommon to find livesttock sales at price of 50% to 70% of the animals value, due to the fact that both the buyer and the seller know that the sale is one of urgency, eroding the bargaining position of the seller and leading to a relatively low price. Low prices in case of an emergency are hard to avoid as it requires someone to actively look for buyers, instead of letting it known by word of mouth. In this way the seller presents a clear signal to any willing buyer that the seller is in need.

13. Greif and Fafchamps extend their analysis to contracts beyond the narrow range of insurance transactions and include all business transactions in their analyses.

14. From a certain perspective, in this case there is also punishment—defaulters are excluded from future insurance—but one that does not require any specific action.

15. An additional reason is that in fishing risks are less covariant than in agriculture.

16. Drèze and others advance a competing explanation in which the decline of mutual solidarity is explained by the decline in patronage relations.

17. It is implicit that the number of participants in the insurance is large, so that by the law of the large numbers the realized income is equal to the expected income.

18. At least if we consider households as dynasties, and if debt is incurred by the household and not by individuals.

19. Interestingly, certain formal insurances against covariate events do precisely this: they write a contract in which the insurance buyer promises to continue to take the insurance for a certain period after the event until the full damage has been recovered through premium payment.

20. Related to this is the impact that spending an extra dollar would have on the Foster, Greer and Thorbecke (1984) squared poverty gap index. An extra dollar spent on a household with a consumption level equal to 50 percent of the poverty line is more than five times more effective than a dollar spent on someone whose consumption level is at 90 percent of the poverty line.

21. The debate over what occurs in response to moderate shortfalls in energy intake is still unresolved (see for instance Dasgupta (1995), Edmundson and Sukhatme (1990) or Osmani (1990)).

22. It is tempting to interpret consumption it in this context in terms of nutritional requirements to fulfil human energy needs (e.g. Dasgupta (1995), but it is preferable to capture under consumption the complex of food and non-food requirements required for the maintenance of health.

23. Each of these schemes has its specific advantages and disadvantages, treatment of which is beyond the scope of this chapter. For an introduction to targeting see van de Walle (1998). Alderman and Lindert (1998) treat the (limited) potential of self-targeted food subsidies. Geographical targeting has been examined for India (Datt and Ravallion 1993), Indonesia (Ravallion 1993), and several Latin American countries (Baker and Grosh 1994). Targeting the landless in Bangladesh is explored by Ravallion and Sen (1995). Family allowances in Hungary are explored by van de Walle, Ravallion, and Gautam (1994).

24. Contingent loans and catastrophe bonds, treated later in this section, provide scope for this.

25. For an elaborate discussion of the possibility of a malaria fund, see M. Kremer (1999).

26. Gautam and others (1994) and Hoogeveen (1999) explore the possibilities for such insurance in India and Zimbabwe respectively and are positive about its potential for implementation.

27. Microfinance schemes can serve as an example. Morduch (1999) indicates that without extensive local experimentation it is difficult to know how best to organize a group-lending program. Experimentation constitutes a large fixed cost, and the rational response is to wait for someone else to bear the costs of experimentation and then to imitate successful procedures. Thus, too little experimentation may be undertaken, and unless some third party (government or donor) catalyzes these programs, too little will be provided.

References

Agarwal, B. 1990. "Social Security and the Family: Coping with Seasonality and Calamity in Rural India." *Journal of Peasant Studies* 17 (3): 341-412.

Alderman, H., and K. Lindert. 1998. "The Potential and Limitations of Self-Targeted Food Subsidies." *The World Bank Research Observer* 13 (2): 213-29.

Antle, J. M. 1987. "Econometric Estimation of Producers' Risk Attitudes." *American Journal of Agricultural Economics* 69 (3): 509-22

Baker, J. L., and M. Grosh. 1994. "Poverty Reduction through Geographic Targeting: Does it Work?" *World Development* 22 (7): 983-94.

Bardhan, P. K. 1983. "Labor-Tying in a Poor Agrarian Economy: A Theoretical and Empirical Analysis." *Quarterly Journal of Economics* 98 (3): 501-14.

Bardhan, P. K., and C. Udry. 1999. *Development Microeconomics*. Oxford: Oxford University Press.

Bauer, P., and F. Paish. 1952. "The Reduction of Fluctuations in the Incomes of Primary Producers." *Economic Journal* 62: 750-80.

Behrman, J. 1988. "Intrahousehold Allocation of Nutrients in Rural India: Are Boys Favored? Do Parents Exhibit Inequality Aversion?" *Oxford Economic Papers* 40 (1): 32-54.

Besley, T. 1995. "Nonmarket Institutions for Credit and Risk Sharing in Low-Income Countries." *Journal of Economic Perspectives* 9 (3): 115-27.

Bhalla, S. S. 1979. "Measurement Errors and the Permanent Income Hypothesis: Evidence from Rural India." *American Economic Review* 69: 295-307.

Bhalla, S. S. 1980. "The Measurement of Permanent Income and Its Application to Saving Behavior." *Journal of Political Economy* 88: 722-43.

Binswanger, H. P., K. Deininger, and G. Feder. 1993. "Power, Distortions, Revolts, and Reform in Agricultural Land Relations." Policy Research Working Papers 1164. World Bank.

Blarel, B., P. Hazel, F. and J. Quigging. 1992. "The Economics of Farm Fragmentation: Evidence from Ghana and Rwanda." *World Bank Economic Review* 6 (2): 233-54.

Borkar, V. V., and V. Nadkarni. 1975. *Impact of Drought on Rural Life*. Bombay: Popular Prakashan.

CSO (Central Statistical Office). 1998. "Technical Annexes for Poverty Analysis Including the Poverty Datum." June. Harare.

Datt, G., and M. Ravallion. 1993. "Regional Disparities, Targetting, and Poverty in India." In *Including the Poor*. Ed. M. Lipton and J. van der Gaag. World Bank.

Deaton, A. 1997. *The Analysis of Household Surveys: A Microeconometric Approach to Development Policy*. Baltimore: Johns Hopkins University Press.

Dercon, S. 1992a. *The Role of Assets in Coping with Household Income Fluctuations: Some Simulation Results*. Oxford: University of Oxford, Centre for the Study of African Economies.

_____. 1992b. *Agriculture and Risk*. Oxford: University of Oxford, Centre for the Study of African Economies.

_____. 1996. "Risk, Crop Choice, and Savings: Evidence from Tanzania." *Economic Development and Cultural Change* 44 (3): 485-513.

_____. 1998. "Wealth, Risk and Activity Choice: Cattle in Western Tanzania." *Journal of Development Economics* 55 (1): 1-42.

Dercon, S., and P. Krishnan. 1996. "Income Portfolios in Rural Ethiopia and Tanzania: Choices and Constraints." *Journal of Development Studies* 32 (6): 850-75.

Drèze J., and A. Sen. 1989. *Hunger and Public Action*. Oxford: Clarendon Press.

Drèze, J., P. Lanjouw, and N. Sharma. 1998. "Credit." In *Economic Development in Palanpur over Five Decades*. Ed. P. Lanjouw and N. Stern. Oxford and New York: Oxford University Press, Clarendon Press.

Ellis, F. 1998. "Household Strategies and Rural Livelihood Diversification." *Journal of Development Studies* 35 (1): 1-38.

Eswaran, M., and A. Kotwal. 1990. "Implications of Credit Constraints for Risk Behaviour in Less Developed Econo-

mies." *Oxford Economic Papers* 42: 473-82.

Fafchamps, M., 1998. "Market Emergence, Trust and Reputation." Stanford University, Stanford, Cal. Mimeo.

Fafchamps, M., and S. Gavian. 1996. "The Spatial Integration of Livestock Markets in Niger." *Journal of African Economies* 5 (3): 336-405.

Fafchamps, M., C. Udry, and K. Czukas. 1998. "Drought and Saving in West Africa: Are Livestock a Buffer Stock?" *Journal of Development Economics* 55 (2): 273-305.

Foster, J. E., J. Greer, and E. Torbecke. 1984. "A Class of Decomposable Poverty Measures." *Econometrica* 52 (3): 761-66.

Gautam, M., P. Hazell, and H. Alderman. 1994. "Rural Demand for Drought Insurance." Policy Research Working Paper 1383. World Bank.

Greif, A. 1993. "Contract Enforceability and Economic Institutions in Early Trade: The Maghribi Traders' Coalition." *American Economic Review* 83 (3): 525-48.

Grimard, F. 1997. "Household Consumption Smoothing through Ethnic Ties: Evidence from Côte D'Ívoire." *Journal of Development Economics* 53 (2): 391-422.

Hazell, P. 1982. "Application of Risk Preference Estimates in Firm-Household and Agricultural Sector Models." *American Journal of Agricultural Economics* 64 (2): 384-90.

Hoddinot, J., and B. Kinsey. 1998. "Child Growth in Time of Drought." Mimeo.

Hoff, K., A. Braverman, and J.E. Stiglitz, eds. 1993. *The Economics of Rural Organization: Theory, Practice, and Policy*, Oxford: Oxford University Press for the World Bank.

Hoogeveen, J. G. M. 1999. "The Puzzle of the Absent Rural Formal Financial Institutions" In *Markets beyond Liberalisation*. Ed. A. Van Tilburg and H. Moll. Amsterdam: Kluwer. Forthcoming.

Hyden, G. 1981. *Efficiency versus Distribution in East African Cooperatives*. East African Literature Bureau, Nairobi.

Jacoby, H., and E. Skoufias. 1997. "Risk, Financial Markets and Human Capital in a Developing Country." *Review of Economic Studies* 64 (3): 335-71.

Jalan, J., and M. Ravallion. 1999. "Are the Poor Less Well Insured? Evidence on Vulnerability to Income Risk in Rural China." *Journal of Development Economics* 58 (1): 61-81.

Johda, N.S. 1978. "Effectiveness of Farmer's Adjustment to Risk." *Economic and Political Weekly* 13 (25).

Kinsey, B., K. Burger, and J.W. Gunning. 1998. Coping with Drought in Zimbabwe: Survey Evidence on Responses of Rural Households to Risk." *World Development* 26 (1): 89-110.

Kremer, M. 1999. "Purchase Pre-Commitment for New Vaccines: Rationale and a Proposed Design." Harvard University, Cambridge, Mass. Mimeo.

Kreimer, A., and others. 1999. *Managing Disaster Risk in Mexico: Market Incentives for Mitigation Investment.* Disaster Risk Management Series 1. World Bank.

Morduch, J. 1999. "The Microfinance Promise." *Journal of Economic Literature.* Forthcoming.

Moscardi, E., and A. de Janvry. 1977. "Attitudes toward Risk among Peasants: An Econometric Approach." *American Journal of Agricultural Economics* 59 (4): 710-16.

Musgrove, P. 1979. "Permanent Household Income and Consumption in Urban South America." *American Economic Review* 69: 355-68.

Newbery, D. 1993. "Implications of Imperfect Risk Markets for Agricultural Taxation." In *The Economics of Rural Organization: Theory, Practice, and Policy.* Ed. Hoff, K., A. Braverman, and J.E. Stiglitz. Oxford: Oxford University Press for the World Bank.

Newbery, D., and J. E. Stiglitz. 1981. *Commodity Price Stabilization.* Oxford: Oxford University Press.

Platteau, J.P. 1997. Mutual Insurance as an Elusive Concept in Traditional Rural Communities, *Journal of Development Studies* 33 (6): 764-96.

Platteau, J. P., and A. Abraham. 1987. "An Inquiry into Quasi-credit Contracts: The Role of Reciprocal Credit and Interlinked Deals in Small-scale Fishing Communities." *Journal of Development Studies* 23 (4): 461-90.

Pyle, A. S., and O. A. Gabbar. 1989. "Household Vulnerability to Famine: Survival and Recovery Strategies among Zasghawa and Berti Migrants in Northern Darfur, Sudan, 1982-1989." African Agriculture: Crisis and Transformation Working Paper Series 2. Social Science Council, Joint Committee on African Studies, New York.

Ravallion, M. 1993. "Poverty Alleviation through Regional Targetting: A Case Study for Indonesia." In *The Economics of Rural Organization: Theory, Practice, and Policy.* Ed. K. Hoff, A. Braverman, and J. E. Stiglitz. Oxford: Oxford University Press for the World Bank.

Ravallion, M., and S. Chaudhuri. 1997. "Risk and Insurance in Village India: Comment." *Econometrica* 65 (1): 171-84.

Ravallion, M., and B. Sen. 1995. "Impacts of Land-Based Targetting on Rural Poverty." *World Development* 22 (6): 823-38.

Ray, D. 1998. *Development Economics.* Princeton, N. J.: Princeton University Press.

Rosenzweig, M. R. 1988. "Risk, Implicit Contracts and the Family in Rural Areas of Low-income Countries." *Economic Journal* 98: 1148-70.

Rosenzweig, M. R., and H. P. Binswanger. 1993. "Wealth, Weather Risk and the Composition and Profitability of Agricultural Investments." *Economic Journal* 103: 56-78.

Rosenzweig, M. R., and O. Stark. 1989. "Consumption Smoothing, Migration, and Marriage: Evidence from Rural India." *Journal of Political Economy* 97 (4): 905-26.

Sachs, J. 1999. "Helping the World's Poorest." *The Economist* (August 14-20): 17-20.

Scott, J. 1976. *The Moral Economy of the Peasant: Rebellion and Subsistence in Southeast Asia.* New Haven, Conn.: Yale University Press.

Stiglitz, J. E. 1993. "Peer Monitoring and Credit Markets." In *The Economics of Rural Organization: Theory, Practice, and Policy.* Ed. K. Hoff, A. Braverman, and J. E. Stiglitz. Oxford: Oxford University Press for the World Bank.

Stiglitz J. E., and A. Weiss. 1981. "Credit Rationing in Markets with Imperfect Information." *American Economic Review* 71: 393-410.

Straus, J., and D. Thomas. 1998. "Health, Nutrition and Economic Development." *Journal of Economic Literature* 36: 766-817.

Udry, C. 1990. "Credit Markets in Northern Nigeria: Credit as Insurance in a Rural Economy." *World Bank Economic Review* 4 (3): 251-69.

Vaughan, M. 1987. *The Story of an African Famine: Gender and Famine in Twentieth-Century Malawi.* Cambridge: Cambridge University Press.

Van de Walle, D. 1998. "Targetting Revisited." *The World Bank Research Observer* 13 (2): 231-48.

Van de Walle, D., M. Ravallion, and M. Gautam. 1994. "How Well Does the Social Safety Net Work? The Incidence of Cash Benefits in Hungary 1987-89." LSMS Working Paper 102. World Bank.

Walker, T. S., and N. J. Jodha. 1982. "Efficiency of Risk Management by Small Farmers and Implications for Crop Insurance." ICRISAT Conference Paper 114. Patacheru, Andhra Pradesh, India.

Wolpin, K. I. 1982. "A New Test of the Permanent Income Hypothesis: The Impact of Weather on the Income and Consumption of Farm Households in India." *International Economic Review* 23: 583-94.

Chapter 12

Financing Disaster Mitigation for the Poor

Krishna S. Vatsa and Frederick Krimgold

Abstract

The growing incidence of disasters correlates strongly with the increasing vulnerability of households and communities in developing countries. Socioeconomic vulnerabilities exacerbate the impact of a disaster and make the process of recovery and rehabilitation very difficult.

Poor households and communities adopt risk-reducing mechanisms to maintain their levels of income and consumption. These mechanisms comprise income diversification, credit and informal insurance arrangements institutionally supported by mutual aid groups, kinship-based networks, credit associations, cereal banks, and rural money-lenders. However, these mechanisms have not proven very effective in dealing with covariate risks of natural disasters.

Investment in mitigation and a strong commitment to the implementation of a participatory mitigation strategy can only reduce the risks and vulnerabilities of poor households. However, mitigation at the household and community levels cannot be accomplished by governments alone. It requires pooling resources, sharing knowledge on hazard mitigation, and community participation.

Providing access to resources to poor households for mitigation investment could be an important way to reduce their vulnerability. The strong potential for households, financial-sector institutions, and governments to pool their resources for risk reduction and mitigation must be explored,. A number of financial services and products may be developed through market- and public-funded institutions. Built-in incentives also should be introduced. They contribute to asset building and protection, and maintain income levels and livelihood of poor households. These instruments may not be universal in application. The specific context of hazard and local institutional and societal capabilities shape these instruments and incentives. At the same time the risk-reducing mechanisms for natural disasters can be effective only if there is a wide participation and the risk pool is sufficiently enlarged. This chapter initiates a discussion among policymakers to explore various ways to pool resources of households and communities, private sector, and governments for mitigation and developing appropriate institutional facilities to channel these resources.

Anywhere it struck, Mitch would have been deadly. But only poverty can explain why it was so deadly. In poor countries, people crowd onto marginal land, in flood plains or on the slopes of menacing volcanoes. They denude the hills, making mudslides more likely. Their flimsy houses have no basements or foundations. Upriver, dams are old, poorly built, infrequently inspected. Poor countries lack the technology to track coming storms, the communication systems to send alarms, the resources to stage large-scale evacuations. There are few helicopters, boats or bulldozers for rescue; scant telecommunications equipment to pinpoint the greatest areas of need; poor or no medical care to save the injured.

—*The Washington Post* (November 1998)
cited in *World Disasters Report* (1999)

Recent discussions in the wake of large-scale natural disasters that called for international assistance in

129

disaster recovery and reconstruction strongly acknowledge that investment in disaster management will not provide commensurate benefits unless it includes a corresponding emphasis on reducing vulnerability of the poor to natural disasters. An appropriate mitigation strategy for the poor calls for strong linkages with poverty alleviation and habitat programs. A sustainable mitigation strategy also requires participation of the poor in all activities aimed at reducing their vulnerability. This chapter, based on a review of relevant literature, presents a case for facilitating participatory disaster mitigation by increasing access of the poor to resources and providing them mechanisms for mitigation. A range of financial instruments could be evolved to support the communities in implementing appropriate disaster mitigation programs. At the same time the policy and institutional contexts for the development of these mitigation mechanisms are extremely important.

The chapter looks at feasibility of financial instruments and mitigation resources that the poor could access to cope with disaster, sustain their consumption levels, and undertake necessary investment in improving their habitat and environment. Since the poor are the main reference group addressed here, the chapter is structured around their risks, fears, uncertainties, losses, and deprivations The chapter is divided into five parts. Part 1 provides global information on the disaster events and the distribution of their impact across countries and income groups. Part 2 deals with issues of poverty and the linkages between poverty and vulnerability. Part 3 discusses the concept of risk, and the role risk reduction plays in shaping economic behavior of the poor. How do the poor identify their risks, and what mechanisms do they adopt for risk-pooling and risk-sharing at the individual and household levels? Part 4 then addresses mitigation concerns of the poor. In addition to the support and assistance the poor receive from governments for vulnerability reduction, how do the poor access financial resources to reduce and mitigate risks of large scale natural disasters? What are the other mitigation instruments that governments, nongovernmental organizations (NGOs), and the private sector could evolve and implement for the poor? Part 5 presents issues for discussion among the stake-

holders comprising international organizations, governments, NGOs, and academia to advance understanding of mitigation requirements and to develop an action plan for disaster risk reduction.

Natural Hazards and Global Distribution of Disasters

In the second half of 1999 natural disasters in different parts of the world provided accounts of overwhelming human suffering and losses. In August northwest Turkey, which is most densely populated and industrialized, was hit by an earthquake of 7.4 on the Richter scale. The official death toll stands at over 17,100 plus some 44,000 people injured, nearly 300,000 homes damaged or destroyed, and more than 40,000 businesses similarly affected. A subsequent earthquake of magnitude 7.2 hit Turkey on November 12 with the confirmed death toll at 815 and 4,946 persons injured. Some 8,944 houses and 1,542 businesses are heavily or moderately damaged. The death toll from the earthquake that struck Taiwan on September 21 stands at nearly 2,300, and approximately 9,000 were seriously injured. According to official figures, the number of persons made homeless as a result of that earthquake is likely to exceed 380,000 (*Situation Reports*, IFRC 1999).

A super cyclone hit the Indian state of Orissa on October 29, causing widespread devastation across eight coastal districts. More than 10,000 people were killed. According to the latest government estimates, 1,714,000 houses and 1,678,000 hectares of cropland were destroyed, and 406,000 heads of livestock perished.

Eleven days of continuous rainfall from December 8 to 19 in Venezuela caused serious flooding and landslides in the Federal District of Caracas, and a number of states. The estimates of deaths vary from an official figure of 1,500 dead to as many as 30,000 according to media reports and other unofficial resources. Over 600,000 persons are estimated to have been directly affected. An initial assessment of damages indicates 64,000 houses damaged and over 23,000 destroyed (*Situation Reports* 1999).

These recent natural disasters continue trends that the decade of the 1990s experienced, related partially to El Nino [DD accent] climatic changes, causing weather-related hazards like floods, drought, and cyclones. The losses due to these natural disasters are mounting, as population grows and human settlements become more dense in hazard- prone areas. Moreover, global urbanization is occurring fastest in areas that are vulnerable to natural disasters. The Pacific Rim, referred to as the "ring of fire" because of its vulnerability to earthquake and volcano, is the fastest urbanizing area on Earth (*World Disaster Report* 1999).

Economic Consequences of Disasters

As the incidence and severity of natural disasters increase, the financing of disaster relief, reconstruction, and rehabilitation has become a serious concern of governments. These disasters upset countries' macroeconomic stability by compelling governments to make allocations for relief and reconstruction efforts. For smaller countries where disaster losses represent a high percentage of the GNP, the impact on the economy is very long term. When governments reallocate funds to meet the exigencies of a disaster, development priorities and allocations fixed through a planning process are thrown into a complete disarray. The support extended by the World Bank, International Monetary Fund, United Nations, and many other international agencies to the countries affected by major natural disasters bear evidence to the macroeconomic difficulties governments face in the wake of these events. Table 1 shows the average estimated damage due to natural disasters by region and type over 10 years.

Human Sufferings of the Vulnerable

According to table 1, the biggest loss reporting region is Asia, followed by the Americas and Europe. The region incurring the least economic damage is Africa. However, these figures could be deceptive. Disasters such as earthquakes, floods, and high wind are estimated to have caused large financial loss, while droughts and famines, which may entail greater human suffering, have resulted in relatively smaller financial loss. These estimates are partially based on the figures provided by the insurance industry, which provides a much higher coverage of assets and properties in developed than in developing countries. In addition the financial value attached to infrastructure in the more developed nations is several orders of magnitude higher than similar structures in developing countries. If we compare the statistics of financial losses reported in table 1 with the statistics of human losses in the table 2, the anomalous situation regarding the distribution of disaster impact across regions becomes clearer.

Since the late 1980s human mortality declined with a greater access to food aid programs, reducing the severity of floods and drought. However, a comparison of these two tables establishes clearly that economic

Table 1 Annual average estimated damage due to natural disasters by region and type, 1988–1997
(thousands U.S. dollars)

Types of disasters	Africa	Americas	Asia	Europe	Oceania	Total
Earthquake	30,920	3,292,886	17,475,437	661,480	125,500	21,586,223
Drought and famine	9,874	314,440	10,575	218,860	520,840	1,074,589
Flood	82,747	2,878,195	8,591,254	8,999,690	34,860	20,586,747
Landslide	0	2,540	38,230	1,630	0	42,400
High wind	59,996	7,569,469	5,846,648	1,453,576	315,823	15,245,512
Volcano	0	1,800	22,089	1,650	40,000	65,539
Other	5,050	781,790	2,377,289	298,569	15,670	3,478,368
Total	188,587	14,841,120	34,361,522	11,635,455	1,052,693	62,079,378

Source: Center for Research on the Epidemiology of Disasters (CRED), Université Catholique Louvain, quoted in *World Disasters Report* 1999.

Table 2 Annual average number of people reported killed by region and period, 1973–1997

	Africa	*Americas*	*Asia*	*Europe*	*Oceania*	*Total*
1973 to 1977	84,413	8,519	68,454	2,318	107	163,811
1978 to 1982	1,436	3,172	16,529	1,406	35	22,579
1983 to 1987	115,269	10,853	17,073	2,302	189	145,686
1988 to 1992	12,272	5,248	63,435	2,352	138	83,445
1993 to 1997	7,919	3,065	19,078	1,996	149	32,206
1973 to 1997	44,262	6,171	36,914	2,075	124	89,546

Source: CRED, Université Catholique Louvain, quoted in *World Disasters Report* 1999.

losses and human sufferings are not directly correlated. Although Africa's economic losses are the lowest among continents, its share of human sufferings as expressed through mortality has been the highest.

Vulnerability and "Class" Disasters

Vulnerability to natural disasters thus assumes a very important dimension when we study the impact of natural disasters on people. During the 1970s a more radical interpretation of disasters emerged which suggested that economic processes could increase the vulnerability of populations to natural disasters and should be considered as causes of disasters in the same way as were the more obvious physical or environmental phenomena. There was a process of marginalization at work, which had a strong spatial implication in terms of pushing the poor into marginal places. Some of these views traced their ideological underpinnings to the dependency theory, and provided a strong critique of the relationship between relief and underdevelopment. Relief merely reinforced status quo, and produced greater marginalization and greater disaster susceptibility. Furthermore, the relief hindered adjustments to future natural hazards and increased dependence (Winchester 1992).

As the concept of vulnerability became central to explaining the incidence and impact of disasters, Westgate and O'Keefe proposed a working definition of disaster event as "an interaction between extreme physical or natural phenomena and a vulnerable human group...(that) results in general disruption and destruction, loss of life, and livelihood and injury." They also provided a definition of vulnerability "as the de-

gree to which a community is at risk from the occurrence of extreme physical or natural phenomena, where risk refers to the probability of occurrence and the degree to which socioeconomic and sociopolitical factors affect the community's capacity to absorb and recover from extreme phenomena." Westgate and O'Keefe also pointed out that the distinction between vulnerability from a hazard environment and vulnerability from socioeconomic status was a false one. They proposed that vulnerability should be a term that embraced not merely risk from extreme phenomena but *the endemic conditions* inherent in a particular society that may exacerbate that risk (Westgate and O'Keefe 1976, cited in Winchester 1992).

Vulnerabilities that manifest themselves at different levels precede disasters, contribute to their severity, impede effective disaster response, and continue afterwards. The most visible area of vulnerability is physical and material poverty. The poor, who suffer serious income fluctuations and have little savings or access to credit and finance in the aftermath of a disaster face, greater hardship than the relatively affluent. There are other vulnerabilities as well, related to social organization and attitudinal attributes. For example, communities that are well organized and cohesive cope with the impact of disaster better than those in which community-based efforts are deficient. Similarly, groups sharing a strong ideology or belief system are more resilient in recovering from a disaster than groups without such shared beliefs (Anderson and Woodrow 1998, pp.10-13).

Since developing countries typically share a greater level of economic and social vulnerabilities, the impact of natural disasters on the population and economy of developing countries is higher compared with developed countries. Even in developing countries it is the poor who lose their lives and assets. The earthquake in Guatemala in 1976, which killed 23,000 people, became known as "class quake" because it singled out the poor communities who lived in the ravines and gorges known to be prone to landslides during an earthquake. These disparities are equally valid for the developed regions of the world. In the 1997 central European floods, Czechs and Poles living along the River Oder suffered far higher losses than their German neighbors on the other bank. Poland is poorer, and years of neglect had undermined its dykes and flood defenses. Very few Poles are insured, and the government had few resources to spare for either compensation or rebuilding (*World Disaster Report* 1999).

Among recent disasters, Hurricane Mitch illustrates how poverty compounds the worst impact of disasters. One of the most destructive storms ever experienced by Central America, Mitch brought torrential rains and mudslides over deforested slopes, leaving 10,000 people dead and eight times as many homeless. Honduras, the country worst affected by Hurricane Mitch, is also the second poorest country in the Western Hemisphere. It has a population growth of 3.1 percent a year. This increase in population combined with poverty and continuing urbanization has led many of its cities to house people in disaster-prone situations on riverbanks and hill slopes. The country's poor health service and other infrastructure and emergency services left it ill-equipped to deal with the aftermath of the disaster. The impact of Hurricane Mitch on Honduras could not therefore be dissociated from the country's development strategy.

Mary Anderson (1990) cites four special circumstances to explain why the costs of disaster recovery are higher in developing than in developed countries:

1. Losses due to disasters as a percentage of national wealth are higher in developing than in developed countries.
2. Disasters and poverty are mutually reinforcing.
3. Frequent incidences of disasters have a negative impact on investment and entrepreneurial incentives that are necessary for development.

4. Disasters have special negative impacts on the nonformal economic sector, and in countries in which this is an important sector, estimates of the costs of disasters are consistently underestimated.

Along with reduction of physical vulnerabilities it is essential to reduce social and economic vulnerabilities that exist in developing countries by building capabilities and organizational and financial mechanisms for risk reduction and risk sharing. Effective risk management implies strengthening governments and communities to grapple with disasters, knowledge of hazard mitigation alternatives, and implementation of mitigation measures. Capacity building is accomplished through public policy interventions, investment at national and community levels, and mitigation incentives. It requires a strategy in which development allocations and disaster spending reinforce each other and achieve complementary goals of poverty alleviation and vulnerability reduction. We shall refer to some of these concerns after we discuss the issues of poverty and vulnerability.

Poverty and Vulnerability

The *World Development Report 1990* (World Bank 1990) addressed the issue of poverty and poverty reduction strategy. This report defines poverty as the inability to attain a minimal standard of living. It measures standard of living in terms of current consumption (including consumption from own production) and supplements it with the quality of life indicators such as nutrition, life expectancy, under-5 mortality, and school enrollment rates. Current consumption reflects households' ability to maintain their standards of living and smooth their consumption through savings and borrowings, despite income fluctuation; therefore, it is a better measure of well-being than income. Another rule of thumb for measuring absolute poverty is per capita income of US$1 per day. By this criterion 1.2 billion people live below the poverty line.

Until the 1970s most poverty measures simply counted the poor as a proportion of the population to derive the headcount ratio. However, this is an unsatisfactory measure of poverty for two reasons. First, it says nothing about how far below the poverty line the income of average poor person is—the poverty gap. The headcount ratio and the poverty gap can easily move in opposite directions. A study for Bangladesh showed that the proportion of population living below the poverty line had declined, yet the remaining poor were, on an average, poorer, implying that the poverty gap had increased. Second, an increase in the income of the poorest of the poor is so important that poverty is said to decline, even if it takes place through a transfer of income from the moderately poor to the poorest (Lipton and van der Gaag 1993). Thus, while the overall number of poor does not decline, the current consumption of the poorest may improve.

Including Vulnerability

Recent attempts at measurement of poverty have therefore recognized the importance of including vulnerability factors. The Human Development Index developed by the United Nations Development Program (UNDP) has been very careful to look at all the factors that contribute to or reduce vulnerability of communities and countries. Emphasizing the distinction between poverty and vulnerability, Chambers argued, "vulnerability...is not the same as poverty. It means not lack of want, but defenselessness and an inability to cope with risks, shocks and stress" (Chambers 1989 cited in Winchester 1992). He cautioned that

> failure to distinguish vulnerability from poverty has bad effects. It blurs distinction and sustains stereotypes of the amorphous and undifferentiated mass of the poor. Poverty is often defined by professionals for convenience of counting, in terms of flows of income or consumption. Anti-poverty programs are then designed to raise incomes or consumption and progress is assessed by measures of these flows. Indicators of poverty are then easily taken as indicators of other dimensions of deprivation, including vulnerability. But vulnerability, more than poverty, is linked with net assets. Poverty in the sense of low income, can be reduced

by borrowing or investing: but such debt makes households more vulnerable. Poor people with a horror of debt appear more aware than professionals of the tradeoffs between poverty and vulnerability—to make more secure—are not for one, the same as programs and policies to reduce poverty—to raise incomes" (Chambers 1989 cited in Winchester 1992).

Seigel and Alwang (1999) have developed an asset-based approach to vulnerability as suggested by Chambers above. This study distinguishes between poverty and vulnerability. Poverty tends to be an ex post state of being. That is, a household is poor if and only if its consumption falls below a level deemed necessary for a minimum level of well-being. A household may move in and out of poverty, but at any point in time, it is classified as poor or not poor. Vulnerability is both an ex ante and an ex post state associated with the probability of falling into a state of destitution. A vulnerable household may have a level of welfare at a point in time that exceeds the minimum level, but under a different state of nature this household will fall below this level (p. 5).

The asset-based approach to vulnerability uses a broad definition of assets covering household-owned assets, community and extra-community assets. Household assets are the stock of wealth used to generate well-being. Households pursue strategies in which their assets interact with community and extra-community assets, both at tangible and intangible levels, to enlarge their risk pool and reduce their vulnerability. The inability of vulnerable households to accumulate assets begins a vicious cycle of inefficient risk management strategy, low return, low consumption, and low saving and investment, and perpetuates their vulnerability.

Vulnerability is a broader and more dynamic concept that includes not only the poor but also those households above the poverty line who risk falling below the poverty line following major shocks. Vulnerability therefore embodies both risk and capacity of households to respond to shocks. The household's command over assets and resources is the most important set of factors influencing vulnerability. Other factors that induce vulnerability are nature and size of shocks, timing and frequency of shocks, and multiplier effects of shocks. Losses that households suffer due to these shocks represent another set of factors. These losses are experienced through deaths, disability and illness, and destruction of assets that include house, crops, cattle, and land.

An important distinction could be made here between wealth destruction and destruction of income opportunities/livelihood, as later directly contributes to vulnerability of a household. Risk strategies available to households for adjusting to these shocks are a final set of factors influencing vulnerability (Winchester 1992). We shall deal with these risk strategies employed by households in greater detail in the part III and IV of the chapter.

A Narrative of Vulnerability

Winchester illustrated the concept of vulnerability by comparing the impact of tropical cyclone in coastal Andhra Pradesh (India) on a wealthy and poor family (cited in Blaikie and others 1994). The wealthy household has six members with a brick house, six draught cattle, and 1.2 ha (3 acres) of prime paddy land. The (male) head of household owns a small grain business for which he runs a truck. The poor family has a thatch and pole house, one draught ox and a calf, 0.2 ha (half an acre) of poor unirrigated land, and sharecropping rights for another 0.1 ha (quarter acre). The family consists of husband and wife, both of whom have to work as agricultural laborers for part of the year, and two children aged 5 and 2. The cyclone strikes, but the wealthy farmer has received warning on his radio and leaves the area with his valuables and family in the truck. The storm surge partly destroys his house, and the roof is taken off by the wind. Three cattle are drowned and his fields are flooded with their crops destroyed. In the poor family the youngest child is drowned, and they lose their house completely. Both animals also drown, and their fields are flooded and the crops ruined.

The wealthy family return and use their savings from agriculture and trade to rebuild the house within a week (cost Rs. 6,000). They replace the cattle and are able to plough and replant their fields after the flood has receded. The poor family, although having lost less in monetary and resource terms, cannot find savings to replace their house (cost Rs. 100). They have to borrow money for essential shelter from a private moneylender at exorbitant rates of interest. They cannot afford to replace the cattle but eventually manage to buy a calf. In the meantime they have to hire bullocks for ploughing their field, which they do too late, since many others are in the same position and draught animals are in short supply. As a result, the family suffers a hungry period eight months after the cyclone.

This anecdote illustrates how access to resources varies among households, and the significance such differences in access have for potential loss and rate of recovery. Those with better access to information, cash, rights to the means of production, tools, and equipment, and the social networks to mobilize resources from outside the households are less vulnerable to hazards, and may be in a position to avoid disaster. Their losses are frequently greater in absolute terms but less in relative terms, and they are generally able to recover more quickly (Blaikie and others 1994, p. 47).

Factors Contributing to Vulnerability

A number of studies dealing with vulnerability to natural disasters have looked at individual, community and extra-community factors contributing to vulnerability of the poor. Aysan (1993) has cited the critical elements of vulnerability to natural disasters as follows:
- Lack of access to resources (material/economic vulnerability)
- Disintegration of social patterns (social vulnerability)
- Degradation of environment and inability to protect it (ecological vulnerability)
- Lack of strong national and local institutional structures (organizational vulnerability)
- Lack of access to information and knowledge (educational vulnerability)
- Lack of public awareness (attitudinal and motivational vulnerability)
- Limited access to political power and representation (political vulnerability)

- Certain beliefs and customs (cultural vulnerability)
- Weak buildings or weak individuals (physical vulnerability).

These forms of vulnerability, characteristic of poor households, arise from the people's inability to protect their livelihood and their relationship with state or other social and political structures on which the people make claims for protection. The impact of a hazard on a person or community depends predominantly on the protection they receive through their own income levels and social and political institutions. So even a small shock or event may affect a highly vulnerable group in a very adverse way, while a low-vulnerability group is little affected by a very strong shock. Terry Canon (1993) has described these components and determinants of vulnerability in table 3.

Modeling Vulnerability

One of the most important theoretical models of the asset-based approach to vulnerability has been provided by the concept of "entitlement" enunciated in *Poverty and Famines* (Sen 1981). Sen developed the "entitlement" approach in the context of famine, the most life-threatening situation for the poor. An individual's "entitlement set," which helps an individual to establish command over food, emanates from all the endowments (assets) at her or his command. A loss of endowments leads to an "entitlement failure" resulting in starvation. The conceptual framework of the "entitlement set" is especially insightful since Sen argued that the entitlement failure need not arise from crop failure. An asymmetry between production and distribution of food, resulting from such seemingly remote factors as an increase in purchasing power in other regions or sectors of the economy, could also change the distribution of entitlements, thus creating a famine. Sen's work therefore focuses on "exchange" or "terms of trade relationship," which made some people and some communities more vulnerable than others. In his view vulnerability to famine is a direct function of relative poverty, and relative poverty is a direct function of a household's ownership of tangible "endowments" (assets) of land, labor, and animals and *the rate at which it can exchange these for food.* Sen supported his arguments with the historical evidence from the Great Bengal famine of 1943, the Bangladesh famine of 1974, and famines in Ethiopia and the Sahel countries in the early 1970s (Ravallion 1997, Winchester 1992).

Jeremy Swift (1989), who drew on Sen's work for providing a recent model of vulnerability, argued that the "entitlement" analysis did not explain a number of problems associated with differential vulnerability within some communities and, on a smaller scale, among households or individuals in the same house-

Table 3 Components of vulnerability

Type of Vulnerability	Components	Determinants
Livelihood vulnerability	Income opportunities Livelihood type Entry qualifications Assets and savings Health Status	Class position Gender Ethnicity Age Action of state
Self-protection	Building quality Hazard protection Location of home/work	Socioeconomic: as above plus technical ability or availability Hazard-specific: return period, intensity, magnitude
Social protection	As above plus Building regulations Technical interventions	As above plus Level of scientific knowledge Level (and characteristics) of technical practice Type of science and engineering used by state and dominant groups

Source: Terry Cannon 1993.

holds. Swift expands the concept of assets to include "stores" of value and "claims" for assistance that can be called on in times of crisis.

Swift's model consists of three types of asset: investment, claims, and stores. Winchester has expanded on Swift's model of vulnerability to include relationships and processes that impinge on households and communities in dealing with their vulnerabilities. He identified the external relationships and processes as being climate, physiography, the social relations of production, and development policies, to which he added the relationship among production, exchange, and consumption (figure 1). Both these groupings directly affect the asset levels of households. These in turn directly affect the risk-reduction and risk-diffusion strategies a household may be able to use (Winchester 1992, p. 63).

The asset-based models include all the variables that influence vulnerability of households. These models also identify market and nonmarket institutions that households could make a claim on to reduce their vulnerability. However, they do not establish a causality between hazards and vulnerability. Blaikie and others (1994) have offered a more dynamic framework in terms of *access to resources* and *characteristic of hazard* for explaining vulnerability. A brief formulation of the access model of vulnerability has been presented below.

"Access" Framework of Vulnerability

Access involves the ability of an individual, family, group, class, or community to use resources that are directly required to secure a livelihood. Access to these resources is determined by social relations of production, gender, ethnicity, status, and age, and is secured through social and legal rights. Shocks of a disaster may so change these rights and patterns of access to

Figure 1 Assets and model of vulnerability

Investments
Human investments
Household members available for work, investments in health and education

Individual productive assets
Land, trees, wells, houses, farming equipment, animals, specialized equipment, domestic utensils

Collective assets
Access to common property resources, soil conservation schemes, water-harvesting, irrigation systems

Claims
Claims on other households in community
Production resources, food, labor, animals

Claims on patrons, chiefs, landlords
Claims on other communities
Claims on government, NGOs
Claims on the international community

Stocks
Food stores
Granaries, fodder

Stores of value
Jewelry, gold

Money or bank accounts

Source: Jeremy Swift.

these resources that some individuals may no longer have access to them, or others may have greater access.

Each household, defined in terms of sharing common eating arrangements, takes up income or livelihood opportunities depending on its skills, resources, and attributes. Each income opportunity has a pay-off in terms of physical product, money, or other services. The mechanisms that set pay-offs for different incomes are of crucial importance in analyzing vulnerability, because they are apt to change radically in a disaster, reducing pay-off to some income opportunities, leaving households without alternatives.

Equally important is how households structure their income opportunities to reduce or mitigate the impact of disaster. These opportunities could mean physical improvements in their habitat, savings, mutual help arrangements through kinship, and community-based networks. Since these income opportunities are rarely spread evenly in geographical space and time, access to resources has a strong spatial and temporal dimension. Access to resources is more relevant in the context of disasters such as earthquakes, floods, and landslides that affect certain locations more frequently, and in extreme climatic events that occur during particular seasons, like floods and storms. For example, cyclones often coincide with the paddy harvest in Andhra Pradesh, with the result that migrant workers find themselves in hazardous places at hazardous times.

A set of social transactions based on social relations of production and structures of domination allocate these resources. One set of transactions takes place within the household itself. These transactions concern allocation of food, provision of education and medical treatment, and absorption of consumption cuts. Gender politics within the household is of great importance here and shows how inadequate it is to treat the household as a homogeneous unit. Another set of transactions is organized through family and kinship-based networks, whereby resource allocation involving shelter, gifts, loans, and employment takes place on the basis of expectations and obligations. Many of these transactions form an important basis of mutual help or individual survival in times of crisis.

Market institutions and common property resources are other sources of social transactions that influence household livelihood and vulnerability. Analyzing these social transaction opportunities gives insight into the longer-term situations of people subject to natural hazards. The analysis also explains why some people differentiated by gender, age, status, and class are more severely affected by disasters than others. It provides a more dynamic characterization of vulnerability.

The nature, intensity, frequency, and duration of the hazard are another set of variables that influence households' access to resources and contribute to their vulnerability. Although the losses suffered by households or communities in a disaster are estimated in relation to their command over resources, the quantum of losses depend on intensity of a disaster and its duration. Various elements that combine to develop a dynamic framework of vulnerability express themselves at different stages in the post-disaster situation. Blaikie and others (1994) have explained the time periods in which the components of vulnerability emerge as contributors and the impact of a disaster manifests itself (table 4).

The components of access framework change in a disaster, extending the impact of disasters on households and communities. Self-protection and social protection measures in these situations become very important for coping with disasters and mitigation. These measures have a strong institutional basis in informal and formal sectors. In the part 3 of the chapter, we deal with some of the institutional arrangements that households engage in for self-protection, while part 4 addresses the institutional forms of social protection against hazards.

Risk and Sources of Vulnerability

"Risk" refers to probability of exposure to events and outcomes, and vulnerabilities determine the impact of an event on individuals, households and, communities. It is important to analyze factors that constitute "shocks" for the poor. Rahman and Hossain (1992), as quoted in Hulme and Mosley (1996), enumerate the following factors as causing "downward mobility pressures":

Table 4 Time periods for components of the access model

Component of the access framework	Typical time period of change after disaster	Example
Class relations Change in political regime	Months or years	Nicaragua (1972) earthquake Portugal (1755) earthquake Ethiopia (1974) famine
Household access profile	Sudden, immediate impact Weeks Weeks or months	Loss of life and house Sale of livestock, jewelry Other assets sold
Income opportunities	Sudden if urban employment is disrupted Usually over months	Rural employment collapses due to drought, flood Taboo foods accepted
Household budget	Immediate impact in sudden-onset hazards Months	Cuts in consumption Reallocations by age' gender Food prices risen and famine
Structures of domination	Immediate impact in sudden disasters Months or years, with episodic food shortages and merchants' high prices	Sharecroppers refuse to give up landlords' share Famine

Source: Blaikie and others 1994.

- *Structural factors* within the economy, particularly demand for labor, demand for products and services of poor people, and seasonality
- *Life-cycle factors*, particularly the proportions of economically active and dependent persons in a household
- *Crisis factors*, such as household contingencies or natural disaster.

The probability of natural disasters' occurrence is highly uncertain and difficult to predict. Risks represented by natural disasters are also a special category of risks referred to as covariate risks, since they affect a large number of people or a large geographical area at the same time, limiting the effectiveness of risk-pooling. High costs associated with large-scale natural disasters and time persistence of their impact are other important factors that seriously circumscribe the effectiveness of risk management strategies adopted by the poor households.

The mass unemployment, soaring inflation, and a drastic fall in the consumption level evidenced during the recent economic meltdown in East and South East Asia are examples of structural factors. In such cases governments have intervened to stabilize consumption levels through unemployment benefits and food subsidies. It is difficult for the poor to understand the underlying causes of economic downturns and insulate themselves against these contingencies. Even preparing for these contingencies could make little difference, as a sharp currency devaluation could wipe out the lifetime savings of the poor.

The poor are, however, sensitive to life-cycle factors arising from old age and infirmity, and seek to insure themselves through a social capital of family ties. Producing more children, bias in favor of male children who are looked on as more productive, and well-entrenched systems of looking after the old in the family are customary social arrangements of securing subsistence in these life-cycle situations.

The poor attempt to contend with crisis factors such as crop failure and drought, two most income-threatening situations for the poor in the farm sector. In fact agricultural communities in developing countries historically have followed informal mechanisms for collective sharing of risks. The sharecropping system is adopted because of its incentive effects and its risk-sharing features. The rental system has greater incentive effects for the tenant, but it forces the worker to bear all the risks. The wage system allows the landlord to reduce his risks, but it may also force him to bear heavy supervision costs. The sharecropping system, therefore, evolved and became institutionalized as a risk-sharing arrangement (Stiglitz 1974).

If these risk-reducing strategies such as income diversification, sharecropping, and seasonal migration are not feasible, the poor are compelled to sell their assets, borrow in the informal credit market, or get food subsidies through government relief programs. The capacity of the poor to hedge against risks depends heavily on the availability of informal mechanisms for risk reduction and government support. It is appropriate here to discuss how the poor perceive their risks, particularly covariate risks, and hedge against them.

Covariate Risks and Limitations of Informal Insurance

An important issue is the extent of covariate risks related to natural disasters. If shocks or adverse events are idiosyncratic, specific to the individual or household, then local risk pooling or insurance may be feasible. Households draw on their traditional risk-coping strategies such as liquidation of assets, borrowing, and reciprocal exchanges within the community. Although these risk-coping strategies have their opportunity costs, they achieve the objectives of securing the minimum threshold of consumption.

On the other hand households are collectively unable to insure against covariate risks of natural disasters. During droughts many households seek credit at the same time, increasing local interest rates. Similarly, there is a contraction of demand and increase in supply of labor, which may drive down local wages. Farmers may sell their assets in a drought year at a lower price but may find it difficult to replenish their assets in the sellers' market in the post-drought year.

To overcome the covariability problem, risk-sharing arrangements must cut across regions that do not experience droughts simultaneously. Few informal arrangements could accomplish this. The traditional risk management strategy is also seriously impeded by cost. For example, diversification pursued to mitigate risks reduces average incomes, too. High interest is the cost to be paid for the credit borrowed in drought years. Storage costs and losses are associated with maintain-

ing food stocks; farmers incur capital losses in liquidating assets; and off-farm work has an opportunity cost (Gautam, Madhur, and others 1994, p. 1).

If the risks are covariate at a local level, there is an incentive for individuals or families to share risks with other individuals facing uncertainties that are likely to be less covariate. Network transactions can provide the means for such insurance schemes. However, as the network expands, costs of information, contracting, and enforcement go up. Thus, there is an incentive to establish social groups with good communication among members. If the group is small, the transaction costs are lower, but so are the insurance benefits.

If insurance benefits are to be increased substantially, the contractual arrangements need to be diversified for different groups, each playing a role in the allocation of particular risks. For example, the village-level mutual work agreements in Africa can be seen as a form of risk pooling and wealth distribution within a village. Yet these work agreements cannot be very effective insurance schemes in dealing with a highly covariate risk of crop failure in semiarid tropics. As a result an individual farmer has to accept a significant part of the yield risk. If the farmer's benefits from the reduced risk exposure are large enough, s/he will prefer explicit insurance arrangements in a privatized and diversified market for a more efficient risk allocation (Bromly and Chavas 1989). However, whether this contingent-claim market through a diversified strategy would be able to adequately address covariate risks of crop failure, especially in the context of semiarid tropical agriculture, remains a difficult question.

Morduch (1998) cites a number of studies from China, India, and Sub-Saharan Africa to show that poor households seek to reduce their risks through informal insurance arrangements. These informal insurance arrangements include drawing down savings, engaging in reciprocal gift exchange, selling physical assets, and diversifying income-generating activities. However, these arrangements provide highly imperfect informal insurance, even against idiosyncratic risks of rural households.

Although there are some warnings about public policy interventions "crowding out" these informal mechanisms, Morduch (1998) suggests that even where informal insurance is well developed, public actions that displace informal mechanisms can yield net benefits. These public actions include creating self-regulating workfare programs and providing a better access to facilities of savings, credit, and crop and health insurance.

Risk Pool and Risk Management Strategies of Poor Households

The effectiveness of risk management strategies is closely linked to the size of risk pool. Siegel and Alwang (1999) describe the risk pool as the group that households can draw on for assistance in managing the impacts of risk. Groups participating in a risk pool may vary in their size and participation. The pool may comprise a few households in a community, the entire community, or a group of communities, and may expand further at the social and geographical levels to include a region, country, or group of countries. Households may access the risk pool through a variety of formal and informal arrangements, which are determined by the nature of risks and transaction costs associated with drawing on the pool.

Poor households typically manage their risks through a small pool. Since a small risk pool could insure relatively fewer households in a community, even idiosyncratic risks within a community could act as covariate risks. The small pool might be a result of widespread poverty in the community or high transaction costs and could determine the extent of vulnerability of a community.

When poor households face the covariate risk of a large natural disaster, they have to contend with the size of the traditional informal risk pool's being much too small to insure large-scale losses. In fact the impact of a disaster is more severe when communities have no access to external mechanisms for mitigating the disaster and internal mechanisms of social ties and networks are overwhelmed by the scale of the event. Poor households cannot recover from the impact of a large disaster in these circumstances unless the size of risk pool is correspondingly enlarged.

On the other hand if the vulnerable households have access to a very large pool, the outcome and impact of a large event could be accommodated. Such is the case with flood insurance in the United States, where the spread of the event may be wide, but the risk pool is also widespread (Siegel and Alwang 1999).

Credit Markets

Where formal insurance markets have not developed and the insurance market is not diverse enough, credit markets are known to play an important role in pooling risks. Risk sharing and credit are linked closely in these situations. Besely has explained these linkages. First, an individual may borrow in lieu of receiving an insurance payment, thus smoothing transitory costs. Second, the distinction between credit and insurance becomes blurred when lenders are willing to relent on some part of the repayment in the event of an unforeseen negative shock to the borrower. Third, the optimal form of contract when information is incomplete and/or enforcement is a problem seems to be a combination of credit and insurance (Besley 1995, p.116).

Udry (1990 and 1994) has shown the importance of credit markets in smoothing production and consumption shocks in a study covering 198 households of four randomly selected villages in the semiarid area of Northern Nigeria. In the credit markets of these villages neither formal sector lending institutions nor specialized private moneylenders participated. Loans in these villages were quite informal, arranged without witnesses or written records. There was widespread participation on both sides of the credit market in these villages. Over the year-long survey 75 percent of the households made loans, and 65 percent of households borrowed. Fifty percent participated as both lenders and borrowers. Households borrowed more when they suffered an adverse shock, and they lent more when their gains were unexpectedly high.

The study showed that households managed their risk through a schedule of repayment dependent on random production and consumption shocks received by both the borrower and lender. Free flow of information in a village and among relatives assisted the process of scheduling repayment and fixing interest rates, and played a direct role in insuring against the risk. Information flow established an understanding that if the debtor household fared well economically, the loan would be repaid with a relatively high interest rate. However, if the household suffered an unexpected negative shock, the repayment period would be longer and the interest rate relatively lower.

An important limitation of a credit market in this kind of a village setting is that while it protects households faced with an idiosyncratic shock, it is ineffectual in dealing with the covariate risks at the village level. Credit market does not go beyond the borders of a village, so it can contribute almost nothing to a household's efforts to protect itself against the impact of a village-level event. However, this study found that idiosyncratic shocks comprise 42 percent of the total shocks experienced by households, as compared with 58 percent of village-level shocks. Therefore, loan contracting among households still takes care of a significant component of the total risk.

That credit contracts in the face of covariate risks are inadequate insurance arrangements has also been demonstrated by a longitudinal study involving six villages of India (Rosenzweig 1988). In contrast to transfer through kinship network, net borrowing by a household depends significantly on the overall economic performance of its village. The study indicated that a 10 percent decrease in village income decreases net loans to each household by 4 percent. While not affecting the household's ability to receive transfers through kinship-based sources, the correlation between a household's fluctuations in income and those of its village neighbors affects its ability to obtain credit. In a covariate adverse shock the implicit insurance-based transfer schemes arranged through kinship ties are much preferred over credit markets.

These credit arrangements for risk management could access both the individual and group-based mechanisms. The reciprocal lending in Nigeria described by Udry and reserved credit capacity, in which the poor households set aside a part of credit availed from any source for their risk management, are examples of credit arrangements at the household level.

Group-based credit arrangements, which are characterized by a joint liability among borrowers are, however, more important for dealing with covariate risks of natural disasters.

A successful example of group-based credit is the Grameen Bank, in Bangladesh. Credit cooperatives, Rotating Savings and Credit Associations (ROSCAs), and Accumulating Savings and Credit Associations (ASCAs) are other important group-based credit programs. These programs aim at meeting the consumption and investment needs of the poor households. However, by pooling the savings of many households or a community, it is also possible to invest in mitigation activities and reduce covariate risks in the short run. Mitigation is enhanced by the fact that, under joint liability, investment is better monitored by the borrowers.

Risk-Reducing vs. Risk-Coping Strategies

Households manage risks in two ways: (1) by adopting means to reduce risk and (2) implementing strategies to cope with risk. These two alternatives represent ex ante and ex post risk management strategies respectively. Risk-reducing strategies comprise activities that result in income diversification such as planting multiple crops, taking up several jobs, diversifying sources of income, and improving housing. These activities change the mix of income-generating activities and increase the asset base. In this way households take steps to guard themselves against income shocks before they occur and ensure income-smoothing.

Risk-coping strategies are aimed at minimizing the welfare loss and smoothing consumption. Households smooth their consumption by a range of personalized and group-based arrangements that include borrowing and saving, depleting and accumulating nonfinancial assets, arranging formal and informal insurance arrangements, and participating in public works program (Morduch 1995, Brown and Churchill 1999).

Great emphasis is placed on risk-coping strategies, as they are aimed at consumption smoothing. Morduch cites a number of studies that point to serious entitlement failures due to inability to smooth consumption.

However, coping strategies have the cumulative impact of social welfare losses. Coping, which could imply distress-sale of assets or acceptance of low-wage labor, can increase inequality. Such coping strategies may lead to more certain income and consumption levels, but the levels are usually very low and unlikely to provide surpluses for investment.

The two strategies for reducing covariate risks of natural disasters are to invest in mitigation and to increase the size of the risk pool. While the first strategy results in ex ante risk reduction, the second strategy is aimed at coping with the losses of a disaster and consumption-smoothing and is ex post in nature. However, segregating the two strategies may not be simple. In many situations both strategies could be at work simultaneously. The first strategy may have multiple benefits. It links mitigation strategy to the poverty alleviation program, diversifies income, generates surplus for investment in mitigation, builds community assets, and reduces risk of natural disasters long term. The risk reduction strategy is in fact an essential prerequisite for an efficient risk-coping strategy based on a large risk pool. Mitigation of economic and physical vulnerabilities in pre-disaster stages reduces the losses of natural disasters, and makes it more feasible for households, financial institutions, and governments to deal with the financial burden of losses. In the next section we shall discuss the not-so-distinct mechanisms of these two strategies of covariate risk management.

Mitigation Mechanisms

Mitigation of hazards focuses on measures to reduce the vulnerability of households and communities, lower the probability of a hazard event, or reduce the impact of a disaster. Mitigation represents typically ex ante measures, and these measures could easily be integrated in normal development activities. There is a strong argument of cost effectiveness associated with investment in mitigation.

Mitigation of hazards must be distinguished clearly from disaster prevention and disaster preparedness. Disaster prevention focuses on the hazard that causes disaster and tries to eliminate or drastically reduce its direct effects. The best example of disaster prevention is the construction of dams or levees to prevent flooding. As a rule prevention is expensive, and results are often less than hoped for. Disaster preparedness on the other hand focuses on developing plans to respond to a disaster once it threatens or has occurred. At its simplest preparedness is an estimation of emergency needs and the identification of resources to meet these needs (Cuny 1983, p. 205).

An appropriate mitigation strategy is developed in the context of not only a hazard but also the surrounding vulnerabilities. As vulnerability arises from a complex socioeconomic process, mitigation acquires a corresponding complexity. Traditionally, mitigation has concentrated on physical and structural measures, with the focus on development of land-use regulations, development of techniques for reinforcing buildings and structures, formulation of building codes, and enforcement.

However, in the last two decades the concept of mitigation has evolved to embody a range of income-diversifying and risk-reducing activities and mechanisms. Introduction of new cropping methods, diversifying income sources through multiple jobs, and insurance are some of the responses to concern for a wider mitigation strategy. Mitigation investment does not, however, preclude the need for recovery assistance and support. Even if the households adopt mitigation strategy and reduce hazard risks, they may not avoid the impact of a disaster altogether. They may still employ coping mechanisms for their consumption needs and require assistance from the government and donors for smoothing their consumption.

Governments may finance mitigation investment, and some mitigation activities may come as a public good. For example, government may subsidize safe siting and disaster-resistant structures or subsidize a disaster insurance program. Alternatively, households and communities may take up mitigation activities using their own resources. Mitigation could also be obtained by pooling both public and private resources, administered through an incentive scheme.

In the context of socioeconomic vulnerabilities prevailing in developing countries, it may not be realistic to expect households and communities to take complete responsibility for mitigation. However, a public-funded mitigation program may run the risk of crowding out private efforts to mitigate risks, or households might tend to engage in riskier behaviors after their risk is reduced (Siegel and Alwang 1999).

Support-led Interventions for Vulnerability Reduction and Mitigation

Appropriate public policy interventions are very important for reducing socioeconomic vulnerabilities. Sen has offered the best argument for vulnerability reduction through "support-led" public interventions, while discussing life expectancy as an important indicator of national economic performance. Income is only one variable among many that affects our chances of enjoying life. Quality of life depends on various physical and social conditions, such as the availability of health care and the nature of medical insurance, public as well as private; basic education; and spread of medicinal knowledge among rural communities (Sen 1998).

Morduch (1998) too recognizes the importance of good governance to vulnerability reduction created by economic uncertainties. Increasing macroeconomic stability, reining in inflation, reducing the tendency to frequently reverse economic policies, securing property rights, improving transport and communications, and creating a stable political environment are some governance issues that insure people against the impact of economic downturns.

Similarly, measures aimed at expanding employment opportunities through public works, ensuring better health and sanitation standards, and stabilizing commodity prices are other public policy objectives essential for reducing households' risks and stabilizing their incomes and consumption.

These arguments lend considerable strength to the advocacy for a wide range of public-funded interventions for making communities in developing countries less vulnerable and more disaster-resistant. The objectives of these interventions are to reduce physical vulnerability and increase access of the poor to financial resources by helping people to relocate to

safer sites, build hazard-resistant houses, and buy life and property insurance. Poor communities that cannot afford mitigation must be supported with safety net assistance. There is now a greater recognition in governments and international agencies of the need to incorporate natural disaster mitigation in development planning. All the development activities may consider: (1) mitigation as a routine, (2) mitigation as a process and input, (3) mitigation as an ongoing operation, and (4) mitigation as part of best practice (Gilbert and Kreimer 1999).

Governments may face strong resistance from pressure groups in implementing a mitigation strategy based on land-use regulations and building code enforcement. Natural disasters have a short span of visibility after which the priority for investment in mitigation takes a back seat. Mobilizing investment in natural disaster mitigation may not therefore be an easy task.

A long-term mitigation strategy can be implemented and institutionalized through a series of steps:
1. Poverty alleviation programs are designed to reduce physical and social vulnerabilities and integrate mitigation components
2. Governments popularize understanding and knowledge of hazard mitigation and provide technical options for achieving it
3. Governments reward compliance with regulatory policies by households and communities.
4. Financial incentives are designed and implemented to encourage mitigation and attract private sector participation in mitigation investment.

In developing countries coverage by the insurance sector to share losses and support mitigation and reconstruction due to natural disasters is very thin. Thus, there is a well-identified need for innovative financial instruments that provide households access to financial resources and reduce, share, and transfer risks at household and community levels. These instruments require a proper institutional and regulatory framework. They also necessitate exploring alternatives to government funds for financing mitigation.

As Morduch (1998) argues, limiting the government's role conserves scarce administrative resources and avoids political conflicts of interest between short-term political exigencies and requirements for longer-term institutional viability. We shall discuss below some of the financial and subsistence resources that could be accessed for coping with and mitigating natural disasters. We will also elaborate on the feasibility of insurance and microcredit as mitigation instruments.

Financial Resources for Mitigation Investment

• *Mitigation/vulnerability reduction fund.* Governments traditionally institute calamity/emergency relief funds for assistance to households in the aftermath of a disaster. Calamity relief funds can also be used as a mitigation or vulnerability reduction fund, which implies investment of resources in the long-term reduction of physical vulnerabilities. It may also be used for subsidizing insurance in an area prone to disasters, or for providing reinsurance. Governments can withdraw this facility once the situation improves enough to make it possible for insurance companies to manage the risk exposure.

• *Self-insurance.* Households can take a conscious decision to share some risk of loss, or the loss can be incorporated in insurance policies through deductibles or limits. By agreeing to share losses due to natural disasters, individuals and the community are more conscious of the need to implement mitigation measures.

• *Government insurance program.* The United States government started flood and crop insurance programs in the1960s. Under the National Flood Insurance Program, private property owners in flood-hazard areas are eligible to purchase federal flood insurance if their locality has qualified through instituting elevation, floodproofing, and zoning regulations. In certain circumstances, when insurance companies are not prepared to provide coverage, governments in developing countries can sponsor mitigation-linked insurance programs. Many developing countries too have introduced crop insurance programs, which have a checkered record so far.

• *Insurance coverage through financial institutions.* One of the most important loss-sharing and risk-transfer instruments has been property insurance. In developed countries property insurance has replaced government assistance for disaster reconstruction. In developing countries, although life insurance is taken on a large scale, property insurance has had a very small market. There is a great potential for increasing property insurance coverage in these countries, as the insurance sector opens up to the private sector and there is increased competition among insurance companies for market share.

• *Microcredit.* Microfinance institutions and rural banks have emerged as important sources of credit to poor and low-income households. Households can use these financial resources for both ex ante mitigation measures and ex post consumption smoothing. However, it is very likely that a microfinance institution would be financially overwhelmed by the demand for credit in the immediate aftermath of a natural disaster affecting a large population or area.

Food Security

One of the important ways in which consumption smoothing among poor households is ensured after a natural disaster is through adequate supplies of food grains. Community-managed cereal banks and government-managed public works programs have been cited as means of ensuring food security for poor households.

• *Cereal banks.* One of the essential purposes of cereal banks is to provide food security for rural communities during drought and/or famine. However, a case study of cereal banks in Burkina Faso, a Sahelian country affected by famine, concluded that the effectiveness of cereal banks for dealing with drought/famine is not so clear as their usefulness for coping with the annual pre-harvest shortfall. Banks that use their collective assets to purchase grain, particularly in surplus regions, or rotate their funds to purchase grain repeatedly, do make a contribution to coping with famine (Woodrow 1998).

• *Public works programs.* In many developing countries public works programs were taken up as a scarcity/drought relief measure. This was a need-based program supported by governments. One of the most important examples of public works program has been the Maharashtra Employment Guarantee Scheme (MEGS) in India, developed as a response to severe drought in 1970-71. MEGS, which aimed at building public and individual assets, has yielded better results in providing income and resources to rural communities. It took care of the basic entitlements by guaranteeing employment to the rural poor, including small and marginal farmers, landless agricultural workers, and rural artisans.

The public works program represents an important social safety net in dealing with situations of mass deprivations. Its effectiveness in protecting poor households from severe shocks is consistent with longer-term goals of economic growth and environmental protection. Public works programs provide employment when households find it difficult to restore their productive assets, entailing irreversible damages to their livelihoods. Employment through these works enables these households to not to draw down their productive assets (Ravallion 1997). Public works programs may also contribute to reduction of physical vulnerabilities through structural measures. MEGS has supported individual asset-building through horticulture plantations on individually owned plots. Whether it could be extended to cover other activities to reduce physical vulnerability at the household level remains to be seen.

However, a number of public works program have been unsatisfactory due to their unspecific targeting and inefficient implementation. Some of these programs were temporarily taken up for the purpose of providing disaster relief, and could never become part of a broad strategy to build new assets and to reduce vulnerability of the poor. Also, public works programs have been more effective in dealing with droughts or famine, and its applicability to dealing with other natural hazards such as floods and earthquakes have not yet been tested.

An important beginning in mitigation may be made with accessibility of finance for reduction of physical vulnerability at the household level. Individual financial mechanisms mainly consist of microcredit and insurance. We shall discuss feasibility of these instruments in dealing with covariate risks of natural disasters.

Natural Disaster Insurance

Freeman and Kunreuther make a strong case for increasing the use of insurance by arguing that the government benefit programs have emphasized equity or "fairness" over efficiency. Government programs generally provide similar benefits at similar costs to all recipients, which may not be based on the individual need for benefits or the individual ability to pay. The government is also not much concerned with risk identification or loss reduction as a basis for specifying benefit levels. The question government normally asks before providing disaster relief benefits is whether the claimant resided within the designated disaster area, not whether the claimant should have avoided living or working in that region in the first place.

On the other hand, private insurance provides better cost efficiency, spreads risk across larger groups, reduces the variance of risk, discriminates between different classes of potential insureds, encourages loss reduction measures as a condition of insurance, and monitors the activities of insureds (Freeman and Kunreuther 1997).

To be sure, these arguments have been made more in the context of the United States, where insurance companies have been able to spread the risk over a sufficiently large number of affluent policyholders settled in a wide and well-dispersed geographical area. Insurance companies have also sought to limit their exposure to catastrophic losses of disasters through purchasing reinsurance, which has a thriving market in developed countries. Other instruments through which insurers and corporations have spread these risks are catastrophe bonds (CATs) and options. The development of computer modeling of natural perils and the growing understanding of catastrophic risk among institutional investors is increasing the market capacity of these new financial instruments (Froote 1998, cited in Kreimer and others 1999).

Developing Countries' Experience

In developing countries typically less than 10 percent of private property is insured (Kreimer and others 1999). The small number of policyholders and the limited geographical area in which insurance companies operate make it very difficult for them to spread their risks. If all the buildings insured by an one insurer are in one area prone to flood or any other natural hazard, and disaster strikes, the loss to the insurance writer may be catastrophic. Even in the United States, after Hurricane Andrew hit, insurance companies suffered heavy losses from the simultaneous destruction over a large part of Florida and Louisiana. Bangladesh and Central American countries, where disasters affect a large part of the country very frequently, may have similar experiences if catastrophic risks to private property are covered through insurance policies.

There are other problems in creating a market in property insurance in developing countries.

- *Government insurance.* One important constraint arises from the fact that governments are looked on as the ultimate insurers, and people expect government assistance for recovery and reconstruction almost as a matter of course.

  Another impediment is the low income and low awareness of target households. A majority of households live in unsafe conditions and do not have the financial or technical knowledge to mitigate their physical vulnerability. Furthermore, the objects to be insured must be both numerous and homogenous enough to allow a reasonably close calculation of the probable frequency and severity of losses. In many developing countries homogeneity is difficult to come by, and calculation of losses due to disasters is a difficult exercise. These conditions create information asymmetry and increase transaction costs in the insurance sector beyond feasible levels.

- *Crop insurance.* The experience of crop insurance programs introduced in a number of countries has been disastrous. High administrative costs, inefficient loss calculation, inadequate premium, and all-inclusive lists of covered hazards are the main rea-

sons that most of those crop insurance programs could not succeed.

- *Disaster insurance.* The Caribbean countries are illustrative. Throughout the Caribbean affordability of natural hazard insurance is perceived to be beyond the disposable income of much of the population. Although statistics are unavailable, it is recognized that most homeowners (perhaps excepting Barbados) do not carry insurance except when required to do so by lending institutions. This is also thought to apply to the majority of small businesses and even, to a significant extent, midsized businesses. Additionally, underinsurance is widespread. In the early 1990s high premium increases and coverage restrictions caused material increases in lapses in policy renewals. The need and demand for insurance protection exist and are not being met, largely because of affordability constraints (USAID/OAS 1996).

Skees, Hazell, and Miranda (1999) list the requirements for an insurance scheme to deal with natural hazards.

1. It is affordable and accessible to all kinds of rural people, including the poor.
2. It compensates for catastrophic income losses to protect consumption and debt repayment capacity.
3. It is practical to implement given limited data available.
4. It can be provided by the private sector with little or no government subsidies.
5. It avoids the moral hazard and adverse selection problems that have bedeviled crop insurance programs.

They suggest that the area-based index contracts, such as regional rainfall insurance, could meet all these requirements. The essential principle of area-based index insurance is that contracts are written against specific perils or events (for example, area yield loss, drought, or flood), defined, and recorded at a regional level (for example, at a local weather station). Insurance is sold in standard units (for example, $10 or $100), with a standard contract (certificate) for each unit purchased called a Standard Unit Contract (SUC). The premium rate for a SUC is the same for all buyers who buy the same contract in a given region, and all buyers receive the same indemnity per SUC if the insured event occurs. Buyers are free to purchase as many units of the insurance as they wish.

Group-based Insurance Programs

Most, although not all, of the above requirements for covering natural disasters are met through group-based insurance programs. The biggest advantage of group-based insurance is that it can enlarge the risk pool and provide insurance at affordable price. Large numbers of policyholders (a) reduce the potential for adverse selection—in which claims are higher than expected because only high-risk households purchase the insurance--and (b) increase the likelihood that the variance of actual claims will be closer to the expected mean used in calculating premiums. Calculating average expected claims requires a sufficiently large number of risks to achieve a statistically significant result. A group-based insurance program with its large number of policyholders and strong familiarity with their risk profiles can better accomplish this.

Selling insurance to group with a membership of 50 to 100 is also a faster and less costly method to develop a customer base than selling one or two thousand individual policies. By enrolling a group of individuals or households to a single contract, the insurance provider reduces the cost of administration and distribution per policyholder. The claims management costs too are lower because the risk profile of a group is more likely to be closer to the insurance provider's expectations that is an individual risk (Brown and Churchill 1999).

Group-based insurance programs have the potential to provide appropriate mitigation incentives to communities. People come together and initiate improvements in their physical surroundings to qualify for insurance benefits. The National Flood Insurance Program administered by the United States government is an important example of group-based disaster insurance program.

Reinsurance

One of the important mechanisms by which insurance providers transfer their risk to worldwide risk-sharing pools is reinsurance. Historically, the reinsurance markets have adopted an implicit financing approach under which losses incurred in one period are "paid back" in subsequent periods through increases in the cost of reinsurance. As a result, reinsurance prices have fluctuated widely, and these fluctuations are passed on to the consumer. Rate increases after natural disasters can be large enough to affect the viability of businesses. Occasionally, reinsurance coverage is canceled altogether after a disaster (Kreimer and others 1999).

Since formal reinsurance tends to be an unreliable instrument, Skees and others suggest that recent developments in global financial markets are making it increasingly feasible to evolve and apply new financial instruments for dealing with covariate risks. For example, catastrophe bonds (CATs) offer innovative ways of packaging the risks assumed by a rainfall insurer to sell in the international financial markets. CATs issued against rainfall events in developing countries could be very appealing to international investment bankers because their risk would be uncorrelated with the risks of most other financial investments. Since El Niño and the Southern Oscillation (ENSO) is a major source of risk, it might be possible to develop an exchange-traded index on ENSO in a major futures market (Skees and others 1999).

Expanding formal-sector insurance coverage to deal with natural disasters, however, is more a pursuit in optimism than the realities in developing countries justify. One may agree with Siegel and Alwang (1999) that formal actuarial insurance is not a panacea for risk faced by poor rural households. Such insurance does not address many sources of risk and subsequent shortfalls in income and consumption. There are social risks that cannot be adequately covered by formal or informal insurance arrangements. Market and social institutions could pool their resources to cover these risks and evolve appropriate protection mechanisms. Mechanisms for strengthening these institutions include provision of information, technical assistance, infrastructure, and legal framework—essential components of a comprehensive mitigation strategy.

Microcredit

One of the limitations of hazard mitigation insurance is that it is primarily an ex post mechanism. It helps policyholders only through sharing and reducing their losses. It does not necessarily encourage investment in mitigation. While some group-based insurance policies are linked to improvement in physical surroundings, there are not many examples of built-in incentives in insurance policies which motivate households to invest in mitigation. On the contrary mitigation may discourage investment, as households may engage in riskier practices after purchasing insurance policies.

It is necessary to evolve financial instruments that enable households to employ ex ante mitigation measures. Banking and housing finance markets in developing countries have not yet extended financial services to poor households for the purpose of building assets. Instead, microfinance organizations have evolved to meet their credit needs. Microcredit could be a potential instrument for providing resources to poor households for mitigation investment.

The need for immediate availability of credit and flexibility of terms innovated the financial instrument of microcredit. The Grameen Bank in Bangladesh pioneered the concept of microcredit in 1976, primarily for consumption and entrepreneurial activities of the rural poor. Important models in other countries include BancoSol, Bolivia; the Bank Rakyat Indonesia; Kredit Desa, Indonesia; and village banks set up in Latin America by the Foundation for International Community Assistance (FINCA) (Morduch 1999). The positive financial and development results these organizations have produced have heralded microcredit as an effective poverty alleviation instrument. It may be argued that mitigation activities are integral to poverty alleviation and thus that microcredit may be an appropriate mechanism for mitigation investment.

One of the distinctive features of microcredit is its basis in group lending. Communities may access resources for building social and physical assets based on a shared perception of their vulnerability. The strong element of peer monitoring in microcredit programs facilitates greater community participation. Microfinance organizations also encourage savings by group members, which may be invested in mitigating hazards at the household and community levels.

A number of microcredit programs also have included government subsidies. If governments provide incentives and subsidies for mitigation, it is feasible to combine it with microcredit that households may access for specified mitigation measures. It is relatively easier for governments to organize technical assistance and other information for mitigation at the group level. Since mitigation requires financial resources, knowledge of hazard, mitigation options, and community efforts, microcredit models can bring together these essential ingredients. In fact there have been a number of case studies of microcredit models used successfully for sanitation and environmental improvements in developing countries.

Microcredit is also an ex post mechanism. A number of studies point its extensive use to meet the consumption needs of poor households. Thus, it could be accessed in when livelihood and consumption are under serious threat. A study of microcredit borrowers in rural Bangladesh suggests that 60 percent of microfinance loans are used primarily for consumption smoothing and repayment of outstanding debts.

A serious constraint to the use of credit for productive purposes arises from lack of adequate skills, education, and information among households. When the credit is largely for the purpose of consumption smoothing, it has a low marginal return to capital, affecting the household's ability to make repayments (Sinha and Matin 1998). It often results in a vicious cycle of indebtedness. To the extent that microcredit is used to smooth consumption, its potential role for mitigation investment is reduced.

Credit requirements for consumption in the immediate aftermath of a disaster may overwhelm microfinance organizations. Geetha Nagarajan (1999) has examined the disaster interventions of microfinance organizations. Although her paper also looks at the possibility of microcredit for mitigation investment, its main concern is handling of households' credit needs by microfinance organizations immediately after a disaster. On the mitigation side microcredit could be used to build capacity through training programs, construction of irrigation and flood control structures, improved housing on safe sites, and emergency preparedness measures. Microfinance organizations could also introduce long-term financial services such as insurance against natural disasters and saving services for a personal safety net.

However, the most pressing credit requirements arise at the relief, recovery, and reconstruction stages, which microfinance organizations find difficult to deal with. Loans could be asked for the immediate consumption needs, replacement of capital assets, house reconstruction, or economic rehabilitation through new investment. Microfinance organizations could also be asked to reschedule payment of old loans. These heavy demands are placed on microfinance organizations at the same time that they face great difficulties due to loss of their clients' economic capacity, operational disruptions, and liquidity shortages resulting from a large number of clients seeking immediate access to their savings.

Microfinance organizations in a post-disaster situation are thus both victims of disasters and potential sources of recovery. In fact, some disaster relief programs have evolved into well-known microfinance organizations, such as the Bangladesh Rural Advancement Committee (BRAC). The effectiveness of microfinance organizations in dealing with these situations may depend on their strategic interventions at different stages of the post-disaster operations, distinguishing clearly between the relief, recovery, and rehabilitation needs of the clients. Their role in the relief stage may necessarily be brief and their functioning as a social safety net very limited in scope. Successful microfinance organizations are required to have a large client-base, thus enlarging the risk pool. They should develop their risk management strategy based on their long-term relationship with clients, adequate information on clients' preparedness, community networks for mitigation, and their own financial and human resources investment in disaster mitigation and preparedness (Nagarajan 1998).

An important means to mobilize investment in mitigation is savings. Households may be given incentives to save and invest these savings in improving their physical assets. Morduch has cited successful examples from Bangladesh and Indonesia of mobilizing savings from poor households (1998). The savings mechanism was also successful in an earthquake reconstruction program in the state of Maharashtra (India) recently. Although the government provided assistance in cash and material to households for seismic strengthening, it also organized self-help groups at the village level and encouraged them to save a part of their earnings. Most of the households participating in the seismic strengthening program invested more money and resources through their own savings than the government assistance they received.

The financial instruments discussed above could be applied for mitigation only in specific contexts of hazards and institutional and societal capabilities. It may be very difficult to standardize an instrument for universal application. Some of these instruments are more relevant for slow-onset disasters, while others may be used for disasters with sudden and cataclysmic impact.

The effectiveness of these instruments as ex ante and ex post mitigation mechanisms may also vary. Some mitigation efforts may be organized through individual/household resources, while community resources are required for another set of mitigation measures. Large mitigation activities must necessarily be publicly funded. A number of financial instruments can be applied in combination, or public subsidy may become an important component of these instruments. It requires a great deal of information, incentives, institutional resources, flexibility, and public commitment to make these financial instruments effective vehicles of mitigation.

Agenda Issues

The preceding discussions present an argument for developing a hazard mitigation strategy that not only deals with the severity of hazard, but also addresses the socioeconomic vulnerability of affected communities. A mitigation strategy that aims at capacity building of communities through infusion of resources, information, and education is a cost-effective and sustainable strategy for risk reduction and mitigation. This chapter also makes a case for increasing the size of the risk pool and evolving varied financial mechanisms for poor households for the same purposes. These mechanisms may be developed and implemented on a wide range from informal to formal.

Increasing the size of the risk pool and administering the pool to mitigate covariate risks requires aggregation of risks and resources. It also requires lowering the transaction costs and increasing the information flow. These aggregations can be accomplished only through the combined effort of government, private sector, and communities.

This chapter makes a case for incentives and regulations through which households and communities pool their risks and either make community-based investments or procure collective insurance for risk reduction and mitigation. Alternatively, government and private sector could pool their resources, which could be used to reduce physical and economic vulnerabilities, and for mitigation activities and a comprehensive risk insurance of poor households.

California, which recently experienced two major earthquakes, Loma Prieta (1989) and Northridge (1994), is a successful example of an active strategy to mitigate earthquake loss promoted through active involvement of government, private sector, and communities. Although there was extensive loss to properties, loss of lives in both the earthquakes together was around 100, a very small figure compared to the death toll in the recent earthquakes in Turkey. Although this success story comes from a developed country, it has important lessons for developing countries.

Let us examine the need for strong financial cooperation between the government and private sector for promoting hazard mitigation mechanisms in developing countries. There are a number of alternatives.

1. The governments may institute and promote market-based mechanisms, through an insurance/vulnerability reduction fund.

2. Insurance companies may increase their coverage and provide a wide range of financial services, taking into account hazard probabilities and community profiles.

3. Households may increase their access to credit and financial assistance on more flexible terms from microfinance organizations. The informal credit sector functions with the formal sector mechanisms to support households in their risk and vulnerability reduction. It could foster greater competition, leading to an increased penetration of financial organizations and availability of credit and insurance to people on better terms.

4. The case for greater public investment in hazard mitigation and the involvement of communities in these mitigation activities may also be evaluated.

The assumptions of a strong public-private partnership and community participation hold good for all the mitigation alternatives mentioned above.

Governments cannot, however, shift their primary responsibilities. They are required to make certain long-term investments for hazard mitigation and habitat improvement. If an area is submerged most part of the year, the government is obligated to invest in flood control and drainage with the involvement of communities, or support the relocation of community. An insurance-based mechanism cannot alleviate peoples' difficulties in these situations. Governments also have the primary mitigation responsibility of enforcing land use regulations and building codes, and carry out mandatory planning role. Similarly, if disaster strikes, the fiscal responsibility for emergency relief, recovery, medical assistance, warning systems, and community shelters rests predominantly with governments.

At the same time poor households need access to private resources for mitigation. Therefore, availability and effectiveness of financial instruments for risk and vulnerability reduction of households is the key issue that needs an immediate attention of all who are concerned with disasters and vulnerabilities. Some of the questions are:

A. What is the relationship of potential disaster impact and adequate risk pool? What are the various ways of enlarging the risk pool for dealing with covariate risks of natural disasters? Is it possible to combine low transaction costs of informal risk-sharing mechanisms with the scale of risk pooling necessary to deal with covariate risks like natural disasters?

B. What is the potential for application of the microcredit model for disaster risk reduction? What incentives do microcredit models offer for risk reduction? Which microcredit models are appropriate for mitigation investment? Can microcredit be accessed at both the individual and community levels for investment in mitigation? Can microfinance networks be utilized to transmit information on risk identification and risk reduction for poor populations in urban and rural areas? Can microfinance be combined with government welfare programs like disaster relief and food for work to finance mitigation investment by and for the poor?

C. How can public insurance regulatory policy be modified to encourage penetration of insurance access in developing economies? Can governments support insurance agencies to provide disaster risk insurance to poor households? What are innovative insurance policies that provide protection to poor households at affordable premiums, without resulting in overexposure of insurance companies? Can government act as a reinsurer?

D. Can microfinance organizations offer microinsurance to the poor households? How can the experience of rural/crop insurance be applied to risk management for urban populations, particularly the poor? What problems arise from moral hazard and adverse selection in dealing with risks of natural disasters?

E. Is individual/household investment feasible for natural-disaster loss reduction? Should such mitigation necessarily be carried out at the community level or regional level? How can effectiveness/execution of individual mitigation be measured or verified in the informal sector? What balance of individual/household, community, and national investment in disaster reduction is appropriate/optimal?

F. How can public subsidy and market incentive be most effectively combined to encourage investment in disaster loss reduction? Can a calamity relief fund/

vulnerability reduction fund act as a risk pool? Is there a difference in the feasible scale of ex ante mitigation schemes and ex post loss finance schemes?

G. Can private profit motive mobilize mitigation for the poor? Is cost/benefit analysis of specific mitigation measures feasible or necessary? How do we deal with loss of life and the irreplaceable loss in the calculation of benefits and costs of mitigation? This chapter attempts to provide a perspective for some of these wide-ranging questions.

References

Anderson, M. B. 1990. "Analyzing the Costs and Benefits of Natural Disaster Responses in the Context of Development." Environment Working Paper 29. World Bank.

Anderson, M. B., and P. J. Woodrow. 1998. *Rising from the Ashes, Development Strategies in Times of Disaster.* Boulder and London: Lynne Rienner Publishers.

Aysan, Y. F. 1993. "Vulnerability Assessment." In *Natural Disasters, Protecting Vulnerable Communities.* Proceedings of the Conference held in London, 13-15 October 1993. Ed. P. A. Merriman and C. W. A. Browitt. London: Thomas Telford.

Besley, T. 1995. "Nonmarket Institutions for Credit and Risk Sharing in Low-Income Countries." *Journal of Economic Perspectives* 9 (3): 115-27.

Blaikie, P., and others. 1994. *At Risk, Natural Hazards, People's Vulnerability, and Disasters.* London and New York: Routledge.

Bromley, D. W., and J. Chavas. 1989. "On Risk, Transactions, and Economic Development in the Semiarid Tropics." *Economic Development and Cultural Change* 37: 719-36.

Brown, W., and C. Churchill. 1999. "Micro-insurance: Providing Insurance to Low-Income Households." Part I. Working Draft. Calmeadow. Washington, D.C. http://www.mip.org.

Cannon, T. 1993. "A Hazard Need Not a Disaster Make: Vulnerability and the Causes of Natural Disasters." In *Natural Disasters, Protecting Vulnerable Communities.* Proceedings of the Conference held in London, 13-15 October 1993. Ed. P. A. Merriman and C. W. A. Browitt. London: Thomas Telford.

Chambers, R. 1989. "Vulnerability, Coping and Policy." *IDS Bulletin* 20:1-7.

Cuny, F. 1983. *Disasters and Development.* New York and Oxford: Oxford University Press.

Freeman, P., and H. Kunreuther. 1997. *Managing Environmental Risk through Insurance.* Boston/Dordrecht/London: Kluwer Academic Publishers.

Froote, K. A. 1999. "Financing of Catastrophic Risk." In *The Limited Financing of Catastrophic Risk: An Overview.* Ed. K. A. Froote. Chicago: The University of Chicago Press.

Gautam, M., P. Hazell, and H. Alderman. 1994. *Rural Demand for Drought Insurance.* Policy Research Working Paper 1383. World Bank.

Gilbert, R., and A. Kreimer. 1999. *Learning from the World Bank's Experience of Natural Disaster Related Assistance.* Disaster Management Facility, World Bank.

Hulme, D., and P. Mosley, eds. 1996. *Finance against Poverty.* Vol. I and II. London and New York: Routledge.

IFRC (International Federation of Red Cross and Red Crescent Societies). 1999. "Situation Reports." http://www.ifrc.org.

IFRC. 1999. *World Disaster Report.* Geneva: International Federation of Red Cross and Red Crescent Societies.

Kreimer, A., and others. 1999. *Managing Disaster Risk in Mexico: Market Incentives for Mitigation Investment.* Disaster Risk Management Series 1. World Bank.

Lipton, M., and J. Gaag, eds. 1993. *Including the Poor.* Proceedings of a Symposium Organized by the World Bank and the International Food Policy Research Institute. World Bank.

Morduch, J. 1995. "Income Smoothing and Consumption Smoothing." *Journal of Economic Perspectives* 9 (3): 103-14.

_____. 1998. "Between Market and State: Can Informal Insurance Patch the Safety Net?" Draft.

_____. 1999. "Microfinance Promise." *Journal of Economic Literature* 37: 1569-1614.

Nagarajan, G. 1998. "Microfinance in the Wake of Natural Disasters: Challenges and Opportunities." Microenterprise Best Practices. Development Alternatives, Inc. Washington, D.C. http://www.mip.org.

Ravallion, M. 1997. "Famines and Economics." *Journal of Economic Literature* 35: 1205-42.

Rosenzweig, M. R. 1988. "Risk Implicit Contracts and the Family in Rural Areas of Low-Income Countries." *The Economic Journal* 98: 1148-70.

Sen, A. 1981. *Poverty and Famines, An Essay on Entitlement and Deprivation.* Oxford: Clarendon Press.

_____. 1998. "Mortality as an Indicator of Economic Success and Failure." *Economic Journal.* 108: 1-25.

Skees, J., P. Hazell, and M. Miranda. 1999. "New Approaches to Crop Yield Insurance in Developing Countries." Draft.

Siegel, P., and J. Alwang. 1999. *An Asset-based Approach to Social Risk Management: A Conceptual Framework.* Social Protection Discussion Paper 9926. World Bank.

Sinha, S., and I. Matin. 1998. "Informal Credit Transactions of Micro-Credit Borrowers in Rural Bangladesh." *IDS Bulletin* 29 (4): 66-80.

Stiglitz, J. E. 1974. "Incentives and Risk Sharing in Sharecropping." *Review of Economic Studies,* 41(2): 219-56.

Udry, C. 1990. "Credit Markets in Northern Nigeria: Credit as Insurance in a Rural Economy." *The World Bank Economic Review.* 4 (3): 251-69,

_____. 1994. "Risk and Insurance in a Rural Credit Market: An Empirical Investigation in Northern Nigeria." *Review of Economic Studies.* 61: 495-526.

USAID/OAS Caribbean Disaster Mitigation Project. 1996. *Insurance, Reinsurance and Catastrophe Protection in the Caribbean.* Washington, D. C.

Westgate, K. N., and P. O'Keefe. 1976. "Some Definitions of Disaster." Disaster Research Unit Occasional Paper 4. University of Bradford, Department of Geography. United Kingdom.

Winchester, P. 1992. *Power, Choice and Vulnerability, A Case Study in Disaster Management in South India.* London: James and James Science Publishers, Ltd.

Woodrow, P. J. 1998. "Cereal Banks in Burkina Faso, Food Security, Drought, and Development." In *Rising from the Ashes, Development Strategies in Times of Disaster Anderson.* M. B. Anderson and P. J. Woodrow. Boulder and London: Lynne Rienner Publishers.

World Bank. *World Development Report 1990.* Oxford: Oxford University Press for the World Bank.

Chapter 13

Moral Dimensions of Risk Transfer and Reduction Strategies

Thomas W. Dunfee and Alan Strudler

An attempt to achieve only an efficient design for a (disaster management) program, without taking into account economic justice or equity, will surely result in the failure of such a ... program.[1]

A Disaster's Deep Scars: Pain from Grand Forks Flood Lingers. Recovery Can Take a Decade.[2]

This chapter examines implications of moral theory for policies of disaster relief and mitigation. We believe that moral theory provides useful insights for determining (1) who should receive relief or be the beneficiary of mitigation, (2) how policies should be implemented, and (3) the role of the World Bank. Moral considerations may also clarify the comparative advantages of alternative strategies for relief and mitigation.

Given time and space constraints, we will consider macro issues of justice, equity, and social norms. We will not consider in detail the more traditional transaction-based issues of moral hazard, except as they have an impact on our broader analysis. Our ultimate focus is disaster relief and mitigation policies for developing countries, but we find it fruitful to begin with a more general discussion of principles of disaster relief. We argue that some of the leading moral theories often applied to these issues, including utilitarian, libertarian, and egalitarian theories, cannot fully answer fundamental questions about the proper scope and content of disaster relief efforts. We then describe a strongly

contextual social contracts approach that we believe offers promise for understanding the moral significance of accidents. We briefly explore the application of the social contracts approach to a distinctive and innovative strategy—catastrophe bonds—and close by listing key issues and concepts relevant to the World Bank's role in disaster relief and mitigation.

Application of Standard Moral Theories to Disaster Mitigation and Relief Strategies

Linnerooth-Bayer and Amendola (1998) offer an analysis of the implications of standard normative theories for disaster mitigation and relief strategies (DMRS). They ultimately conclude that "notions of what is fair are socially contingent" and that "(t)here is no single, universally valid set of moral principles that can inspire effective personal, institutional, or national commitments to a fair distribution of social burdens, including those from natural disasters" (p.11). We find their conceptual geography useful but need to explore their claims and conclusions. Adopting more traditional vocabulary, preliminarily we will characterize the theories they discuss as libertarian, utilitarian, egalitarian, and corrective justice. We will disagree with Linnerooth-Bayer and Amendola about certain implications of these theories for disaster relief and also with their position that there are no manifest universal ethical principles relevant to DMRS.

Egalitarianism

From an egalitarian view DMRS may be justified if they bring a society closer to an ideal of equality. Egalitarian theories differ in their conception of the content of equality: some favor equal distribution of resources; others favor equal distribution of welfare; still others favor equal distribution of opportunity (Sen 1987). But these ideals often are connected. Promoting equality of welfare requires attention to the distribution of resources. An initial limitation of the former is that the account of equality assumed by the analyst may be at a strong variance with the cultural norms of a given society. For example, consider the implications were an outside agency to insist on imposing on the United States the view of equal distribution of wealth. Surely there would be strong resistance to its implementation, and any such program would be seen as illegitimate by many. Similarly, in a Muslim society a norm of equal distribution of opportunity may be seen as problematic.

A second problem is that each of the particular approaches to equality has problems with its own internal logic. For simplicity, we will take as our representative account of equality one that focuses on equality of welfare. In reality, do disaster relief policies advance egalitarian values? Not necessarily. Other things being equal, we would expect that a program that would most promote an egalitarian ideal would direct resources toward the worst-off people in society. Even if a disaster relief program somehow succeeded in treating all disaster victims equally from a social policy perspective, respect for equality also requires taking into account claims for equality that might be made on behalf of members of society who are not accident victims. Disaster victims often are not the worst-off people in a society.

In the United States disaster relief programs arose in part in response to needs expressed by middle and upper income classes (Landis 1998). Even today, American flood insurance and hurricane insurance policies sometimes are criticized for diverting money from the homeless and others whose needs are more acute than the average disaster relief victims. Saul Levmore (1996) argues that this phenomenon is not an idiosyncratic feature of the American system but part of the inevitable logic of government-sponsored disaster relief. Levmore also argues that disaster relief benefits do not go to the most needy people in a society but to comparatively affluent people who are better organized and more articulate.

In a developing country should we expect that disaster relief benefits would go to the poorest? Unless that expectation is justified, we must look beyond egalitarian values to locate a rationale for disaster relief programs. In the poorest countries, there may be many homeless and indigent people whose needs persist independent of losses caused by natural disasters. This fact raises a doubt about whether respecting the ideal of equality is consistent with protecting people against the prospect of disaster. No one in a culture is more needy than its homeless. From an egalitarian perspective, why invest in bonds or insurance now to aid people who at worst might become homeless, when so many are already homeless? Egalitarian values seem to provide only the shakiest of foundations for disaster relief policy. Or, to put matters less contentiously, there is no direct tie between egalitarian values and disaster relief. It would be useful if we could find a moral value that more specifically justifies disaster relief.

Welfare Maximization

On a welfare-maximizing or utilitarian account (Kagan 1998), disaster relief programs are justified if their net aggregate social utility exceeds that of alternative programs, including programs that involve no disaster relief. Disaster relief programs reallocate resources within a society, either through ex ante investment in insurance, bonds, or mitigation, or through ex post expenditures on repair.

Both ex ante and ex post programs redistribute resources within a society. Why should shifting resources around result in increasing total aggregate utility? There are at least three reasons. First, the marginal value of resources directed ex post at accident victims may exceed the marginal value of resources directed at others because of peculiarly acute needs of accident victims. Second, resources directed ex post at accident victims may be put to a more constructive use than resources directed to others. For example, if disaster relief is directed at agriculture or other basic industry that has been undermined by disaster, it may contribute significantly to the aggregate good. Third, ex ante investment in preventing or mitigating disasters may involve a much smaller investment than the net present value of the disaster, both to society and to the individuals protected. If one considers the marginal value of aiding accident victims, given that their needs are more acute than those of many others in society, it may seem to follow that aid should be provided to disaster victims. Here doubts can be raised that are similar to doubts with the egalitarian framework. Why help accident victims when one might instead provide relief to the more needy homeless or indigent?

Carrying the efficiency argument to its extreme evokes the traditional rights-based objections to efficiency approaches. Given constraints on resources, the most efficient form of mitigation may be to provide longer-lived, healthier communities greater protection against disasters while providing less protection to communities with poorer health and shorter life spans. After all, their losses will be less when measured by their economic value. As with egalitarian approaches, an emphasis on welfare maximization may be at odds with strongly ingrained cultural and social norms of many communities. The expressions of outrage that occurred in reference to Lawrence Summers' memorandum, written while he was chief economist of the World Bank, which reflected some of these ideas ("the economic logic behind dumping a load of toxic waste in the lowest-wage country is impeccable; "I've always thought that under-populated countries in Africa are vastly *under* polluted" is evidence of the existence of contrary social norms.[3] Brazil and other developing countries were strong contributors to the chorus of criticism that accompanied disclosure of the memo in the *Guardian*.

Libertarianism

Libertarians see respect for liberty rights and respect for property rights as core concepts in morality (Nozick 1974). While libertarians do not deny that it is good

to help people, including victims of disasters, they insist that it is wrong to do so in ways that violate individual rights. The legitimacy of disaster relief depends on how it respects these rights. From a libertarian view the downside of disaster relief is that it forcibly transfers wealth to disaster victims and risks violating the property rights of people from whom wealth is taken to provide that relief. A common response to libertarianism is to say that it is harsh and that it undervalues rights to welfare against rights of liberty and property (Nagel 1995). Why should the property rights of the relatively well off be regarded as morally more important than the welfare rights of accident victims?

While critics of libertarianism may be skeptical about the preference that the theory shows for property rights and liberty rights against other rights, Linnerooth-Bayer and Amendola (1998) suggest a softening argument. Disaster victims of course cannot be held responsible for the earthquakes or hurricanes that caused their suffering. But they can be held responsible, the libertarian may argue, for choices about whether to mitigate or to expose themselves to harm. To the extent that disaster victims suffer harm because of their own choices not to mitigate, the libertarian may say that the person assumes the risk of that harm, and other people should not be regarded as responsible for his or her plight. In a prosperous nation this libertarian argument will seem more plausible than in a poor nation, where mitigation efforts may seem less accessible.

Most writers find the libertarian arguments unreasonably harsh (Nagel 1995). Still, these arguments are important because they remind us of issues that must be faced by any adequate moral theory of disaster relief. A crucial question for libertarians is whether a person sometimes has the right to live in a risky place. If a person has a right to live in a place, there may be a correlative right to do so without being considered to have assumed the risk of natural disasters.

Corrective Justice

If neither egalitarian, libertarian, nor welfare maximization values fully explain disaster relief policy, might other moral values do better? The growing literature in the ethics of accident policy may prove helpful (Coleman 1992). This literature emphasizes the importance of distinguishing between two realms of justice: distributive justice and corrective justice. Distributive justice concerns the distribution of social and economic goods across a society, and may plausibly be regarded as including egalitarian, libertarian, and welfare maximization frameworks.

Corrective justice concerns making adjustments for harms and wrongs that individuals do to one another. In recent years theorists have used concepts from corrective justice to explain the ethics of accident policy. When society compels one individual to compensate another for harm done, it is a matter of corrective justice rather than distributive justice. Corrective justice is invoked to justify restoring people to the position they were in before suffering an accident.

If the concept of distributive justice provides little hope for an explanation of disaster relief policy, perhaps the concept of corrective justice will prove more promising. After all, the concept of corrective justice is used to explain the ethics of providing accident relief, and disaster relief is a form of accident relief. But here the problem is that corrective justice ordinarily works by requiring those who cause accidents to pay for the harm they brought about. In disaster relief, however, it is nature itself that brings about accidents. It is nonsense to suppose that nature might pay for its accidents. On the other hand, to the extent that damage from accidents can be blamed on shoddy construction and design in bridges, dams, and buildings, corrective justice may suggest some remedial action for accident victims. It seems implausible, however, that all damage from natural disasters can be blamed on shoddy construction and design. So corrective justice seems on the surface to provide no more hope than does distributive justice as an explanation of disaster relief policy.

The corrective justice framework serves as a reminder that harms individuals suffer may have moral significance that merits response independent of considerations about distributive justice. When we decide that a person deserves compensation for harm she suffered in an ordinary traffic accident, it may be because

we think that accident victims deserve relief no matter where they stand in the distributive scheme. Nevertheless, the corrective justice model is not adequate for purposes of analyzing accident relief, because, as we have noted, it pertains to what individuals owe one another for harm they cause. It makes no sense to speak of nature, which causes the harm of natural disasters, doing anything to harm anybody.

An Alternative Approach: Social Contracts

In this section we discuss whether a social contracts-based approach derived from the field of business ethics provides insights for understanding the moral implications of disaster mitigation and relief strategies. A recent application of social contract theory to business ethics emphasizes (1) the role of legitimate ethical norms within communities and (2) the primacy of manifest universal ethical principles. This application is called Integrative Social Contracts Theory (ISCT) (Donaldson and Dunfee 1999, 1995, 1994). It emphasizes identifying moral norms which represent a consensus within a specific community pertaining to the propriety of particular actions based on aggregate attitudes and behaviors of individuals.

A community is defined in ISCT as a self-defined, self-circumscribed group of people who interact in the context of shared tasks, values, or goals and are capable of establishing norms of ethical behavior for themselves. In the context of a given ethical decision nation states, nongovernmental organizations (NGOs), corporations, subsidiaries, even departments or informal units within an organization, along with partnerships, professional groups, and trade associations, all may be ISCT communities. Thus, the World Bank, countries in which disaster occurs, and relief-providing agencies all may be among the many communities relevant to an analysis of DMRS.

In focusing on communities, ISCT recognizes that norm-governed group activity is a critical component of economic life. These communities are recognized as having a substantial moral free space in which to develop their own internal moral rules. Within the context of DMRS it is to be expected that communities, particularly nation states and NGOs, will have moral norms that require consideration and respect. Examples could include community norms pertaining to a duty to aid those in need, societal preferences concerning allocation of resources among differing categories of needy within the community, and the significance of a failure to take steps to avoid or lessen harm.

With the realistic assumption that communities do indeed develop problematic norms supporting racial and gender-based discrimination as well as other appalling practices, ISCT recognizes a limited set of universal principles that constrain the relativism of community moral free space. Accordingly, to be obligatory, a community norm must be compatible with manifest universal ethical norms, called "hypernorms" in ISCT. Hypernorms are defined as principles so fundamental to human existence that we would expect them to be reflected in a convergence of religious, philosophical, and cultural beliefs. As expressed by Michael Walzer (1992), they would be a thin "set of standards to which all societies can be held— negative injunctions, most likely, rules against murder, deceit, torture, oppression and tyranny." Community norms that are compatible with hypernorms are considered obligatory. In ISCT terminology such obligatory norms are called "legitimate."

It will often be the case that multiple legitimate norms applicable to the same ethical judgment conflict. This may happen when a transaction crosses two distinctly different communities, as is often the case in global business transactions, and would typically be the case in reference to DMRS. To resolve problems of this type, ICST specifies a loose set of six priority rules:

1. Transactions solely within a single community that do not have significant adverse effects on other humans or communities should be governed by host community norms.
2. Community norms for resolving priority should be applied, so long as they do not have significant adverse effects on other human beings or communities.
3. The more extensive the community that is the source of the norm, the greater the priority that should be given to the norm.
4. Norms essential to the maintenance of the economic environment in which the transaction oc-

curs should have priority over norms potentially damaging to that environment.
5. Where multiple conflicting norms are involved, patterns of consistency among the alternative norms provide a basis for prioritization. Well-defined norms should ordinarily have priority over more general, less precise norms.
6. Community moral free space is thus circumscribed by manifest universal ethical norms and principles and is subject also to the influence of norms of other communities.

Authentic norms that pass these screens are characterized as "legitimate" and become ethically obligatory. Although developed to deal with fundamental questions of business ethics, we believe that ISCT provides important insights regarding DMRS. The following implications of ISCT for DMRS are briefly discussed in turn:

- DMRS must be compatible with the legitimate moral norms of communities they affect.
- DMRS must be compatible with hypernorms.
- DMRS should be designed to support the development of essential background institutions in communities they affect.

DMRS Must Be Compatible with the Legitimate Moral Norms of the Communities They Affect

Many types of moral norms relevant to DMRS may be held by communities. Such norms may be expected to vary among communities and to change over time. All DMRS must be designed in a manner that is sensitive to such norms, and where they are legitimate they must be given appropriate respect. Pragmatically speaking, whether DMRS are compatible with community norms may have a major impact on the success of the strategies. The significant success of the microcredit arrangements implemented in Bangladesh by the Grameen Bank may be due in large part to their connection to important authentic norms in the communities in which the loans were made. The women in these communities had close-knit relationships conducive to cooperative endeavors. By requiring that loans be made to groups that could provide mutual support, Grameen built on these norms and created an environment that maximized payback.

A number of plausible moral norms that may be held within a disaster-affected community should be given consideration in the design of DMRS. For example, concepts of what constitutes a fair distribution likely vary among countries. A Muslim society may want the manner of distribution to complement, and certainly be compatible with, Islamic norms defining appropriate methods for providing assistance. An Asian society may prefer that families, not individuals, be the focus of the definition of need. A developing country may prefer that emphasis be given to education, job creation, and the building of long-term infrastructure, as opposed to compensating individuals for lost private property.

Norms of this sort may be particularly relevant to the desirability, even the ultimate effectiveness, of strategies, such as the cash-for-work programs advocated by Martina (1998a, b) to relieve famine. If a Muslim society believes that certain types of work are inappropriate for women and as a consequence women may be excluded from opportunities for work-based relief, work-for-food or work-for-cash programs may not produce adequate assistance. It should be expected that there will be local norms prescribing when it is appropriate to intervene and provide relief. A society may have sympathy-based norms that support the providing of relief to victims of natural disaster regardless of the impact on property rights or other forms of welfare assistance.

The occurrence of a particular disaster may generate event-specific norms supporting relief. Disasters often are accompanied by sympathetic media coverage of individual suffering that may influence attitudes and behaviors pertaining to the propriety of providing relief. The headline at the beginning of this article is just one recent example of literally thousands that have appeared over the years generating sympathy for victims of disasters. The recent tornado in Oklahoma City in the United States produced enormous amounts of sympathetic media coverage, which probably helped to reinforce community norms that special aid should be provided to those who have suffered this loss. Decisionmakers ignore such norms at their peril.

Linnerooth-Bayer and Amendola (1998) report that the prime minister of Poland was forced to apologize after stating that uninsured flood victims had only themselves to blame for their plight and that they were not entitled to government help (p.16). As they noted, helping neighbors in a time of need may be a cherished community value.

It may be that such norms may seem to be irrational when viewed by other decision criteria or when evaluated under particular moral theories. A society may have norms distinguishing among types of disasters: earthquakes may be seen as justifying less of an intervention than floods, or vice versa. There may be a wide variety of logics among communities in reference to norms pertaining to DMRS. Communities are entitled to follow their own preferred forms of moral logic (so long as they do not violate hypernorms), which may be religion-based.

Communities may also be likely to have norms pertaining to the scope of a duty on the part of individuals to mitigate their losses, at least in reference to certain types of potential natural disasters. In some communities those who fail to take relatively easy and low-cost steps to mitigate against readily foreseeable losses may be seen as unworthy recipients of ex-post disaster relief. Other communities may not recognize an obligation to mitigate.

There may also be local preferences concerning the respective roles of the private and public sector, which could have an impact on the delivery of relief services under a DMRS. In Muslim or socialist countries, there may be a strong preference for having certain functions performed by the public sector even with a loss of efficiency. Thus, even though a government based insurance system may be arguably less efficient than the private sector (Priest 1996), a government system may be seen as legitimate while a private scheme is not.

Saul Levmore (1996) suggests that even though disaster relief programs that involve government action are generally inefficient, the public feels some enthusiasm for them because of the sympathy it feels for actual and prospective accident victims. It is plainly Levmore's view that accident policy disrespects the discipline of the market because it is influenced by irrational emotions. We suggest, instead, that such a policy may reflect community moral judgments that cannot be reduced to pure market concerns. Appeal to community moral norms of this type can support the adoption of DMRS for reasons wholly outside of Priest's and Levmore's analytical frameworks. Both disasters and the mere prospect of disasters possess moral significance worth taking seriously apart from pure considerations of efficiency and redistributive equity. There is nothing unusual or irrational about the idea that morality requires an action independent of the welfare or distributive justice consequences of that action. One can appreciate, for example, the moral wrongfulness of both slavery and punishing the innocent independently of thinking about their general welfare or distributive justice implications. We suggest further that consideration for hypernorms generally involves the possibility of respecting requirements about how we treat people, where these requirements must be understood independently of concerns about general welfare and general distributive equity. For example, the fact that a private sector scheme produces substantial profits for wealthy shareholders may be seen as illegitimate.

Authentic local norms may reflect very powerful societal beliefs and, when they involve preferences that fall within the realm of moral free space, should be given great consideration. For example, a society may prefer that where malnutrition exists, priority be given to reducing child mortality rates. Martina describes an enormous success in Chile with policies based on such preferences (1998b, p. 328).

Two problems inhere in a social contracts approach emphasizing the role of local legitimate norms. First is the difficult question of how to identify the norms with sufficient certainty to be able to rely on them for critical policy decisions. Survey techniques and reliance on public sources of information are both useful in identifying norms. A key characteristic of a legitimate norm is that many people in the community believe it exists and are able to express it in words. Common reference to the norm in the media could be another marker. We note that it is common to speak of certain national social contracts, and references may be found in the media to the terms of such understandings. Although we recognize the challenges associated with designing competent opinion surveys for identifying broad group norms of proper behavior, particularly in developing countries, we believe that such surveys can offer important insights regarding issues directly relevant to DMRS.

The second major problem is that norms with reference to particular issues associated with DMRS may not exist within a relevant community, particularly the country suffering the losses from a natural disaster. There are many reasons why this may be so. Whenever wealth transfer is at issue, the haves and have nots may be expected to have differing views of what is a just arrangement. Societies differ greatly in cohesiveness and extent of shared values. On many issues the range of differing preferences held by various groups within a given society may be such that no single norm can be identified. In the ISCT approach if there are no relevant local community norms, then the decisionmaker (in many cases, an entity such as the World Bank), is entitled to act within its own moral free space so long as its actions are compatible with hypernorms.

Often norms may conflict among communities. Norms pertaining to a duty to mitigate risk may vary between the country suffering the loss and the agencies providing the resources for ex post compensation. The citizenry of the loss-incurring country may think it unfair to punish those who failed to insure against loss or take steps to mitigate loss. For example, a judgment of unfairness may be based on the recognition that humans tend to act irrationally regarding low-probability risk; therefore, it is unfair to impose sanctions for falling prey to a common mistake in human reasoning (Kunreuther 1994). Communities providing the resources for relief may instead emphasize the deterrent effect of punishing a failure to reduce risk.

Other examples relevant to DMRS may be found in North/South industrial/developing country conflicts. The victims in a developing country may hold a norm that wealthier countries have a special obligation to respond to their needs because the wealthier countries benefited from practices that increased the probability of a natural disaster for the developing country or enhanced their losses therefrom. For example, methods of mining of natural resources may have increased the chances of flooding or crop failure. This prior history may produce conflicting views concerning what constitutes fair levels of compensation.

So long as both sets of the conflicting norms are compatible with hypernorms, then either may have a legitimate claim as a source for moral guidance. Relevant factors among the set of priority rules of thumb relevant to determine which norms should be emphasized include the extent to which one set of norms is more consistent with norms of other communities, and the clarity and specific nature of the norms at issue.

All DMRS Must Be Compatible with Hypernorms

Several hypernorms may come into play in the development of DMRS. Donaldson and Dunfee (1999) suggest that it is more efficient to attempt to identify hypernorms relevant to the context of a given decision rather than to establish ex ante a full list of hypernorms. Depending on the specific DMRS and the context of its application, there may be several candidate hypernorms that should be considered. We briefly describe a few candidates for relevant hypernorms.

One candidate hypernorm is to respect the equal dignity of all human beings, recognizing a basic right to life and subsistence. Given the circumstances, such a hypernorm, might require that when a disaster has pushes people below minimal subsistence, those who have resources available at reasonable cost and risk to prevent death and extreme suffering have a moral obligation to provide such assistance ex post, regardless of efficiency considerations.

For example, the injury and death rates from disasters are much higher in developing countries than in industrialized countries. Using a welfare maximization analysis, one might be tempted to note the shorter life spans of those in developing countries and to allocate resources on that basis, preferring the "more valuable" lives of long-lived citizens in the developed countries. Such a policy would be inconsistent with the candidate hypernorm respecting human dignity and worth. In reference to the Summers memorandum, Hausman and McPherson ultimately conclude that "exporting pollution would be morally objectionable ... because it is unfair and it callously fails to show equal concern for people who happen to be born in poor countries" (p. 207). Their reference to an obligation to "show equal concern for people" implies the existence of a hypernorm of this type.

One specific implication of this hypernorm may become relevant if, as has apparently been the case, World Bank mitigation policies end up focused on just a few borrowers (Gilbert and Kreimer, p. 19). The reasons why just a few countries account for much of the expenditure of resources become relevant. Is it because those countries are more willing to adopt the concept of mitigation? Or does it relate to the type of disasters to which they are prone, or to other factors beyond their control? If the latter, it may raise questions of equity among potential borrowers. It may also invoke the potential hypernorm of autonomy discussed below.

Another candidate hypernorm potentially relevant to DMRS is one condemning coarse public sector corruption. (Donaldson and Dunfee 1999; Dunfee, Smith, and Ross 1999.) Corruption disrupts capital and consumer markets, interferes with representative government, weakens essential background institutions, causes government to be used against and not for its citizens, and contributes to poverty and suffering. It is also widely condemned in religion proscriptions and violates the tenets of many moral theories. Corruption is particularly appalling in the context of disaster relief, as for example, when it diverts foodstuffs intended to eliminate famine, or diverts and resells for personal profit emergency medical supplies. Recently in Puerto Rico, several public officials pled guilty to, and the Governor has been accused of, embezzling $2.2 million in aid intended for the treatment of AIDS victims (Dunfee and Hess, forthcoming).

The enormous diversions of national resources into private accounts that occurred in places such as Indonesia and Nigeria are matched by allegations against the members of the European Commission and even the questionable claim that the World Bank is a "beehive of corruption" (*Financial Times* 1999). Mobuto Sese Seko of then-Zaire reportedly amassed one of the world's largest fortunes by diverting much of the foreign aid sent to alleviate misery in his beleaguered country (Dunfee and Hess, forthcoming).

The anti-corruption hypernorm would require that the development of DMRS must be cognizant of the potential for corruption, particularly in the case of ex-post disaster relief. Such programs are often ad hoc and locally directed and therefore susceptible to the diversion of funds. Corruption may be more prevalent in the case of large public works projects, and any attempt to direct funds from social services where there is less chance of wrongdoing should be carefully monitored.

A third candidate hypernorm would involve an obligation to respect human autonomy, in a manner similar to analysis by John Rawls (1971). Rawls argues that policies that show respect for autonomous decision-making, rather than promote individual utility, should be the objective in institutional design. One of the most attractive functions of a just social institution, on Rawls' account, is its ability to buffer the vicissitudes of what he calls the "natural and social lottery." This is Rawls' phrase for the accidents of a person's biology and environment. On Rawls' account, then, to the extent that outcomes reflect reasonable choices rather than accidents of birth, social circumstance, or genetic endowment, what happens to a person is mere luck. So long as feasibly consistent with a fair allocation of resources, social institutions should be arranged so that they increase the prospects that what happens to a person is the outcome of reasonable autonomous choice and not mere luck.

Rawls' idea that fostering human autonomy is an important social concern is quite plausible. It implies that it is valid to have social policies protecting against bad luck. On this Rawlsian view, it makes sense that disaster relief policy in some advanced economies, including that of United States, protects people who are not among the poorest people in the country. There is independent value attaching to protecting people from bad luck, and natural disasters are bad luck. Similarly, for poorer countries there is a moral reason to provide people with relief from disasters apart from welfarist and egalitarian considerations. But such reason might be balanced against other values, including equality, utility, and respect for libertarian rights.

An additional factor complicates measuring the relevance of Rawlsian autonomy-based consideration to disaster relief policy. To the extent that people suffer from natural disasters as a result of their own choice, not as a matter of luck, based on autonomy-based reasoning, one may argue that people are owed, at most, diminished compensation for their accidents. In other words people had the choice to protect themselves, and they failed to take it. So autonomy-based reasons may not always require relief. Context is important.

DMRS Must Support the Development of Necessary Background Institutions and Authentic Norms in Local Communities

Both developed and developing countries may have serious problems of incompetence and inefficiency. Priest (1996) details problems with the U.S. Federal Emergency Management Agency (FEMA) in which gross misallocation of resources occurred. Disasters are exacerbated by failures in crime control and by the inadequacy of local public health and social services institutions. Incompetence and/or corruption often contribute directly to human suffering when for example, incompetence results in the distribution of HIV infected blood, the building of defective bridges and buildings, or the distribution of ersatz drugs resulting in the deaths of many children (Dunfee and Hess, forthcoming.). Most DMRS require the existence of local institutions capable of reasonable efficiency in distributing goods and services to those in need.

At the same time, the DMRS themselves may influence the development or improvement of necessary institutions. Donaldson and Dunfee describe a hypernorm of necessary social efficiency relating to the need for institutions and for coexistent duties enabling people to achieve basic or necessary social goods, for example, those thought to be desired by all people such as health education, housing, food, clothing, and social justice (Donaldson and Dunfee 1999, chap. 5).

The hypernorm of necessary social efficiency requires that trust and the elements of essential cooperation be developed within a society. It is here that the issues surrounding moral hazard are relevant. Those who make false or overstated claims weaken the fabric of trust within a society. Such actions also limit the ability of insurers to correctly price their products, as when insureds are able to hide relevant information from insurers or to hide actions that enhance risk exposure. Similarly, insureds may be able to conceal their failure to take expected mitigating steps. If the DMRS are designed without reference to moral hazard problems, they may encourage problematic practices, which can have a rippling effect with far reaching consequences.

An Application: Catastrophe Bonds

Thus far we have suggested how a social contracts-based approach may provide a contextual understanding relevant in assessing DMRS. We now apply these ideas to a particular type of potential DMRS, catastrophe bonds (CATs). CATs are a capital market device that supplements the existing, but constrained, reinsurance market. CATs specify a particular risk and term. They tend to pay a superior rate of return necessary to compensate for the risk of reduction or total loss of principal that may result from the occurrence of the designated natural disaster. CATs presumably could be used to finance relief for major natural disasters, even those affecting developing countries. The manner in which they might work in reference to natural disasters is quite open at this point. Presumably there are a variety of options in terms of who might issue and purchase CATs and how payments might be made in case of a natural disaster. Depending on the manner in which they are used, a variety of authentic or hypernorms might become relevant. Here are a few suggestions of issues to consider and authentic norms to identify:

1. If the World Bank were to subsidize the issuance of CATs, subsidization would necessarily involve the use of resources that could otherwise be used for disaster relief, mitigation projects, or even responding to the needs of the world's poor. If the Bank were to subsidize a capital market device, perhaps even providing excess profits to wealthy private investors, this might be perceived as inappropriate in relevant communities.

2. To the extent that the terms of a CAT bond influence the manner in which payments will be made, or relief provided, they would need to be consistent with relevant community norms. Furthermore, if the payments were made in a manner in which corrupt government officials could divert them for their own personal benefit, they would violate the putative hypernorm against contributing to coarse public sector corruption.

3. The manner in which interest is paid, particularly in the case of a government issuer, may conflict with authentic norms of some potentially participating countries, for example, strict Muslim nations.

4. The availability of insurance, whether catastrophe bonds or other forms, raises a question of the entitlement for ex post relief of those who fail to insure against natural disasters. If such a form of mitigation is readily available at a reasonable price, does it then become mandatory? Are countries then at risk to be denied the opportunity to take the position that they would prefer to spend the insurance premium money (or its equivalent) for current social welfare programs? If so, should they be punished for such a choice by being denied all or a portion of available ex post relief funds?

5. There are various options as to how CATs might be sold. If they are available to individuals, they may violate local norms concerning the propriety of condoning or encouraging risky behavior on the part of individuals.

Conclusion: Implications for DMRS Strategies

As we have emphasized, decisionmakers cannot ignore local norms when devising DMRS. No matter how attractive it may seem for policymakers to alter patterns of disaster mitigation in developing countries, for example, it would be presumptuous and inefficient to violate local sensibilities about acceptable conduct. It is inappropriate to rely on a single moral or economic theory as the basis for justifying a DMRS strategy. Aspects of moral and economic theories, particularly those with a Western rights or justice bias, may be inconsistent with the values and cultural moral norms of relevant communities.

What should be done when policymakers' conception of optimal economic conduct conflicts with local norms and practices? When DMRS cross cultures, particular attention should be given to ascertaining the existence of local norms that may influence the selection of those entitled to relief assistance or the manner in which relief is provided. While we insist that local norms, at least when they are consistent with hypernorms, must be respected, we also observe that local norms sometimes change in morally acceptable ways. If a change in norms is not imposed by outsiders, but instead freely adopted by the local community, it may be acceptable change. Finding morally acceptable disaster relief programs is therefore not simply a matter of discovering the right answers to policy questions, but is sometimes a matter of working with local communities to cooperatively construct economically beneficial practices that local communities find morally acceptable. Often the task of risk policymakers is not to prescribe "right answers" for local communities but to assist these communities in creating change: new answers and new locally acceptable norms for new problems.

Finally, we have suggested that there may be manifest universal moral principles relevant to DMRS. Typically, they will be consistent with the tenets of multiple moral theories and religions. These principles may require that disaster relief be provided even when efficiency considerations would support a refusal to provide relief.

Notes

1. Martina 1998b, 329.
2. Cover story *USA Today*, May 11, 1999.
3. See Haussman and McPherson 1996, p. 9 and chaps. 2 and 14.

References

Coleman, J. 1992. "The Mixed Conception of Corrective Justice." *Iowa Law Review* 77: 427-44.

Donaldson, T., and T. W. Dunfee. 1994. "Towards a Unified Conception of Business Ethics: Integrative Social Contracts Theory." *Academy of Management Review* 19: 252-84 .

_____. 1995. "Integrative Social Contracts Theory: A Communitarian Conception of Economic Ethics." *Economics and Philosophy* 11: 85-112.

_____. 1999. *Ties That Bind: A Social Contracts Approach to Business Ethics*. Boston: Harvard Business School Press.

Dunfee, T. W., and D. Hess. 2000. "The Legitimacy of Direct Corporate Humanitarian Investment." *Business Ethics Quarterly* 10: 95-109.

Dunfee, T. W., N. C. Smith, and W. T. Ross. 1999. "Social Contracts and Marketing Ethics." *Journal of Marketing* 63: 14-32.

Financial Times. 1999. "World Bank to Brush up Its Image." Feb. 10.

Gilbert, R., and A. Kreimer. 1999. *Learning from the World Bank's Experience of Natural Disaster-Related Assistance*. Washington, D.C.: World Bank.

Hausman, D. M., and M. S. McPherson. 1996. *Economic Analysis and Moral Philosophy*. Cambridge, UK: Cambridge University Press.

Kagan, S.. 1998. *Normative Ethics*. Boulder: Westview Press.

Kunreuther, H. 1994. "Protection against Low-Probability High- Consequence Events." Working Paper 94-03-01. The Wharton Risk Management and Decision Process Center, Philadelphia, Pa.

Landis, M. L. 1998. "Let Me Next Be Tried by Fire." *Northwestern University Law Review* 92: 967-1034.

Levmore, S. 1996. "Coalitions and Quakes: Disaster Relief and Its Prevention." *University of Chicago Roundtable* 3: 1-34.

Linnerooth-Bayer, J., and A. Amendola. 1998. "Global Change, Catastrophic Risk and Loss Spreading." Manuscript.

Martina, A. 1998a. "Searching for Principles to Guide the Design of Effective Disaster Mitigation Policy in Developing Countries: Part 1." *The Journal of Interdisciplinary Economics* 9: 201-38.

Martina, A. 1998b. "Searching for Principles to Guide the Design of Effective Disaster Mitigation Policy in Developing Countries: Part 2." *The Journal of Interdisciplinary Economics* 9: 293-348.

Nagel, T. 1975. "Libertarianism without Foundations." In *Other Minds*. Ed. T. Nagel. New York: Oxford University Press.

Nagel, T. 1991. *Equality and Partiality.* New York: Oxford University Press.

Nozick, R. 1974. *Anarchy, State, and Utopia.* New York: Basic Books.

Priest, G. 1996. "The Government, the Market, and the Problem of Catastrophic Loss." *Journal of Risk and Uncertainty* 12: 219-56.

Rawls, J. 1971. *A Theory of Justice.* Cambridge, Ma.: Harvard University Press.

Sar, D. W. 1996. "Helping Hands: Aid for Natural Disaster vs. Aid for Ordinary Homeless." *Stanford Law and Policy Review* 7: 129-45.

Sen, A. 1987 "Equality of What?" In *Liberty, Equality, and Law.* Ed. S. M. McMurrin.

Sen, A. 1993. "Capability and Well-Being." In *The Quality of Life.* Ed. M. Nussbaum and A. Sen.

Walker, M. 1992. "Moral Minimalism." In *The Twilight of Probability: Ethics and Politics.* Ed. W. R. Shea and G. A. Spadafora.

Chapter 14

Risk Transfer and Finance Experience in the Caribbean

Jan C. Vermeiren

This chapter is based on the experience gained from the Caribbean Disaster Mitigation Project (CDMP), a six-year, US$5.0 million project executed by the Organization of American States (OAS) with financing from the Office of Foreign Disaster Assistance of the U.S. Agency for International Development (OFDA/USAID). The purpose of the project was to establish sustainable public/private disaster mitigation mechanisms that measurably lessen loss of life, reduce potential damage, and shorten the disaster recovery period. The project was completed in December 1999, but many of the activities and institutional arrangements that were pilot-tested and established under the project remain firmly in place.

One of the objectives of the CDMP was to promote natural hazard damage mitigation and the use of loss-reduction incentives in the Caribbean property insurance industry. Soon after its inception in 1993 the project assisted national insurance associations in several of the Caribbean states in organizing meetings and technical conferences to address issues facing the industry, and to explore how the industry could play a more effective role in reducing property risk in the region. Whereas these meetings regularly counted received strong participation and support from the local representatives of the industry, little headway was made in mounting joint efforts to improve the quality of risk assessment and underwriting. The project soon discovered that one of the main reasons for this was that the local insurance companies and agencies retain little of the risk.

The Caribbean property insurance industry is characterized by a proliferation of general agency units representing foreign companies sharing the market with a relatively small number of Caribbean-owned companies. Industry experts agree that the number of agencies and companies is disproportionately large for the small volume of property risk underwriting in the region. In addition, the portion of the catastrophe risk retained by the companies in the region is small, estimated at approximately 15 percent, with the remainder being ceded to reinsurers outside the region. As a consequence, competition for agency fees and reinsurance commissions tends to drive the underwriting practice, often at the expense of a sound appreciation of the underlying risk.

Caribbean Reinsurance Crisis of 1993–94

Rates for property insurance in the Caribbean started creeping up in 1989, triggered by reinsurance losses caused by Hurricanes Gilbert (1988) and Hugo (1989). Then in August 1992 came Hurricane Andrew followed by winter storms in Europe. These events created an extremely tight reinsurance market, which peaked in 1993 and continued through 1994. Prices reached levels of 200 percent to 300 percent above those of 1989 and prior years. Several companies refused to extend coverage to the Caribbean, and those that did imposed a 2 percent deductible on the insured value. Primary insurers and agencies in the region, highly dependent on the reinsurers, had no option but to pass on the increases to property owners.

The dramatic increase in the cost of primary insurance generated widespread complaints from the housing and commercial sectors throughout the region. It also put a temporary hold on several large tourism and commercial projects under development. Responding to the concerns expressed by key sectors in their economies, CARICOM heads of government first addressed the regional catastrophe insurance crisis at their fourteenth regular meeting in the Bahamas in July 1993. At their request a multidisciplinary Working Party on Insurance and Reinsurance was established in 1994 to explore potential actions by government and private sector to address the issues involved in maintaining adequate catastrophe insurance coverage in the Caribbean.

Late in 1994 the Organization of American States (OAS), as executing agency for the CDMP, responded to a request from the chairman of the CARICOM Working Party and assisted in preparing a working paper on Catastrophe Protection in the Caribbean. The paper guided the working party.[1] The paper addresses industry performance, retention of risk at a regional level, and opportunities for reducing risk. The World Bank joined in this effort, specifically to study mechanisms to establish a regional catastrophe risk fund.

CARICOM Report on Insurance, Reinsurance, and Catastrophe Protection

The working party submitted its report to the CARICOM heads of government on February 29, 1996.

The report's recommendations cover the following areas:

1. Improving financial management in the industry, including increasing the minimum capital requirements.
2. Strengthening the role of insurance regulation and requiring companies to provide more timely, detailed, and accurate financial reports.
3. Creating a regional reinsurance mechanism to increase risk retention, including arrangements to establish pre-event catastrophe reserves.
4. Reducing risk exposure through disaster mitigation and vulnerability reduction programs aimed at public infrastructure and residential properties.

The CARICOM ministers of finance reviewed the report in a subsequent meeting and endorsed its recommendations. However, by that time the urgency that had led to the creation of the working party had disappeared. New capital had entered the reinsurance market, and reinsurance rates had come down to a level somewhat above the pre-1993 rates. The political will necessary to effect such changes as introducing a stronger regulatory framework and requiring more effective financial management and reporting of the industry faded away.

Nevertheless, one promising development subsequent to the completion of the Working Party report was the establishment of a Caribbean Association of Insurance Regulators, an institutional framework that could play a critical role in rationalizing the Caribbean insurance industry in the future. The CARICOM Secretariat also continued to pursue progress in this area. It called on the World Bank and the OAS to provide the technical assistance to implement the recommendations on establishing a regional reinsurance program mechanism and strengthening disaster mitigation and vulnerability reduction programs.

The World Bank obtained internal funding to study the feasibility of a Caribbean Catastrophe Reinsurance Fund, using as a model the private-sector-financed funds in California and Hawaii. In carrying out the study, the Bank held regular consultations with regional institutions and governments, in particular those of the Organization of Eastern Caribbean States (OECS). CARICOM finance ministers were kept informed and continued to endorse the Bank's initiative.

On completing its study, the Bank prepared an initial proposal for a loan program for the OECS states that combined the establishment of a regional risk management and financing mechanism with investment in mitigation and emergency preparedness measures. The impact of Hurricane Georges in September

1998 generated new urgency. The mitigation financing component was substantially expanded to include financing reconstruction for the countries affected by the hurricane and strengthening lifeline infrastructure and emergency response capacity. As part of this adjustment, the risk management component was changed to a contingency line of credit available to participating countries should a severe natural hazard strike them during the program period.

In July 1999 three OECS countries signed loan agreements under the OECS Emergency Reconstruction and Disaster Mitigation loan and credit program. Two more are expected to sign by mid-2000. In parallel the Bank is continuing to prepare a separate program covering the risk management and insurance component at the regional level.

With resources from the CDMP, the OAS pursued those recommendations of the working party's report that concerned risk reduction in public sector infrastructure, housing, and commercial properties. Specific activities carried out by the CDMP included

- Assisting several Eastern Caribbean governments and Belize with the introduction of a national building code based on the OECS model code
- Training building inspectors from several countries in enforcement
- Building capacity in the Caribbean Institute for Meteorology and Hydrology to assess coastal hazards from storm surge and wave action
- Launching, with the CDB, school/shelter retrofit program for OECS countries
- Training staff of the national disaster offices and planning agencies in hazard assessment and formulation of national disaster mitigation plans.

Key elements of the disaster mitigation methods and institutional capacity building techniques that were pilot-tested under the CDMP have been included in the World Bank's OECS Emergency Reconstruction and Disaster Mitigation loan and credit program. In addition the Office of Foreign Disaster Assistance of USAID, the agency that financed the CDMP, is providing grant funding for several projects designed to build on the experience gained under CDMP. The goals are to strengthen institutional capacity for disaster mitigation and vulnerability reduction at national and regional levels in the Caribbean.

Incentives for Risk Reduction: A Pilot Experience

How natural hazard damage mitigation and catastrophic insurance could strengthen each other recently was investigated by Kleindorfer and Kunreuther.[2] The authors contend that in theory all interested parties concerned with losses from natural hazards should view risk reduction measures as favorable. However, the reality is that few property owners adopt mitigation measures voluntarily; few insurers provide incentives to encourage owners to do so; and cost competition prevents developers, designers, and contractors from building safer structures.

The authors identify three types of public-private partnerships that can encourage mitigation: (1) well enforced building codes, (2) provision by banks of long-term loans for mitigation, with the cost of the loan being offset by premium reductions, and (3) lower deductibles and/or lower premiums offered by insurers for those who invest in mitigation.

Design of Pilot Program in Barbados

As part of the CDMP activities aimed at establishing partnerships with the insurance industry, in collaboration with one of the largest Caribbean-owned property insurers, the OAS has supported just such a risk-reduction initiative based on premium reduction. In summer 1997 Barbados-based UNITED Insurance Company (UIC) began a program in which homeowners and businesses can qualify for significant reductions in insurance premiums by retrofitting homes and buildings to better withstand hurricane-force winds. This leading Caribbean property insurer was the first to respond to the recommendation by the CARICOM Working Party on Insurance and Reinsurance in 1994 for the Caribbean insurance industry to more proactively promote hazard mitigation.

UIC's innovative program provides incentives to policyholders in the form of premium reductions ranging from 25 percent to 40 percent to apply measures designed to safeguard their properties against the perils of hurricanes. The company contracted a leading consulting engineering firm in Barbados to produce two technical booklets, "Making Your Home Hurricane Resistant," aimed at homeowners; and "Professional Guide to Performance-based Design Upgrade for Hurricane Resistant Construction," aimed at commercial property owners.

Owners of residential properties can use the first booklet as a do-it-yourself guide, following the simple instructions and graphics to apply the hurricane-resistant construction improvements. The second booklet, which applies to commercial structures, is more technically complex and requires the assistance of an engineer to implement the specified retrofitting interventions.

For UIC's scheme to yield benefits to the primary insurer, several conditions need to be in place. First, the primary insurer has to be able to ensure the quality of the retrofit work undertaken by the property owners. When such work is applied to a sufficient number of risks in the company's portfolio, the company can expect its aggregate catastrophe Probable Maximum Loss (PML) to be lower. UIC uses two distinct methods to ensure the quality of the retrofit work: a self-declared certification in the case of residential owners, and certification by the engineer contracted to supervise the retrofit work in the case of commercial properties.

Second, with information to substantiate a lowered PML, the primary insurer must negotiate lower rates for the proportional treaties and excess of loss cover from the reinsurers. For the insurance company to benefit from this scheme, savings realized from lower reinsurance premiums and lower incurred claims on the retained risk should exceed the reduced premium income.

A year after the program was first launched in Barbados, it became evident that its penetration was less than what had been expected. An evaluation carried out by UIC's management and CDMP identified the following factors as possible causes for the lack of success: (1) low perception of risk by the population. The last serious storm to affect Barbados had been Hurricane Janet in 1955; (2) a soft catastrophe insurance market, which encouraged commission-driven competition by smaller insurance agencies, thus undercutting the premium reductions offered by UIC without requiring retrofitting; (3) deficiencies in the promotional effort, particularly the lack of a more user-friendly presentation of the guidelines for property owners.

Presently, Barbadian property owners and insurers demonstrate indifference to taking hurricane vulnerability reduction measures. UIC competitors offer premium discounts merely to retain business. For meaningful program penetration to be feasible it will take a significant hardening of the catastrophe peril insurance market. Despite these issues UIC has decided to continue its incentive program in Barbados in low gear until the market materially hardens.

Redesign of Pilot Program in Antigua and Barbuda

In light of it Barbados experience UIC requested assistance from CDMP in designing a new program to launch in Antigua and Barbuda. The program incorporates the lessons learned in Barbados and includes features that provide reasonable assurance that the same limitations will not be encountered in the new market.

Antigua and Barbuda was selected for several reasons. The country has suffered the impact of hurricanes more frequently and more recently than Barbados, starting with Hugo in 1989, followed by Luis in 1995, and Georges in 1998. Since the decision to launch a new program in Antigua and Barbuda was taken, Hurricanes Jose and Lenny struck the country in 1999. As a result, public understanding of extreme weather related risk is much greater, and the market for catastrophe insurance is much firmer. Antigua's needs for hurricane vulnerability reduction measures are particularly acute with the current high premium rates driven by scarce and expensive reinsurance. Furthermore, UIC invited two other companies with major holdings in Antigua and Barbuda to join the program. One has formally joined, and the other has agreed to support the initiative. The three companies together underwrite almost 80 percent of the property insurance in the country.

Consultation between the partners of this program led to the following design characteristics for the program to be implemented in Antigua and Barbuda.

1. *Promotion and marketing.* Revision of the existing retrofit manuals, and dissemination of new, more user-friendly manuals. Preparation and circulation of advertisements via television, radio, and newspapers.
2. *Training and workshops.* Various core groups were identified for training and information dissemination. Included are government agencies, associations of builders, architects and engineers, financial institutions, and the Chamber of Commerce.
3. *Demonstration projects.* To generate practical how-to information, it is proposed to carry out a demonstration retrofit for one private dwelling and one commercial structure. The demonstration will be filmed, and an edited and narrated video-tape will be used as training material.
4. *Survey/certification of retrofitted risks.* An effective survey of the properties undergoing retrofit work is seen as being of crucial importance. The mechanism for carrying out the surveys and certification is awaiting final design, with the involvement of the engineers who will be responsible for this aspect.

The program was launched in Antigua in July 1998 by ANJO Insurance, agents for UIC. To date it has been offered exclusively to residential owners. As of February 2000, nearly 100 homeowners have joined the program, of whom approximately 35 percent are new clients.[3] A preliminary analysis of the damage claims generated by the participating homeowners following Hurricanes Jose and Lenny indicates that insured losses from this group are lower as a proportion of total risk than the losses experienced by the nonparticipating policyholders. To date, the company has not experienced any competition aimed at undercutting the premium reduction without requiring an investment in retrofitting. The company also continues to pursue collaboration with other companies operating in the national market to implement the training, demonstration, and certification components of the program.

Market Penetration

Given the lower levels of disposable income in the Caribbean compared to Europe or North America, the penetration of property insurance is also relatively lower. In a 1997 study undertaken for the World Bank, the Insurance Information Institute estimated that 30 percent of the "insurable" residences in the CARICOM countries do not have property insurance.[4] Self-built, informal housing traditionally is considered uninsurable. However, the absence of insurance coverage for a sizable portion of Caribbean society is not the only problem, as William Tomlin, a Barbados- based insurance broker, made clear in his presentation to a meeting of the International Decade of Natural Disaster Reduction (IDNDR) in 1993, shortly after the dramatic increase in reinsurance costs.[5]

Tomlin noted that as a consequence of the tightening of the reinsurance markets, primary insurers were forced to impose a 2 percent deductible clause in their policies, passing a significant portion of the catastrophe risk to their policyholders without any option of purchasing it back. Furthermore, due to the high cost of insurance, many policyholders started deliberately underinsuring or not insuring a large portion of their risk. Since the crisis of 1993-1994, primary insurance rates have come down, but they still are about 100 percent above their pre-crisis level. The 2 percent deductible is still in force, and the habit of underinsuring is still largely in place.

Reducing Risk in the Informal Housing Sector

Safer homes are a key element in building disaster-resistant communities. Many factors play a role in ensuring that housing can withstand the effects of natural hazards. Builders and artisans who construct and repair homes bear a direct responsibility for the success or failure of these structures. Many others, however, supply an important context for safe home construction.

In the formal sector, incorporation of natural hazard damage mitigation guidelines in the local building code, and proper enforcement of that code, can significantly increase housing safety during hazardous events. In the informal sector, training local builders in the minimum requirements of safer home construction can institutionalize damage mitigation techniques in the construction of lower-income housing, typically the most vulnerable. Availability of funds to support home construction, retrofitting, and improvement can also affect the adherence to hazard-resistant building techniques in design and construction work.

Home construction in the lower-income segments of Caribbean society is normally a continuous process whereby the original, often very modest, structure is expanded and improved periodically when household savings and short-term credit permit the owner to do so. Since homeowners rarely seek insurance for their property, other means of risk management need to be found.

Recognizing that informal housing represents a substantial part of the existing housing stock, the CDMP formed a partnership with the Cooperative Housing Foundation (CHF), a United States-based nongovernmental organization (NGO) with wide experience in low-income housing programs, to introduce a program to address safety of construction in this sector. Focused on the OECS countries, the Hurricane Resistant Home Improvement Program is being implemented by National Development Foundations in Antigua and Barbuda, Dominica, and St. Lucia. Replication by the St. Kitts and Nevis Development Foundation is in the planning stage.

Lower-income families stand most to lose when their homes are damaged by a natural hazard because much of what they own is tied up in their home and belongings. Winds of tropical-storm strength (63 to 119 km per hour) can be expected to affect the Windward Islands on the average once every 10 years.[6] Leeward Islands are somewhat more exposed and can expect category I hurricane-strength winds (120 to 153 km per hour) for the same return period. Thus, a home not properly constructed to resist these wind forces can be expected to lose its roof once every 10 years, resulting in significant damage.

With technical assistance from the CDMP and CHF, the National Development Foundations in three of the OECS countries acted as the local implementing agencies. They embarked on the Hurricane Resistant Home Improvement Program in their countries with a national awareness campaign and outreach program targeted at selected communities. Local carpenters and construction artisans, who traditionally are engaged by householders in the targeted communities, are trained in applying safe construction techniques in which emphasis is put on protecting the roof and all openings, such as windows and doors.

The technology consists of simple, time-tested construction techniques using appropriate materials: strong connections (at the ridge board, between the joists and the top plate, between the floor and the foundation, at the foundation footing); long, strong screws/nails; hurricane straps, and strong roofing materials. The essence of these training programs is captured in two simple documents produced by the local implementing agencies: "Basic Minimum Standards for Retrofitting"[7] and "Making the Right Connections: A Self-Guided Manual of Safe Construction Techniques."[8]

Traditional finance systems (commercial banks, savings and loans) generally are unable or uninterested in lending to low-income working families due to the small size of the loan, insufficient collateral, and lack of credit history. In recognition of this limitation, CHF assisted the local implementing agencies of the Hurricane Resistant Home Improvement Program to establish a revolving loan fund, which provides low-income families with small loans for home improvement combined with hurricane-resistant retrofitting. During the initial phase of the program, a typical loan would be under EC$5,000.00 (US$1,750.00), and the monthly payment could not exceed 25 percent of household monthly income.

Seed funding for the revolving loan funds has been provided by CDMP and CHF at concessionary rates. Loans to the homeowners are made at market rates, enabling the local implementing agencies to use the spread to defray their administrative costs. A key variable in determining the viability of the program is the volume of the loan portfolio, which depends directly on the size of the revolving loan fund. Two of the local implementing agencies were successful in attracting substantial amounts of local funding for their revolving loan fund, enabling them to reach a loan volume that makes their operation sustainable.

A comprehensive description of the program and practical guidelines for local implementing agencies can be found in the CDMP publication, "Hurricane Resistant Home Improvement Program: A Toolkit."[9]

Introducing Property Insurance
in Nontraditional Markets

As noted earlier, the informal housing sector in the Caribbean traditionally is not a market for individual property insurance. There is, however, a potential to exploit group insurance arrangements, using some of the many NGOs or civic service groups that assist this sector of society in meeting its housing needs.

The National Research and Development Foundation (NRDF) of St. Lucia has been the most successful of the local implementing agencies of the CDMP Hurricane Resistant Home Improvement program in the Eastern Caribbean.[10] The number of home improvement loans on NRDF's books as of December 1999 was 195, for a total value of EC$1,886,378.00, amounting to approximately EC$9,700.00 or US$3,600.00 per loan. To feed the revolving loan fund, the foundation was able to contract loans at rates from 4 percent to 5.5 percent from three local commercial banks, as well as from government's National Insurance Scheme.

NRDF management long had expressed concern over the lack of access to property insurance among the clients of its home improvement program. Through a St. Lucia broker, the NRDF was able to obtain a Homeowners Comprehensive Group Plan underwritten by a Caribbean subsidiary of a United Kingdom-based insurance company. The insurance coverage became effective in 1998. All recipients of home improvement/retrofit loans must purchase insurance under the group plan. NRDF project officers have been trained by the insurer in valuation of the properties, and their estimates are accepted by the insurer. Premium rates charged to the owners range from 0.60 percent for concrete block homes to 1.05 percent for homes constructed largely or entirely of timber.

Linking Property Insurance with Construction
Quality Control

The Homeowners Comprehensive Group Insurance plan achieves more than merely transferring part of the catastrophe risk affecting the households participating in a hurricane-resistant home improvement program. Since the insurance is offered only to those who participate in the program, it is in effect treating the program's investment in retrofitting as a condition of access. The Hurricane Resistant Home Improvement program, as operated by the NRDF of St. Lucia, offers an excellent example of linking property insurance to the quality of the risk.

Linking property insurance to the quality of construction has been practiced for many decades by what are called the highly protected risk carriers, such as Industrial Risk Insurers or Factory Mutual. The extra investment in loss prevention made by the owner as a condition to obtain coverage from this class of insurers is rewarded by a significant reduction in the premium. Several large commercial and industrial risks in the Caribbean have been underwritten in this way.

Another example is the way construction review is institutionalized in France, including its overseas departments. Hurricane Luis, which hit St. Martin in September 1995, caused substantial damage and disruption to the island's infrastructure and economy. There was, however, a significant difference in the degree of damages suffered by the two distinct parts of the island. The Dutch side suffered a more substantial impact on its infrastructure and commercial buildings, and took longer to recover than the French side.

A comparative analysis of how both sides fared under the impact of the hurricane was carried out by Tony Gibbs, a consulting engineer based in Barbados with a keen interest in quality design and construction.[11] The objective was to discover whether differences in the administration and practice of construction in the two parts of the island could lead to different levels of damage. The following factors on the French side were identified as possible causes for this difference:
- Better attention to conceptual design
- Greater consistency and uniformity of standards of design for hurricane and earthquake resistance

- Involvement of *bureaux de controle* in the design and construction process.

The "bureaux de controle," or technical inspection services, are independent engineering firms licensed by the state. They can be contracted to check the quality of design and construction of buildings and can issue a formal certification that a building meets the necessary standards. Their involvement in construction in France or any of its territories is brought about by the Spinetta Act of 1978. This law requires that owners of buildings that can be used or occupied by others are required to obtain insurance to cover the appearance of defects for 10 years after handing over the building (decennial insurance). As a condition for underwriting such risks, the insurance company requires that a technical inspection service firm review the design and construction and certify the building. The owner selects the technical inspection service, with the agreement of the insurer, and pays for the service.

Decennial insurance covers only damage caused by what are referred to as hidden defects. A prudent owner usually will take out fire and perils insurance in addition. Typically, hidden defects are found in a structure built with inappropriate material, deficient workmanship, or below building code standards. An effective way to minimize hidden defects is to ensure compliance with the code and regulations applicable in the construction locality, including the standards and regulations required to make a building resistant to natural hazards.

It is ironic that decennial insurance, which is not catastrophic insurance, had a significant impact on reducing catastrophe losses in the side of St. Martin in which it was systematically applied. Structures built with the benefit of a quality control system imposed as a condition for insurance (on the French side) do perform better than those that did not benefit from such an approach to risk management (on the Dutch side).

Conclusion

Property insurance in the Caribbean has several different faces, and its most common face is not pretty. The standard product offered by the insurance industry to the average property owner is expensive; more than half of the premium paid by the insured is allotted to commissions, profit, marketing, and administrative expenses. The underwriter pays little attention to catastrophe risk, and the industry does not offer the insured any incentive to reduce that risk. A substantial part of society is uninsured, and this applies not only to the lower income sectors but also to a large majority of government-owned properties.

Yet, other aspects of property insurance in the Caribbean demonstrate the industry's capacity to increase the awareness of risk and contribute to risk reduction. The homeowners' comprehensive group plan in St. Lucia and the use of technical inspection services by French property insurers in St. Martin exemplify a more proactive role for and by the industry. These two programs as well as the highly protected risk programs have in common the fact that insurance is used to introduce a critical element of control over the quality of the design and construction, the strongest determinant of a property's catastrophe risk.

The agencies that finance infrastructure projects in the region, be they national development banks, private sector banks, or multilateral financing agencies, are in a position to change the face of the property insurance industry in the Caribbean. If the beneficiary countries are to maintain positive growth in the face of increased losses from natural disasters, a concerted effort is needed to minimize failure of infrastructure due to the effects of natural hazards. In almost every case such failures have economic and financial consequences to national economies that far exceed the cost of repairs and reconstruction.

As a minimum, for the explicit purpose of protecting the client and themselves from catastrophic risk, lenders should require that infrastructure projects be insured as a condition for the loan. To protect their assets, underwriters of this risk should want a certification that the structure is designed and built in accordance with appropriate standards and good practice. The certification would be issued by an independent technical inspection service. Only through a loss-prevention partnership of the owner, lender, and insurer will the value of the insurance industry as a potential contributor to loss reduction be realized.

Notes

1. Organization of American States. 1996. "Insurance, Reinsurance and Catastrophe Protection in the Caribbean." USAID/OAS Caribbean Disaster Mitigation Project. Washington, D.C.

2. Kunreuther, H., and P. Kleindorfer. 1997. "The Complementary Roles of Mitigation and Insurance in Managing Catastrophic Risk." Paper presented at the Public-Private Partnership 2000 Conference on Uncertainty of Managing Catastrophic Risk. Washington, D.C.

3. Information provided by Glenford Turner, ANJO Insurance, St. Johns, Antigua and Barbuda.

4. Insurance Information Institute. 1997. "Property Insurance in the Caribbean Community (CARICOM)." Report prepared for the World Bank. Washington, D.C.

5. Tomlin, W. 1993. "Economic Implications of Disaster Impacts." Presentation at the meeting of the International Decade of Natural Disaster Reduction, Port of Spain, Trinidad and Tobago. October.

6. Organization of American States. Forthcoming. *Atlas of Probable Storm Effects in the Caribbean Sea.* OAS/USAID Caribbean Disaster Mitigation Project. Washington, D.C.

7. Organization of American States. 1997. "Basic Minimum Standards for Retrofitting." OAS/USAID Caribbean Disaster Mitigation Project. Washington, D.C.

8. Organization of American States. 1997. "Making the Right Connections: A Self-Guided Manual of Safe Construction Techniques." OAS/USAID Caribbean Disaster Mitigation Project. Washington, D.C.

9. Organization of American States. 1997; rev 1999. "Hurricane Resistant Home Improvement Program: A Toolkit." Washington, D.C.

10. Information provided by Bryan Walcott, Executive Director, National Research and Development Foundation, St. Lucia.

11. Gibbs, T. 1996. "The Role of Independent Design and Building Checking Agencies in Disaster Prevention." In *STOP DISASTERS* IV (30): 18-19.

Chapter 15

Incentives for Mitigation Investment and More Effective Risk Management: The Need for Public-Private Partnerships

Howard Kunreuther

This chapter focuses on the type of incentives necessary to encourage the adoption of mitigation measures to reduce disaster losses.[1] The word "mitigation" will be treated synonymously with "loss prevention." Most risk mitigation measures (RMMs) have the following characteristics. There is an upfront investment cost (C) incurred by either a property owner or the government. The expected benefits (B) from the loss prevention measure are the reduction in losses weighted by the chance that a disaster will occur during some prespecified length of time (T). The value of T is often the expected life of the property.

The following two hypothetical scenarios illustrate two RMMs that can be undertaken either by residents or government.

Scenario 1: Robert Shaker resides in a home in California and is considering reducing the losses from a future earthquake by bolting the structure so that it is on a solid foundation.

Scenario 2: The Honduran government is concerned with damage to one of its water treatment plants from flooding and wishes to mitigate future damage to the structure from a major river in the country.

The next section probes more deeply into Scenario 1 by examining the decision processes of homeowners with respect to the adoption of RMMs in the United States. The chapter then turns to an analysis of Sce-

nario 2 by considering the opportunities facing governments in developing countries regarding the adoption of RMMs. This is followed by a discussion of how insurance and new financial instruments can be linked with mitigation to encourage its adoption. The chapter then indicates the importance of improving risk estimates to encourage the adoption of cost-effective RMMs and makes the case for a public-private partnership to increase the adoption of mitigation measures and provide funding for loss recovery. The concluding section suggests directions for future research.

Adoption of RMMs by Homeowners

The empirical data on studies of mitigation adoption in hazard-prone areas of the United States suggest that individuals are not willing to invest in RMMs despite the rather large damage that either they and/or their friends and neighbors suffered from recent disasters. For example, after Hurricane Andrew in Florida in 1992, the most severe economic disaster in the United States, most residents in hurricane-prone areas appear not to have made improvements to existing dwellings that could reduce the amount of damage from another storm (Insurance Institute for Property Loss Reduction 1995).

Measures, such as strapping a water heater with simple plumber's tape, can normally be done by residents at a cost of under $5 in materials and one hour of their own time (Levenson 1992). This RMM can reduce damage by preventing the heater from toppling during an earthquake, creating gas leaks and causing a fire. Yet these and other mitigation investments are not being adopted by residents in earthquake-prone areas. A 1989 survey of 3,500 homeowners in four California counties subject to the hazard reported that only between 5 percent and 9 percent of the respondents in each of these counties adopted any loss reduction measures (Palm and others 1990).

Why the Limited Interest?

There are a number of reasons why a homeowner will decide not to invest in loss prevention measures:

Underestimation of probability. Some individuals may perceive the probability of a disaster causing damage to their property as being sufficiently low that the investment in the protective measure will not be justified. For example, they may relate their perceived probability of a disaster (p) to a threshold level (p*) unconsciously set, below which they do not worry about the consequences. If they estimate p < p*, then they assume that the event "will not happen to me" and take no protective actions. This decision to ignore events where p < p* may be justified by individuals who claim that there is a limited amount of time available to worry about protecting themselves against hazards. By setting a threshold level, p*, individuals can devote their attention to events for which p is sufficiently high to be a source of worry and concern. Such a rule is also easy to explain and justify to others because of its simplicity.

Short-term horizons. Individuals may have relatively short time horizons over which they want to recoup their investment in an RMM. Even if the expected life of the house is 25 or 30 years, the person may look at the potential benefits from the mitigation measure only over the next 3 to 5 years. He or she may reason that they will not be residing in the property for longer than this time and/or that want a quick return on investment before adopting the measure.

Aversion to upfront costs. If people have budget constraints, they will be averse to investing in the upfront costs associated with protective measures because they feel they cannot afford these measures. It is not unusual to hear "We live from payday to payday" when a person is asked why a household has not invested in protective measures.

Expectation of disaster assistance. Individuals may have little interest in investing in protective measures if they believe that they will be financially responsible for only a small portion of their losses should a disaster occur. If their assets are relatively limited in relation to the potential loss, these individuals may feel they that they can walk away from their destroyed home without being financially responsible. Similarly, if residents anticipate liberal disaster relief from the government should they suffer damage, they have less reason to invest in an RMM.

In summary, many property owners are reluctant to invest in cost-effective RMMs, because they misunderstand information on the potential benefits, feel they will have to pay only a portion of the cost if a disaster occurs, and/or do not have financial resources. In addition they may not have knowledge of these measures and may fear that the contractor will not do the job properly. Such nonadoption behavior may be exacerbated by developers who may believe (perhaps correctly) that they are unable to recover the costs of RMMs in increased selling prices for the structures (Kleindorfer and Kunreuther 1999).

Adoption of Mitigation by Governments

For public-sector agencies to determine whether it is worthwhile to invest in a specific mitigation measure, they will want to undertake some type of benefit-cost analysis. Consider the decision on whether a government agency in Honduras should floodproof a water treatment plant to prevent future damage to the building. One first needs to determine the costs associated with a specific set of mitigation measures. These include the relevant materials as well as the person power and time associated with making the plant more flood resistant. It is not easy to specify precise figures for these expenditures, so it is useful to put bounds around the estimates to reflect the degree of uncertainty surrounding them. This will enable the government to evaluate the desirability of a particular mitigation measure under a wide variety of cost assumptions.

Estimating the Direct Benefits of a Mitigation Measure

Mitigation measures reduce the direct and indirect impacts to the region following a disaster. Both of these effects need to be specified in evaluating the floodproofing of a water treatment plant. To undertake such an analysis, it is necessary to assess the flooding hazard. Hydrologists and engineers need to determine the probability that the river in question will rise to certain levels and estimate the resulting direct damage to the water treatment plant with and without floodproofing. They can then construct a probability-damage matrix in a framework such as the one depicted in table 1.

If the only losses incurred from flooding were the costs of repairing the water treatment plant, it would

Table 1 Probability-damage matrix to water treatment plant

Flood height of river	Probability of flood height	Damage with floodproofing	Damage without floodproofing

Data to be supplied by user

be a relatively simple matter to calculate the expected benefits from the mitigation measure. One would compare the damage to the plant for floods of different heights with and without flood proofing the structure. The reduction in damage associated with each flood height would be multiplied by the probability of this type of flood occurring. One would sum all the figures to obtain the expected benefits from floodproofing for any given year.

It is then necessary to consider the number of years that the plant would be operational, and discount each future year's benefit to the present time period by using some agreed discount rate. This would enable one to determine the expected discounted benefit of floodproofing the plant. The mitigation measure would be considered attractive if the total costs of floodproofing the water treatment plant were *less* than its expected discounted benefits.

An Example

For simplicity, and without loss of generality, assume that there is only a single type of flood that can occur on the river and that the probability of such an event and the resulting losses are constant over time. We can characterize the problem as to whether the government should mitigate the water treatment plant by defining the following terms:

C = upfront cost of mitigation measure

p = annual probability of flood (for example, $p = 1/100$)

L = damage to water treatment plant without floodproofing (for example, $L = 500$)

L' = damage to water treatment plant with floodproofing (for example, $L' = 300$)

d = annual discount rate (for example, $d = .10$)

T = relevant time horizon (for example, $T = 10$ years).

The decision as to whether to invest in an RMM is determined by comparing the cost of mitigation (C) with the expected discounted benefits [$E(B)$]. Assume that if a flood occurs on the River within the T year time horizon, the water treatment plant will be restored to its predisaster condition. Then [E(B)] can be characterized as follows

$$E(B) \sum_{t=1}^{T} p\,(L - L'))/(1+d)^t \qquad (1)$$

To illustrate with a simple example, consider the figures presented with the notation above. Equation (1) now becomes

$$E(B) = \sum_{t=1}^{T=10} (1/100)(500-300)/(1.10)^t \qquad (2a)$$

$$E(B) = \sum_{t=1}^{T=10} 2/(1.10)^t = 12.3 \qquad (2b)$$

On average the mitigation will yield 2 worth of direct expected benefits each year, so that over the 10-year time horizon, it will yield total discounted expected benefits of 12.3. If the mitigation measure costs less than 12.3, it is cost effective for the government to floodproof the structure based on an analysis of directed expected benefits. If the water treatment plant were expected to last for more than 10 years, E(B) would of course be greater than 12.3.

Indirect Benefits of Mitigation Measures

Over time floods and other disasters produce indirect or secondary impacts—such as family trauma and social disruption, business interruptions and shortages of critical human services—which need to be considered in evaluating specific mitigation measures. The costs of some indirect impacts are easy to quantify, such as the expenditures associated with providing bottled water to residents because the water treatment plant is not functioning. Other indirect impacts are less easy to determine and quantify. For example, how does one put a value on the loss of "community" associated with wholesale destruction of neighborhoods, on stress on families due to loss of homes, or on fear and anxiety about having another home destroyed in a future flood (Heinz Center 1999)?

In evaluating the benefits of a specific mitigation measure, it is important to consider these indirect impacts. Here are a few examples that one would want to take into account when undertaking such an analysis of floodproofing a water treatment plant:

- Provision of bottled water and toilet facilities to those residences who are not able to receive water because the treatment plant has been damaged. The need for these provisions may last for a number of days or weeks, so the cost could be extensive. If the water treatment plant were functional because of floodproofing, this would be an added benefit of investing in this measure.

- If businesses were interrupted because of the damage to the water treatment plant and the lack of fire protection, as in the Midwest floods of 1993, this would be an additional indirect cost of the flood. Businesses forced to close temporarily have immediate cash flow problems. Employees lose work, and customers who must go elsewhere for goods and services may not return when the business reopens. Other businesses require a certain amount of commercial activity in their geographic area to prosper (Heinz Center 1999).

If a functioning water treatment plant could have prevented some of these business interruptions, these would be considered an additional benefit of floodproofing the structure. To the extent that other businesses in Honduras not affected by the disaster fill the gap caused by nonfunctioning businesses, this is a transfer rather than a loss. If Honduras needs to rely on imports from other countries because their own businesses cannot provide goods and services, this is a loss to Honduras.

The above examples illustrate what economists term *externalities* associated with damage to a particular facility. The damage to the water treatment plant created a set of losses to residents and businesses specifically because they could not receive pure water. Suppose there were some people who drank contaminated water because they were not able to get their normal water supply and as a result contracted some disease. The hospital costs and loss of work time from their drinking impure water would be an additional cost of the damaged water treatment plant.

Financial Incentives to Encourage Mitigation

Role of Insurance

Insurance can be used as an incentive for encouraging governments and private citizens to invest in mitigation measures. More specifically, if a private insurer were to offer coverage against repairing damage to the water treatment plant, it would base its premium on the figures in the probability-damage matrix specified in table 1 above.

By using the example in Section 3, one can *illustrate* how insurance could be used to encourage the government to floodproof its water treatment plant. Assuming that an insurer would provide full coverage, it would pay for repairing the entire damage to the plant if a flood occurred. If the government decided not to floodproof the water treatment plant, the actuarially fair insurance rate would be determined by multiplying the probability of a flood (that is, 1/100) by the resulting damage to the plant (that is, 500). The resulting rate would be 5. If the plant were floodproofed, the actuarially fair rate would be 3 (that is, 1/100 x 300). This means that the expected annual reduction in damage from investing in mitigation is 1/100 (500-300) = 2. Thus, the insurer could reduce its premium for flood coverage by 2 to reflect the expected annual reduction in claims it would have to pay the government for repairing damage to the water treatment plant.

Role of CAT Bonds

Many developing countries do not have active private insurance markets. In these cases governments may need to rely on other ex ante risk transfer mechanisms to provide them with financial protection against disaster losses. Catastrophe or CAT bonds represent an alternative to insurance for offering funds to aid the recovery effort. CAT bonds also can provide an incentive to encourage the adoption of cost-effective mitigation measures by lowering the interest rate that the government will have to pay for purchasing these bonds.

Consider the following scenario to motivate the analysis of the supply and demand of CAT bonds. The Honduran government wants to obtain 500 worth of protection against the possibility of damage to one of its water treatment plants from floods in the next year. The chances that a flood will occur and cause damage of 500 is estimated by experts to be 1 in 100. There is a 99/100 probability that there will be no damage to the water treatment plant. This provides an opportunity for an institutional investor to purchase a CAT bond whose payoff is tied to the flood losses to the water treatment plant.

To illustrate the terms of such a CAT bond, we use a simple one-period model as described in a recent Goldman Sachs Fixed Income Research report (Canabarro and others 1998).[2] The investor is assumed to buy the Honduras CAT bond at the beginning of the risk period at par (100). At the end of the risk period (1 year in this case) the investor will receive an uncertain dollar amount. With probability 1/100, the government will incur damage of 500 to its water treatment plant. This will trigger losses on the bond in which case the investor would lose all his or her principal (that is, 100). The other 99 percent of the time, the investor gets back her principal plus interest, which will normally be above the market rate to reflect the risk of losing its principal.[3]

For the Honduran government to issue these bonds to private investors, it will have to pay a high enough return to private investors to cover the risk of flood damage to the water treatment plant. Suppose that the risk-free interest rate is 5 percent. The Honduran government wants to determine how high an interest rate (r) it should charge so that the investor will get the same expected return as if his money were in a risk-free security.

To determine r, the investor knows that with probability .99 it will get an annual return of .05 on its investment, and with probability .01 it will have to pay for the damage to the plant. Alternatively, the investor can receive a .05 return on a risk-free security. Let A be the amount of the bond to cover the water plant be damaged. To determine the value of r, the investor computes

.99 r (A) - .01 (A) = .05 (A)

r = .06/.99 = .0606

The expected benefits of investing in a mitigation measure can now be easily determined. If the water treatment plant were not mitigated, the Honduran government would have to issue a bond with a value of A=500 to reflect the costs of repairing the water treatment plant following a disaster. The annual expenditure on the bond in terms of interest payments by the government would be .0606(500. =30.3). If, on the other hand, the plant had been floodproofed, a bond of only 300 would be issued, and the annual expenditure would be .0606(300) =18.2. The Honduran government could save 12.1 (30.3-18.2) per year by mitigating the water treatment plant.

One challenge in issuing the type of catastrophe bond described above is the ability of the Honduran government to verify the damage to the water treatment plant. In the above example the government issued a bond under the assumption that it knew that the damage would respectively be 300 and 500 with and without floodproofing. In reality it is difficult to estimate these figures, and there may be an incentive for the public agency operating the water treatment plant to distort the damage, so that it would receive the maximum amount of payment for repairing damage.

This problem of *moral hazard* can be dealt with by relating the payouts from CAT bonds to an objective index (for example, flood height) rather than to actual damage. There may be some *basis risk* associated with these type of bonds to the extent that the actual losses differ from those predicted by the index. Recent catastrophe bonds issued to insurers have been based on an index, but there has not been any actual experience to evaluate the nature of the basis risk. Details on the nature of these type of bonds and a comparison with nonindexed bonds and/or reinsurance can be found in Doherty (1997), Freeman (1999), Croson and Kunreuther (1999), and Insurance Services Office (1999).

In many countries, such as Honduras and other parts of Central America, where the government can-

not easily afford the premium on insurance or the interest on the CAT bond, there may be an important role for organizations who provide loans to developing countries, such as the World Bank. More specifically, the World Bank could serve as a broker by purchasing these bonds from developing countries at a subsidized interest rate and issuing them to private investors at higher rate. This would enable the countries to obtain the bonds at low cost to them while protecting the World Bank's investments in these countries for health, education, and general welfare. Funds for these purposes could easily be diverted to disaster recovery if the country did not have other sources of relief, such as from a CAT bond.

By having an organization such as the Bank as the broker between investors and the developing country at risk, it might also avoid or reduce the stigma that might arise if private individuals or institutions were to collect high interest rates from poor countries through CAT bonds.[4] Furthermore, the issuance of a CAT bond by the World Bank would require the Bank to provide subsidized disaster assistance, a role it felt it had to play following the 1977 Polish floods (World Disaster Report 1998).

Improving Risk Estimates to Encourage Mitigation

An important step in encouraging property owners and government to adopt loss prevention measures is to improve estimates of the risks associated with natural disasters. There are two principal reasons why the relevant interested parties, such as insurers, reinsurers, investors, and organizations such as the World Bank, will benefit from improved estimates of the risk associated with these events.

First, by obtaining better data on the probabilities and consequences of these events, insurers will be able to more accurately set their premiums and tailor their portfolios to reduce the chances of insolvency. Second, providing more accurate information on the risk also reduces the asymmetry of information between insurers and other providers of capital such as reinsurers, the financial investment community, and lending organizations such as the Word Bank. These groups are more likely to obtain and supply capital if they are more confident in the risk estimates provided to them.

In setting rates for catastrophe risks, insurers traditionally have looked backward by relying on historical data to estimate future risks. This procedure is likely to work well if there is a large data base of past experience that forms the basis for extrapolation into the future. However, low-probability-high consequence events generally have a relatively small historical data base. In fact, many technological and environmental risks are associated with new processes, so that past performance data are lacking. One thus has to rely on scientific modeling and epidemiological data to estimate these risks.

Fortunately, there is considerable scientific work undertaken in the areas of natural, technological, and environmental hazards to provide estimates of the probabilities and consequences of events of different magnitudes.[5]

Advances in information technology have encouraged catastrophe modeling, because they enable simulation of a wide variety of scenarios that reflect the uncertainties in these estimates of risk. For example, it is feasible to evaluate the impact of different exposure levels by insurers on both expected losses as well as maximum possible losses by simulating a wide range of estimates of seismic events using the data generated by scientific experts. Similar studies can be undertaken to evaluate the benefits and costs of different building codes and loss prevention techniques (Insurance Services Office 1996).

Today a growing number of catastrophe models have been used to generate data on the likelihood and expected damage to different communities or regions from disasters of different magnitudes or intensity. Each model uses different assumptions, different methodologies, different data, and different parameters to generate its results. Hence, they have highlighted the need for a better understanding as to why these models differ and for attempts to reconcile these differences more scientifically.

Policy Implications: Need For A Public-Private Partnership

This section suggests ways that the public and private sectors can work together to reduce future losses from natural disasters. Specifically, I proposed three public-private partnership programs to encourage cost-effective risk mitigation measures and provide funds to cover losses from catastrophic disasters: (1) building codes, (2) premium reductions linked with long-term loans for mitigation, and (3) broadened protection against catastrophic losses.

In the many developing countries that lack a well-functioning private insurance market, governments could play an important role by providing protection against future damage from disasters through a tax on property owners. If the tax rate reflected the hazard risk, it would play a role similar to insurance, and the phrase "tax-rate reduction" would replace "premium reduction" as part of the proposed program.

Role of Building Codes

Building codes mandate that property owners adopt mitigation measures. Such codes may be desirable when property owners would otherwise *not* adopt cost-effective RMMs, because they either misperceive the benefits from adopting the RMM and/or underestimate the probability of a disaster occurring.

Suppose the property owner believes that the losses from an earthquake to the structure is 20, but the developer knows that it is 25 because the home is not well constructed. There is no incentive for the developer to relay the correct information to the property owner because the developer is *not* held liable should a quake damage the building. If the insurer is unaware of how well the building is constructed, this information cannot be conveyed to the potential property owner through a premium based on risk. Inspecting the building to see that it meets code and giving it a seal of approval would provide the property owner with more accurate information.

One way to encourage the adoption of cost-effective mitigation measures is for banks and financial institutions to provide a seal of approval to each structure that meets or exceeds building code standards. The success of such a program requires the support of the building industry and a cadre of qualified inspectors to provide accurate information as to whether existing codes and standards are being met. Insurers may want to limit coverage to only those structures that are given a certificate of disaster resistance.[6]

Cohen and Noll (1981) provide an additional rationale for building codes. When a building collapses it may create externalities in the form of economic dislocations and other social costs that are beyond the economic loss suffered by the owners. These externalities may not be taken into account when the owners evaluate the importance of adopting a specific mitigation measure. For example, if a building topples off its foundation after an earthquake, it could break a pipeline and cause a major fire that would damage other homes not affected by the quake itself. In other words there may be an additional annual expected benefit from mitigation over and above the reduction in losses to the specific structure adopting this RMM. All financial institutions and insurers responsible for these other properties at risk would favor building codes to protect their investments.

If a family is forced to vacate its property because of damage that would have been obviated if a building code had been in place, this additional cost that needs to taken into account when determining the benefits of mitigation. Suppose that the household is expected to need food and shelter for 50 days at a daily cost of 10. After a disaster occurs, the additional expense from not having mitigated is 500. If the annual chance of the disaster occurring is p =1/100, the annual expected extra cost to the taxpayer of not mitigating is 1/100 x 500 = 5. This gives rise to an expected discounted cost of over 56 for a 30-year period if an annual interest rate of 8 percent were used. Should there be a large number of households that need food and shelter, these costs could mount rapidly.

In addition to these temporary food and housing costs, the destruction of commercial property could cause business interruption losses and the eventual bankruptcy of many firms. The impact on the fabric of the community and its economic base from this destruction could be enormous (Britton 1989). In a study estimating the physical and human consequences of a major earthquake in the Shelby County/Memphis, Tennessee area, located near the New Madrid fault, Litan and others (1992, pp. 65-66) found that the temporary losses in economic output stemming from damage to workplaces could be as much as $7.6 billion based on the magnitude of unemployment and the accompanying losses in wages, profits, and indirect "multiplier" effects.

Premium or Tax Reductions Linked
with Long-term Loans

Premium or tax reductions for undertaking loss prevention methods can be an important first step in encouraging property owners to adopt these measures. The basic rule in this case is simple: if the premium or tax reduction is less than the savings in expected claim payments due to mitigation, it is a desirable action for the insurer or government to promote the measure .

Suppose homeowners are reluctant to incur the upfront cost of mitigation due to budget constraints. One way to make this measure financially attractive to the property owner is for the bank to provide funds for mitigation through a home improvement loan with a payback period identical to the life of the mortgage. For example, a 20-year loan for $1,500 at an annual interest rate of 10 percent would result in payments of $145 per year. If the annual premium reduction from insurance or the tax reduction by the government reflected the expected benefits of the mitigation measure and was greater than $145, the homeowner would have lower total payments by investing in cost-effective mitigation than by not doing so (Kunreuther 1997).

Many poorly constructed homes are owned by low-income families who cannot afford the costs of mitigation measures on their existing structure nor the costs of reconstruction should their house suffer damage from a natural disaster. Equity considerations argue for providing this group with low-interest loans and grants for the purpose of adopting cost-effective RRMs or of relocating to a safer area. Since low-income victims are likely to receive federal assistance after a disaster, subsidizing these mitigation measures can also be justified on efficiency grounds.

Broadening Protection against Catastrophe Losses

New sources of capital from the private and public sectors could provide insurers, reinsurers, and governments with funds against losses from catastrophes. They range from capital market instruments to insurance pools to federal solutions.

With respect to capital market solutions, in the past couple of years investment banks and brokerage firms have shown considerable interest in developing new financial instruments for protecting against catastrophic risks. Their objective is to find ways to make investors comfortable trading new securitized instruments covering catastrophe exposure, just like the securities of any other asset class. In other words catastrophe exposure would be treated as a new asset class (Insurance Services Office 1999).

In June 1997 the insurance company USAA floated act-of-God bonds that provided it with protection should a major hurricane hit Florida. A 2-year CAT bond was put together by Swiss Re Capital Markets and Credit Suisse First Boston in July 1997. [Ding—Credit gets an accent grave: /]The loss triggers were tied to California insurance industry earthquake losses based on the Property Claims Insurance index for the state. Since that time there have been a number of other CAT bonds issued in Japan and other countries (Insurance Services Office 1999).

Turning to the role of the public sector, Lewis and Murdoch1996. developed a proposal that the federal government offer *catastrophe reinsurance contracts*, which would be auctioned annually. The Treasury would auction a limited number of excess-of-loss (XOL) contracts covering industry losses between $25 billion and $50 billion from a single natural disaster. Insurers, reinsurers, and state and national reinsurance pools would be eligible purchasers.

Another proposed option is for the government to provide protection against catastrophe losses. Governments could purchase CAT bonds from either the private sector or organizations such as the World Bank to obtain the needed capital to cover these large losses. In countries in which there are active private insurance industries, insurers would be assessed premium charges in the same manner that a private reinsurance company would levy a fee on insurers for providing protection to them against large losses.

Conclusions and Suggestions for Future Research

This chapter makes a case for the importance of cost-effective mitigation and new sources of funding for loss recovery from natural disasters that takes advantage of recent developments in information technology and the emergence of new financial instruments.

There are a set of open questions as to the types of incentives insurers and government can provide to individuals who invest in loss-mitigation measures, and what types of financial instruments can supplement or replace traditional insurance and reinsurance coverage. A strategy for undertaking research in this area would involve the analysis of the impact of disaster of different magnitudes on a set of structures, industrial plants, or their equipment.

To determine expected losses and the maximum probable losses arising from worst case scenarios, it may be necessary to undertake long-term simulations. For example, one could examine the impacts of earthquakes of different magnitudes on the losses to a community or region over 10,000 years. In the process one could determine expected losses based on the probabilistic scenario of earthquakes as well as the maximum possible loss during this period based on a worst-case scenario.

By constructing large, medium, and small *representative* insurers with specific balance sheets, types of insurance portfolios, premium structures, and a wide range of potential financial instruments, through simulation one could examine the impact of different disasters and accidents on the insurer's profitability, solvency, and performance. Such an analysis might also enable one to evaluate the risks associated with different types of financial instruments provided to different-sized insurers with a given portfolio. These data could be used to determine the return an investor would require to provide capital for supporting each instrument. The selling prices of different types of financial instruments would reflect both the expected loss and variance in these loss estimates to capture risk aversion by investors. One could also examine the role of the government in regulating rates and providing protection against catastrophe losses.[7]

Two very important outcomes would emerge from such simulations. It should be possible to rank the importance of different financial instruments for different types of firms. Small firms may prefer finite risk products while larger ones may want to rely on excess loss reinsurance due to a more attractive price for a prespecified amount of protection. These simulation results could be compared with analytic studies of the performance of these instruments. If there are major differences, it would be important to understand why they exist. Second, investors could determine whether the market price that emerged from this simulation would be sufficiently attractive for them to provide investment capital to support certain instruments.

Future studies could examine the following issues:

- *Regulatory issues.* What impact would rate restrictions on premiums that insurers are allowed to charge in hazard-prone areas have on the availability of coverage and their incentive to encourage mitigation?
- *Uncertainty issues.* There is considerable uncertainty in estimating the probability of disasters of different magnitudes occurring and the magnitude of the resulting losses. How can one incorporate these uncertainties in an analysis of which mitigation measures are cost effective?
- *Tradeoffs between reinsurance and mitigation.* How much reinsurance would have to be purchased to provide sufficient protection to the insurer as a function of the amount of mitigation in place?
- *Impact of mitigation on capital market instruments.* How will loss-reduction measures impact on the abil-

ity of the insurance industry to provide coverage without relying extensively on funds from the capital market? Will mitigation reduce the uncertainty of future losses, so that these new financial instruments could be more easily marketed to investors?

This is a very exciting time for the private and public sectors to explore new opportunities for dealing with catastrophe risks. Each country will have its own set of institutional arrangements to develop a strategy for reducing future losses and having adequate funds for recovery. If insurance and new financial instruments such as CAT bonds can be used as catalysts to bring key interested parties to the table, they will serve an important purpose in helping society deal with the critical issue of reducing losses and providing protection against natural disasters.

Notes

1. The author gratefully acknowledges support from National Science Foundation (NSF) Grant #CMS97-14401 to the Wharton Risk Management and Decision Processes Center at the University of Pennsylvania. Discussions with Paul Freeman, Alcira Kreimer, Fred Krimgold, and Joanne Linnerooth-Bayer were very helpful in providing a perspective on the importance of these issues to developing countries.

2. Note a one-period model ignores issues of multiple cash flows, applicable reinvestment rates, and the term structure of interest rates. Actual CAT bonds, for example, often make coupon payments semi-annually.

3. See Bantwal and Kunreuther (1999) for details on catastrophe bonds and discussion as to why the interest rates are so high.

4. The contrasting argument is that if the World Bank were to subsidize the interest rate on CAT bonds, subsidization would necessarily involve the use of resources that otherwise would be used for disaster relief or responding to the pressing needs of the world's poor (Dunfee and Strudler 1999).

5. For example, with respect to earthquakes, a discussion of new advances in seismology and earthquake engineering can be found in Federal Emergency Management Agency (1994) and Office of Technology Assessment (1995). Regarding technological hazards, the Wharton Risk Management and Decision Processes Center is compiling a very comprehensive

data base on the impact of large-scale catastrophic accidents on health and safety risks (Kleindorfer, Lowe, and Rosenthal 1997). With respect to environmental risks to health, such as groundwater contamination, data bases have been assembled that open opportunities for providing insurance protection on risks that recently had been considered uninsurable by firms in the industry (Freeman and Kunreuther 1997).

6. For details on ways to make communities disaster resistant see CUSEC 1997.

7. An example of the application of such an approach to a model city in California facing an earthquake risk can be found in Kleindorfer and Kunreuther (1999).

References

Bantwal, V., and H. Kunreuther. 1999. "A CAT Bond Premium Puzzle?" Working Paper. Wharton Risk Management and Decision Processes Center, University of Pennsylvania, Philadelphia, Pa.

Britton, N. R. 1989. "Community Attitudes to Natural Hazard Insurance: What Are the Salient Facts?" In *Natural Hazards and Reinsurance: Proceedings of Sterling Offices College*. Ed . J. Oliver and N. R. Britton. Lidcombe, NSW: Cumberland College of Health Sciences. 107-21.

Canabarro, E., and others. 1998. "Analyzing Insurance-Linked Securities." Goldman Sachs & Co. New York. October.

Cohen, L., and R. Noll. 1981. "The Economics of Building Codes to Resist Seismic Structures." *Public Policy* (Winter): 1-29.

Croson, D., and H. Kunreuther. 1999. "Customizing Reinsurance and CAT Bonds for Dealing with Natural Hazard Risks." Paper presented at IIASA Conference on Global Change and Catastrophic Risk Management. Laxenburg, Austria. June 6-9.

Doherty, N. 1997. "Financial Innovation for Financing and Hedging Catastrophe Risk." Paper presented at the Fifth Alexander Howden Conference on Disaster Insurance. Gold Coast, Australia. August.

Dunfee, T. W., and A. Strudler. 1999. "Moral Dimensions of Risk Transfer and Reduction Strategies." Paper presented at the World Bank Conference on Issues for a Consultative Group for Global Disaster Reduction. Paris. June 1-2.

Federal Emergency Management Agency. 1994. *Assessment of the State-of-the Art Earthquake Loss Estimation*. Washington, D.C.: National Institution of Building Sciences.

Freeman, P. 1999. "Risk Transfer and Developing Countries." *Journal of Environment and Development*.

Freeman, P., and H. Kunreuther. 1997. *Managing Environmental Risk through Insurance*. Boston: Kluwer and Washington, D.C: American Enterprise Institute.

Heinz Center for Science, Economics, and the Environment. 1999. *The Hidden Costs of Coastal Hazards: Implications for Risk Assessment and Mitigation*. Washington, D.C.: Island Press.

IFRC (International Federation of Red Cross and Red Crescent Societies). 1997. Section Four: The Year in Disasters. *World Disasters Report 1998*. Geneva: IFRC.

Insurance Institute for Property Loss Reduction. 1995. *Homes and Hurricanes: Public Opinion Concerning Various Issues Relating to Home Builders, Building Codes and Damage Mitigation*. Boston, Mass.: IIPLR.

Insurance Services Office.1996. *Managing Catastrophic Risk*. New York, N.Y.: Insurance Services Office.

Insurance Services Office. 1999. *Financing Catastrophe Risk: Capital Market Solutions*. New York, N.Y.: Insurance Services Office.

Kleindorfer, P., and H. Kunreuther. 1999. "The Complementary Roles of Mitigation and Insurance in Managing Catastrophic Risks." *Risk Analysis* 19: 727-38.

Kleindorfer, P., and H. Kunreuther. 1999. "Challenges Facing the Insurance Industry in Managing Catastrophic Risks." In *The Financing of Property/Casualty Risks*. Ed. Kenneth Froot. Chicago: University of Chicago Press.

Kleindorfer, P., R. Lowe, and I. Rosenthal. 1997. "Major Event Analysis in the United States Chemical Industry: Proposed Studies Using the EPA RMP*Info Data Base." Wharton Risk Management and Decision Process Center, University of Pennsylvania, Philadelphia, Pa. Mimeo.

Kunreuther, H. 1997. "Rethinking Society's Management of Catastrophic Risks." *The Geneva Papers on Risk and Insurance* 83: 151-76.

Kunreuther, H., and R. Roth, Sr., ed. 1998. *Paying the Price: The Status and Role of Insurance against Natural Disasters in the United States*. Washington, D.C.: Joseph Henry Press.

Levenson, L. 1992. "Residential Water Heater Damage and Fires Following the Loma Prieta and Big Bear Lake Earthquakes." *Earthquake Spectra* 8:595-604.

Lewis, C., and L. Murdock. 1996. "The Role of Government Contracts in Discretionary Reinsurance Markets for Natural Disasters." *Journal of Risk and Insurance* 63:567-97.

Litan, R., and others. 1992. *Physical Damage and Human Loss: The Economic Impact of Earthquake Mitigation Measures.* New York: Insurance Information Institute Press.

Loewenstein, G., and D. Prelec. 1992. " Anomalies in Intertemporal Choice." *Quarterly Journal of Economics* 107: 573-97.

Office of Technology Assessment.1995. *Reducing Earthquake Losses.* Washington, D.C.: USGPO.

Palm, R., and others. 1990. *Earthquake Insurance in California: Environmental Policy and Individual Decision Making.* Boulder: Westview Press.

Chapter 16

Catastrophe Insurance and Mitigating Disaster Losses: A Possible Happy Marriage?

Robert E. Litan

Natural disasters are inevitable. Losses from them are not. Provided the right incentives are in place, individuals, businesses, and governments can mitigate losses of disasters, although they almost certainly cannot eliminate them.

Catastrophe insurance can play a role in generating an appropriate degree of mitigation—that is, policies and actions whose expected benefits outweigh their costs. This is not apparent at first blush. The availability of insurance entails a well-known moral hazard: knowing they have the insurance, insureds have less incentive to avoid losses than they would without coverage. Providers of insurance recognize this problem and seek to minimize it by requiring deductibles (so that insureds bear a certain amount of initial loss before they collect on their policies) and by tying the premiums they charge to the risks of loss. In turn, if government policymakers allow premiums to truly reflect risks—a major qualification—then insurance can provide incentives in the form of lower premiums for homeowners and businesses to take precautions to minimize their catastrophe losses.

This chapter addresses the prospects for using insurance to promote mitigation against catastrophes in the developing world. There are several significant challenges to doing so. Insurance against catastrophe risks entails particular problems, spelled out below, even for developed economies such as the United States (with which the author is most familiar). But for developing countries the problems are compounded by the shortage of adequate loss and frequency data that permit the estimation of appropriate premiums for insurance and reinsurance against catastrophe risks. In addition, because insurance is likely to be a luxury good over some range of income—that is, demand for it increases faster than income—it is not surprising that insurance generally, even for noncatastrophe risks, is not widely used or available in developing and emerging market countries.

For these reasons, policymakers concerned about mitigating catastrophe losses in developing country markets probably will need to emphasize more direct measures, such as land use planning and zoning controls, and possibly judicious use of subsidies. Nonetheless, over the longer run insurance may play a role. This chapter attempts to provide a framework for thinking how that might be possible.

Special Problems Insuring against Catastrophe Risks

Insurance is well suited to spread the risks of frequent low-consequence events, such as auto accidents, fires, and routine storm damage to residential and commercial property, and major health expenditures by individuals. Using the law of large numbers, actuaries can predict with reasonable accuracy the likely payouts from a given insured population. Insurers take those estimates of expected losses, factor in the rates of return they can earn on loss reserves, and then set premiums at levels that can provide adequate compensation for the capital that must be devoted to bearing the risks of providing the insurance.

The law of large numbers can easily break down, however, when confronted with infrequent, but very large, catastrophes—such as major hurricanes or earthquakes. Because these events are infrequent, it may be difficult to calculate their probability. In the case of hurricanes in particular, historical weather patterns may not be predictive at all of future losses. Earthquakes tend to have more regular cycles, but these cycles may be hundreds or thousands of years in duration, and geologists often do not know precisely when the last major earthquake along particular fault lines may have occurred. An additional complication is that, at least in the United States, population and construction has grown disproportionately faster in regions of the country that are exposed to especially high catastrophe risks (for example, coastal areas, which are susceptible to hurricanes, and California, which is exposed to earthquakes). As a result historical losses from events of a given magnitude are no longer reliable indicators of likely losses should the same or similar events occur in or near the same locations.

But even if catastrophes and their losses could be accurately predicted, insurers and reinsurers confront another major problem known as "timing risk": the catastrophe may occur before the insurer has built up sufficient reserves to reimburse all of the claimants for all of their losses. If insurers or reinsurers could borrow against future premiums into perpetuity, they would be able to bridge the timing risk. This is not possible, however. Lenders will not finance insurers once they have been forced into insolvency. Knowing this, insurers may purchase reinsurance to cover very large losses to which they may be exposed. But reinsurers, too, face timing risk and thus charge premiums that are multiples of expected losses. Insurers that are unwilling to pay those high reinsurance rates go naked, running the risk of insolvency in the event of very large catastrophe losses.[1]

Two of the states in which catastrophes pose perhaps the largest risks—California and Florida—have stepped into the breach with their own programs designed to make insurance coverage for catastrophes more affordable and thus more available.

California has established an earthquake fund (the California Earthquake Authority, or CEA) that offers coverage directly to residents (and is marketed by insurance companies). The fund is financed by insurers—whose liability for catastrophes is capped—and by layers of bonds and reinsurance. The price of the reinsurance coverage (sold to Berkshire Hathaway) demonstrates the existence of timing risk: it reportedly is at least five times expected loss. The coverage provided by the fund originally was capped at $10 billion (and has since been lowered somewhat), with any losses above that threshold prorated between policyholders and the fund. As a result, even those California homeowners who buy earthquake coverage from the CEA bear significant risks. They may not collect 100 cents on the dollar if they suffer losses during a very costly earthquake. In addition the typical earthquake policy carries large deductibles, on the order of 10 percent or more of the value of the house.

Florida has adopted a different program, one that theoretically covers all homeowner losses from hurricanes above the relevant deductible, and instead shifts the risk of large losses to insurers. In Florida hurricane coverage is a mandatory part of homeowner policies (in contrast to California, where earthquake coverage simply must be *offered*). The state operates a reinsurance pool for insurers doing business in the state (who face restrictions to keep them from leaving). Primary insurers *must* purchase the reinsurance for hurricane losses in excess of $3 billion. If the state fund runs out of money, insurers are assessed after the fact to make up the difference, with the fund having the authority to borrow $6 billion to tide it over in the meantime. At this writing the Florida fund would have insufficient resources to cover the costs of another hurricane the size of Andrew, which cost insurers more than $15 billion, and certainly insufficient to cover the $50-100 billion costs of the megastorms recently projected for the next decade by Dr. William Gray, one of America's leading hurricane forecasters.[2]

That is not the only problem with the Florida system. As in a number of other states residential property insurance rates in Florida are tightly regulated. (In most states the rates are filed by the insurers but not subjected to a regulatory ceiling.) Although hurricane losses are not likely to obey historical patterns, Florida regulators nonetheless continue to use historical experience, rather than more recently developed models used by insurers, to set rates. As a result, property insurance rates in Florida almost certainly are suppressed by regulation below actuarially appropriate levels. This regulatory practice not only inhibits insurers from recovering the costs of future claims but also dampens incentives for mitigation, especially location away from coastal areas.

Enter the Capital Markets

The high cost of reinsurance and the limited coverage of the state funds has led to growing interest in the United States in the capital markets as a source of financing for catastrophe risks. In recent years a number of insurers—USAA, St. Paul, among others—have issued "CAT bonds." CATs, or catastrophe bonds, are debt instruments whose principal and/or interest is subject to reduction and even cancellation in the event of large catastrophe losses either to the company or based on some regional or national index. (The latter types of triggers are less susceptible to manipulation by the insurers and thus should be preferred by investors over company-specific triggers.) In addition a number of corporations reportedly are interested in issuing their own CAT bonds, bypassing the insurance market altogether.

When CAT bonds initially were offered in 1998, they carried interest rates that were well above the risk-free rate—for example, 500-600 basis points on CAT bonds with principal subject to cancellation. Now that investors have greater familiarity with the bonds, the interest rate premium reportedly has fallen to the 200-300 basis point range.

Still, the CAT bond market is relatively immature. As of mid-1998, there were only six CAT bond issues outstanding, worth a total of $1.1 billion.[3] Many investors—even large institutions—are not familiar or are uncomfortable with the bonds. Accordingly, CAT bonds still carry interest premiums implying a cost to the issuer that is several multiples of expected loss. This no doubt discourages some insurers from issuing the bonds.

From the investor side, the key question is what will happen to demand for these bonds when the cancellation-triggering events actually occur. Defenders of the bonds assert that the market can and will withstand the shock because investors—typically institutions—put only small portions of their portfolios in the bonds. Indeed, they should do so, according to the investment bankers' pitch, since the returns on the bonds are not correlated with those available in the equities markets or with general interest rate movements.

Skeptics about CAT bonds (I count myself as one) respond that thin and relatively untested markets are subject to contagion and redlining once investors get burned. The recent flight of investors from Asian currency markets provides a good example. In the case of CAT bonds—especially those that cancel the principal in the event of a large loss—investors who counted on superior returns could find themselves out their entire investment, or a significant portion thereof, if the triggering catastrophe occurs. Portfolio managers who bought the bonds for institutions would then be forced to explain to their superiors why they purchased a security that had the potential for becoming become worthless. No doubt they would be reminded that even the junk bonds of troubled companies typically do not suffer a loss of 100 cents on the dollar. Some of those who bought the bonds would find, therefore, that they had made a "career-ending" decision.

Accordingly, there is a significant risk that the CAT bond market could evaporate or shrivel significantly once investors are hit with a big loss. Indeed, the more weather forecasters of such repute as Dr. Gray forecast large hurricane losses, the more nervous CAT bond investors may become—and thus begin to demand higher interest rate premiums to compensate them for the risk.[4]

Government-Supplied Reinsurance

For all the reasons given, both reinsurance and CAT bonds—at least in the United States—continue to be priced at several times expected loss, reflecting timing risk. For this reason, many primary insurers lack reinsurance for very large losses and thus remain exposed to insolvency in the event of major catastrophes.

It has been claimed recently that the property-casualty industry nonetheless is well-capitalized and could easily withstand very large losses. Total surplus (the equivalent of shareholders' capital, which is available to absorb losses beyond those set aside in loss reserves) stood at $250 billion at year-end 1998, more than total annual premiums in the industry.[5] The total figures are misleading , however. They include surplus backing all lines of property-casualty insurance, not just those relating to property. Monoline property insurers by definition cannot benefit from surplus backing other lines of insurance. Multiline insurers also often offer different coverages through separate companies, so they too may be legally constrained (and restricted by their regulators) from using the surplus dedicated to one line to subsidize or bail out another.

The imperfect insurance market for large-scale losses in the United States therefore has several implications:

- Where they can, primary insurers limit their coverages for large-scale events —such as in California, where deductibles for earthquake insurance are high and where the state plan requires insureds to bear losses pro rata above the threshold of coverage supplied by the CEA. Insurance is thus less available than it otherwise might be.

- Well-capitalized insurers that can withstand large catastrophe losses are exposed not only to claims of their own policyholders but also to paying claims owed by insurers that may be rendered insolvent by such events. This is because state guaranty plans designed to protect policyholders when their insurers fail assess healthy insurers after-the-event if the total losses exhaust the resources in the funds.

- Taxpayers in the United States also are exposed to future tax liabilities to cover disaster payments by the federal government, which so far has provided them following every major disaster. These tax liabilities might be avoided if more private individuals and businesses purchased insurance than is now the case. In addition, in a truly large disaster, even

the remaining solvent insurers may find their surplus positions so weakened that the government might find it necessary to provide some subsidy to shore up their balance sheets. The federal government collects no premium revenue from the taxpaying public or the insurance industry, however, to defray the costs of these possible payments. This not only shortchanges the government but also reduces incentives for mitigation by potential catastrophe victims.

A few countries (France and Japan, for example) have recognized these problems by having the government step in to supply catastrophe insurance directly. I will not discuss those plans here for two reasons: I know little about them and I do not believe they are relevant for developing countries, which, in the absence of large-scale international assistance, lack the resources to finance them. Instead, I will briefly summarize the response in the United States, where the Congress at this writing is considering legislation (H.R. 21) that would authorize the federal government to sell catastrophe reinsurance.

The main rationale for government-provided reinsurance is that unlike private insurers, government does not face a timing risk. It can issue bonds safe in the knowledge that the revenues from future tax collections will be sufficient to service the debt.

The proposal currently being considered in the House Banking Committee is illustrative of where the debate in the United States now stands. Briefly, the proposal would enable the Treasury to sell two types of reinsurance contracts: individually negotiated contracts to state catastrophe plans (such as those in California and Florida) and regional loss contracts auctioned to primary insurers. Both types of contracts would be proportional excess-of-loss contracts. In other words they would cover 50 percent of losses over some threshold, currently defined as one-in-one hundred year losses, or those with less than 1 percent annual probability of occurrence. The dollar level of the 1 percent threshold, of course, would vary from state to state and region to region. A special commission would be established to advise the Treasury on what minimum rates should be set on the contracts, which could be no less than twice expected losses plus an allowance for administrative expenses. The proposal would cap the total amount of annual coverage offered under the plan, which is currently $25 billion.

In principle, because the reservation price of the reinsurance would be twice the expected loss, the House proposal should entail no federal subsidy. However, the official budget scorekeeper in the United States, the Congressional Budget Office (CBO), has expressed skepticism about the ability of the commission to accurately estimate expected losses based on existing models and believes that the commission and the Treasury would be subject to political pressure to keep rates below their actuarially fair levels.[6] Accordingly, CBO believes the plan would involve some subsidy (of undetermined amount). This assumption is important, because Congress may be reluctant to endorse any proposal that "scores" on the budget.

At this writing the fate of the catastrophe reinsurance proposal is unclear. Nor is it clear what impact a major disaster in the meantime would have on the bill's political prospects. On one hand, a large-scale event would dramatize the need for the legislation. On the other hand, such an event would highlight the federal government's financial exposure for large payments if the program were in place. It thus could dampen support (notwithstanding the fact that the catastrophe most likely would trigger large federal disaster payments in any event).

Applications to Developing Countries

The mitigation of catastrophe losses in developing countries arguably is even more important than in the developed world. Developed economies generally are more resilient in the face of natural disasters. Their building codes typically are more stringent. Typically, fallback mechanisms or redundancies are in place. As a result even very costly hurricanes, earthquakes, or droughts barely affect gross domestic product in developed countries (The Kobe earthquake in Japan, given its size, may be an exception.) In contrast, natural disasters in developing countries can have devastating impacts, measured not only by the value of wealth destroyed and human suffering and deaths but also by the loss in real output for several quarters, or even years, following the event.

The contrast between developed and developing countries is also evident when it comes to insurance. Given their relatively low per-capita incomes, insurance—even for routine losses, let alone catastrophic events—is not widely demanded or available in many developing or emerging market countries. Insurance may also be difficult to provide because many individuals and even firms in these countries lack formal titles to their property and thus have no formal proof of their holdings.[7]

Developing countries face special hurdles when it comes to catastrophe coverages, whether in the primary or reinsurance markets. Seismological, weather, and property data are even spottier for developing countries than for the developed world. In addition it is difficult, if not impossible, for insurers to diversify catastrophe risks in small countries, whether developed or developing. This contrasts with the United States, where insurers doing business nationwide can offset losses from, say California, against net income generated by policies written in other states.

The problems unique to catastrophes spill over into the ordinary primary insurance market. If the underlying data and loss models are poor and the opportunities for diversification are limited, then insurers either will refrain from offering insurance even to cover ordinary property losses, or if they provide the insurance, it will be on terms that exclude losses from hurricanes, earthquakes, and other natural disasters and at high prices with high deductibles. To the extent national regulators inhibit insurers from following any one or a combination of these latter strategies, insurers have strong incentives to avoid offering coverage altogether.

Role for the International Financial Institutions in Promoting Catastrophe Insurance

The impediments to the development of catastrophe insurance in developing countries, and thus the use of insurance markets to provide incentives for mitigation, therefore would seem insurmountable. This may well be true in the short run. But it does not have to be the case over the longer run, especially if the international financial institutions (IFIs), specifically, the World Bank and perhaps the regional development banks, provide the right kind of assistance to developing countries.

At a minimum it seems appropriate and necessary that the IFIs assist the development of geographically coded data bases on property values, as well as research aimed at establishing more precise probabilities of major disasters. Depending on the sophistication of insurance markets, it may also be useful to support data collection and loss projection projects for more routine losses. The information generated from these projects should not remain proprietary, but should be made widely available to actual or potential insurers, who can then choose to supplement the data as they believe appropriate.

A more ambitious project—one that is not feasible until the data collection and modeling effort is further down the road—might be to assist developing countries that alone, or ideally in concert with neighboring countries, offer reinsurance for high-end catastrophe risks to primary property insurers doing business in these countries. The reinsurance program could be modeled on the proposal now being discussed in the United States, but with appropriate modifications to suit the preferences of each country. Given the problems of diversification for small countries, the IFIs should give strong preference to multicountry consortia, which would permit a broader sharing of the risks and the costs.[8]

The purpose of the reinsurance program would be to provide primary insurers with the financial tools to manage their own risks and thus to enhance the availability of insurance they offer to local residents. At the same time, however, if the insurance is to be effective in promoting mitigation, countries must resist the temptation to suppress rates. Some rate regulation may be necessary if local insurance markets are dominated by one or two firms. But in the more usual case where there are a number of competitors, a hands-off approach to rate regulation is in order.

Mitigation in the Meantime

Since the further development of insurance as a device for both compensation and mitigation most likely is some years off for developing countries, other measures to promote mitigation are appropriate and necessary in the meantime. Two deserve mention.

The more traditional "command and control" approach to mitigation, and one that should entail relatively little government cost, is to develop and enforce land use regulations and building codes. To the extent possible new buildings should not be constructed in high-risk areas. This is probably easier to accomplish in the case of earthquake risks (few people want to live on or close to a fault line if they can help it) than for hurricane risks, which are highest in coastal areas, where many people want to live and commercial developers want to build (to service tourists).

Building codes, meanwhile, are an important means of mitigation. But as the damage wrought by Hurricane Andrew in Florida demonstrated, codes alone are insufficient; enforcement is critical. Another role for the IFIs might to assist governments in hiring and supervising inspectors, so they are not subject to bribes. In addition, the codes themselves must be suited to the risks of loss in each country. Other factors being equal, higher-risk countries should have tougher codes.

There may also be incentive-based approaches to mitigation that the IFIs might encourage, but these may require financial assistance to individual governments. In particular, I have in mind suggestions made by Howard Kunreuther that governments subsidize loans to residents and businesses that invest in mitigation or purchase homes or buildings designed to withstand earthquakes and hurricanes. Here, too, however, inspection and enforcement is necessary. Without proof that the mitigation measures actually have been implemented, the subsidies will amount to little more than handouts.

Concluding Thoughts

Insurance-based incentives for mitigation of catastrophe risks in developing countries may not yet be ready for prime time. However, the IFIs can take steps now—notably, the support of data collection and modeling efforts—that can lay the foundation for the development of a viable general-purpose insurance market, and perhaps later the development of catastrophe insurance and reinsurance. In the meantime the IFIs should work with local governments to enhance mitigation efforts in other ways.

Notes

1. Reinsurance rates have come down significantly over the past several years—to the point at which a recent survey article by *The Economist* suggests that reinsurers are chasing too much risk. Nonetheless, my understanding is that reinsurance prices still remain well above expected losses, confirming the existence of timing risk.

2. Dr. Gray made this projection in testimony before the Housing Subcommittee of the House Banking Committee on April 28, 1999.

3. "Catastrophe and the Capital Markets," *Wharton Alumni Magazine* (Summer 1998), pp. 7-12.

4. CAT options are another instrument that insurers theoretically may use to hedge against some of their catastrophe exposure. However, the market for these options—which were introduced on the options exchanges in the early 1990s—has not yet taken off and remains very thin.

5. "Capital Punishment," *The Economist*, January 16, 1999.

6. The experience with state rate regulation in Florida, which as already noted has suppressed property insurance rates, would appear to support CBO's skepticism. However, unlike the Florida regulators who have rejected the use of models in favor of historical loss experience in setting rates, the federal catastrophe proposal implicitly embraces models for rate-setting. Moreover, the final premiums for the regional contracts would be determined by the market through auction, not through regulation.

7. The well-known Peruvian economist Hernando De Soto wrote about this problem in his widely acclaimed *The Other Path*. De Soto has prepared a new book, *The Mystery of Capital*, devoted specifically to the absence of property titles in the developing world. It will be released in September 2000.

8. In principle, it might also be appropriate to encourage the development of a CAT bond market in developing countries. However, I have doubts about that approach for two reasons. First, for reasons already given, I have doubts about the long-term viability of CAT bonds in the United States, let alone for other markets. Second, and perhaps more important in the short run, capital markets in general are not deep in developing countries. These countries need first to further develop markets in plain-vanilla government and corporate debt. CAT bonds, if they do prove viable in the developed world, can always come later. They probably would be offered first in U.S. and European markets before being offered to investors in developing and emerging market countries.